Portfolio
Assessment

A Handbook for

Preschool and Elementary

Educators

Sue C. Wortham,
Ann Barbour &
Blanche Desjean-Perrotta

with Peggy Apple and Sandy Enders

Association for Childhood Education International
17904 Georgia Ave., Ste. 215, Olney, MD 20832
800-423-3563 • www.udel.edu/bateman/acei

Anne W. Bauer, *Editor/Director of Publications*
Bruce Herzig, *Assistant Editor*
Debbie Jordan Kravitz, *Production Editor*

Copyright © 1998, Association for Childhood Education International
17904 Georgia Ave., Ste. 215, Olney, MD 20832

Library of Congress Cataloging-in-Publication Data

Wortham, Sue Clark, 1935-
    Portfolio assessment: a handbook for preschool and elementary
educators / Sue C. Wortham, Ann Barbour, Blanche Desjean-Perrotta.
      p. cm.
    Includes bibliographical references.
    ISBN 0-87173-145-2 (pbk.)
    1. Portfolios in education. 2. Educational tests and
measurements. I. Barbour, Ann. II. Desjean-Perrotta, Blanche.
III. Title.
LB1029.P67W67   1998
372.127--dc21
                                              98-20427
                                                  CIP

Table of Contents

Chapter 1——Introduction

WHY PORTFOLIO ASSESSMENT? 7

UNDERSTANDING PERFORMANCE AND PORTFOLIO ASSESSMENT 8

WHY TEACHERS ARE MOVING TO PERFORMANCE AND PORTFOLIO ASSESSMENT 8

    Concerns and Questions Teachers Have About Portfolio Assessment 9

CURRENT TRENDS AND ISSUES IN PORTFOLIO ASSESSMENT 10

A LOOK AT THE CONTENTS OF THE BOOK 11

Chapter 2——The Basics of Portfolio Assessment

INTRODUCTION 15

PURPOSES FOR PORTFOLIOS 15

TYPES OF PORTFOLIOS 16

    Evaluative 16

    Working 16

    Showcase 16

    Archival 17

SELECTION CRITERIA FOR PORTFOLIO COMPONENTS 17

    Teacher Contributions 17

        Anecdotal Records 18

        Checklists 18

        Rating Scales 18

        Teacher's Notes 18

        Conference Notes 19

        Tests 19

        Program Goals, Objectives, or Standards 19

    Child Contributions 19

        Attitudinal Surveys or Interest Inventories 20

        Logs and Journals 20

        Literacy Development Samples 20

        Project Work Documentation 20

        Written Justifications for Selection of Products 20

        Videos and Audiotapes 20

        Self-Reports 21

        Computer Disks 21

    Parent Contributions 21

        Questionnaires and Forms 21

        Work Samples from Home 21

        Comments on Portfolios 21

        Teacher-Parent Dialogue Journals 21

        Notes from Informal Conversations 21

        Parent-Teacher Conference Notes 21

CONTAINERS AND STORAGE 22

ORGANIZING PORTFOLIOS 22

    Keys to Organization 25

        Balancing 25

        Dating 25

        Annotating 26

        Table of Contents 26

        Color Coding 26

USING CONTENTS FOR ASSESSMENT 26

CONCLUSION 27

Chapter 3——Portfolio Assessment for Infants, Toddlers, and Preschoolers: Bridging the Gap Between Data Collection and Individualized Planning

Introduction 31

Portfolio Assessment 32
   Establishing the Portfolio 32
   The Process 33

Steps for Individualized Planning Based on Portfolio Assessment 34
   Stage 1: The Program Planning Process 34
   Stage 2: The Individualized Planning Process 37
   Stage 3: The Integration Process 42

Conclusion 44

Chapter 4——A Model of Portfolio Assessment in Prekindergarten Through Primary Grades

Introduction 45
   The Setting: Multiage Classrooms in an Inner City Elementary School 45
   The Decision Process: Selecting Portfolio Assessment 46
   Restructuring Curriculum and Instruction for Portfolio Assessment 46

Steps in Using Portfolio Assessment 47
   Establishing a Program Philosophy 47
   Developing Teaching and Learning Strategies for Multiage Classrooms 48
   Establishing Class Organization and the Environment 49
      Class Organization 49
      Organizing the Classroom Environment 49
   Establishing the Curriculum 51
   Designing Assessment 54
   Initiating and Refining Portfolio Assessment 54
      Determining the Purposes for the Portfolio 54
      Determining the Format for the Portfolio 55
   Determining Assessment Strategies To Be Used 55
      Observation 56
      Interviews 57
      Work Samples 58
      Performance Examples 58
      Teacher-designed Assessments 58
      Portfolio Conferencing 59
   Establishing Procedures for Data Collection and Interpretation 59
   Establishing How Results of Portfolio Assessment Will Be Shared 59
   The Learning Process in Getting Started 60

Conclusion 60

Chapter 5——Portfolio Assessment in Elementary Mathematics and Science

Introduction 63
   Curriculum Framework 63
      Program Goals 63
      Performance Standards 64
   Assessing Student Achievement 65

Organizing the Portfolio 66
   Purposes for the Portfolio 66
   Selection of Portfolio Format 66
   Suggestions for Types of Materials and Data 67
   Suggested Timelines 71

Assessment Strategies to be Used 72

Checklists and Rubrics 73

Interpretation of Portfolio Contents 81

CONCLUSION 81

Chapter 6——Project Portfolio Assessment in Multiage After-School Programs

INTRODUCTION 83

A BRIEF OVERVIEW OF THE PROJECT APPROACH 83

Five Features of the Project Approach 84

Group Discussion 84

Field Work 84

Representation 84

Investigation 84

Display 84

Phases in the Life of a Project 86

Phase I 86

Phase II 86

Phase III 86

The Role of Assessment in Project Work 86

THE NEWSPAPER PROJECT 87

Phase I of the Newspaper Project 88

Developing the Portfolios 89

The Teacher's Portfolio 89

The Children's Portfolios 90

Phase II of the Newspaper Project 90

Preparing for Field Work 91

Teacher Assessment During Field Work 91

Field Work Follow-up 91

Long-term Multi-stage Work 93

Portfolio Assessment 94

Teacher Assessment of Portfolios During Phase II 94

Informal Evaluation-Sharing Portfolio Contents Through Display 96

Phase III of the Newspaper Project 97

Concluding the Work 97

Portfolios and the Culminating Event 98

The Newspaper Project's Culminating Event 98

CONCLUSION 98

Chapter 7——Conclusion

THE DECISION TO USE PORTFOLIO ASSESSMENT 101

PHILOSOPHICAL BASES FOR USING PORTFOLIO ASSESSMENT 102

SELECTING THE PURPOSE FOR THE PORTFOLIO 102

CRITERIA FOR SELECTING ASSESSMENT STRATEGIES 102

COLLECTING, INTERPRETING, AND REPORTING DATA 103

A FINAL WORD 103

SUGGESTED RESOURCES 103

Appendices

APPENDIX A, FORMS FOR CHAPTER 2 105

APPENDIX B, FORMS FOR CHAPTER 3 109

APPENDIX C, FORMS FOR CHAPTER 4 121

APPENDIX D, FORMS FOR CHAPTER 5 139

APPENDIX E, FORMS FOR CHAPTER 6 151

About the Authors

Sue Wortham is Professor of Early Childhood and Elementary Education, The University of Texas at San Antonio.

Blanche Desjean-Perrotta is Assistant Professor of Early Childhood and Elementary Education, The University of Texas at San Antonio.

Ann Barbour is Associate Professor, Division of Curriculum and Instruction, Charter School of Education, California State University at Los Angeles.

Peggy Apple is Associate Professor and Chairperson, Department of Child Development, San Antonio College.

Sandy Enders is Assistant Professor, Department of Child Development, San Antonio College.

Introduction

This book is a guide for educators who want to begin using portfolios in their classrooms. It is a response to the trend toward using portfolios to reflect the development and learning of children more accurately, and to plan instruction that better extends the child's current level of learning and interests. Portfolio assessment is thought to be more effective than the traditional assessment methods—those that are associated with report cards and letter grades.

The authors of this handbook share a philosophy about how children develop and learn. They believe that children are active learners who construct their own understanding through interaction with concepts and information. As constructivists, the authors believe that children are capable of taking responsibility for their own learning and are capable of planning and implementing learning activities and projects. To take advantage of these capabilities, both learning and assessment should be authentic; that is, they should be meaningful for the student. In this sense, the learner both constructs and uses knowledge in a realistic context. Children demonstrate how they apply knowledge through work that reflects their performance. To be consistent, assessment must measure what children understand and can use. As will be described in the following sections, portfolio assessment provides strategies that complement this constructivist approach to learning.

Not all teachers who use portfolio assessment are constructivists, however. Teachers who either are required to or prefer to use traditional objective tests and grades also might use portfolio assessment as part of their assessment strategies (Guskey, 1994). Teachers who do not embrace the constructivist philosophy might use portfolio assessment to incorporate both process and product criteria in grading student work. The authors of this book prefer to use portfolio assessment that is authentic, demonstrates student performance, and reflects individual student interests.

WHY PORTFOLIO ASSESSMENT?

Portfolios are merely one component of authentic assessment. Portfolios report children's accomplishments resulting from performance-based assessment. Therefore, before proceeding any further, it is important to clarify the meaning of performance assessment and examine how portfolios fit into the assessment process. In the next section, authentic and performance assessment will be defined and the role of portfolios in performance assessment will be discussed.

Sue C. Wortham

UNDERSTANDING PERFORMANCE AND PORTFOLIO ASSESSMENT

Performance-based assessment reflects what a person can do. In contrast to measuring what children know, as found in formal measures, performance assessments measure how students can *apply* the knowledge they have acquired (Pierson & Beck, 1993). Performance can be observed by the teacher; thus, performance assessment is based on observation and judgment (Blum & Arter, 1996).

Other terms are associated with performance assessments. One, *alternative assessment*, refers to strategies for assessment that are alternatives to standardized tests. Work samples, interviews, and teacher observations are among the options that can be used to understand what a student knows or has accomplished (Maeroff, 1991).

Another term that is frequently used is *authentic assessment*. Authentic assessments must have some connection to the real world or to a simulation of the real world (Bergen, 1993/1994). A child who performs an experiment with water and evaporation and can discuss the results is demonstrating authentic learning, as contrasted to the child who reads information about evaporation in a textbook and demonstrates what she has learned by completing a worksheet. Authentic assessment, then, is a part of performance assessment because the student demonstrates application of learning through an activity that includes performing a task to demonstrate what is understood.

How does the portfolio relate to performance assessment? A portfolio is a collection of student work that displays what the child has learned. The portfolio can have samples of the student's writing, photographs of a class project, a written book report, and/or a videotape of a game designed by the student and used by other students. The contents are examples of how the student performed in demonstrating application of knowledge.

The portfolio is, however, more than a collection of student work. It is also a tool for interpreting student learning in order to plan further instruction and learning experiences for the child (Stone, 1995). Furthermore, a portfolio of student work can help students to develop a sense of ownership of their learning and can encourage self-analysis as they reflect about their work (Conley, 1993).

Why are teachers moving to performance assessments that are reported and interpreted through portfolio collections? As will be discussed in the next section, these teachers are part of an education reform movement that has affected both instructional and assessment practices during the last decade.

WHY TEACHERS ARE MOVING TO PERFORMANCE AND PORTFOLIO ASSESSMENT

Teachers are dissatisfied with the emphasis on standardized tests and concerned about the related pressure to teach to ensure higher test scores. This trend toward increased importance of test results has affected curriculum and instruction in elementary schools. Consequently, educational programs are dominated by meager curriculum content and by instructional and assessment strategies that stress improvement in the basic skills measured on standardized tests (Darling-Hammond & Wise, 1985; McNeill, 1988; Shepard, 1989). Much of the classroom assessment that is congruent with standardized tests stresses knowledge and facts that are measured in isolation.

As elementary school educators change their goals for student learning, assessment strategies must come into alignment. In the past, teachers used assessment for grading, assigning children into instructional groups, or identifying low-performing students for special programs. Current trends in assessment are moving away from a "sorting" approach towards a "real life" approach. Students need to know how to learn, how to acquire information, and how to use information to find solutions to real-life situations (Arter & Bond, 1993). As instructional goals become more process-oriented and less skill-driven, assessment strategies are changing to reflect them.

The use of standardized tests with young children is particularly inappropriate and frustrating. Amspaugh (1990) reported her frustrations with preparing 1st-graders for a standardized test. Both the time spent preparing the children to take the test and the long-term pressure on teachers and children were totally at odds with the goal of helping children become lifelong learners. Not only are the tests inappropriate for young children's developmental levels, but the reliability and validity of test results are in question (National Association for the Education of Young Children, 1986).

Performance assessment as applied through portfolios provides a contrasting view of a child's progress. Instead of a one-time picture of what a child knows, a portfolio provides a multifaceted view of what the child understands and can use. Moreover, the portfolio reflects growth and progress over time, which facilitates planning by the teacher and student for future learning goals and experiences. Portfolios empower students to become involved in self-evaluation and reflection and to have input into their own learning (Tierney, n.d.).

The most significant reason that teachers are turning to performance assessment and portfolios is to improve learning. Teachers and students can set their own goals for the child's learning, as well as choose suitable assessments to glean information about student progress (Shepard, 1995). Assessments can be authentic in that they are contextual; they emerge from classroom work. Assessment within a meaningful context is particularly relevant when instruction and learning evolve through integrated curriculum. Likewise, assessment is integrated into the learning process, rather than standing as a separate activity that reduces time for learning activities (Valencia, 1990).

To summarize, teachers are moving to performance and portfolio assessment because they are seeking information about the child's development and learning in all domains and content areas. They want a longitudinal portrait of the child and documentation of change, rather than an assessment of a limited range of skills at a particular time. They want information about individuals and groups of children that will inform their instructional planning. They want a method that can include the child in evaluation and planning. Finally, they want a vehicle that they can use to communicate with parents about what their child is learning, the processes and activities the child uses to learn, and how the child's portfolio reflects his or her accomplishments. Performance and portfolio assessments are continuous and dynamic and can be shared by teachers, learners, and parents.

Concerns and Questions Teachers Have About Portfolio Assessment. Teachers who are new to the idea of using portfolios for performance-based assessment usually have questions about how difficult it will be to use them. Two questions concern the time needed to maintain portfolios: "How much time does it take to keep up with portfolios?" and "How do teachers manage their time so that portfolios can be used appropriately?"

Another frequently asked question is, "How is assessment different when portfolios are used?" Teachers want to know if they will need to learn new assessment strategies and if everything they are doing now has to be replaced if they are going to implement portfolios.

Also, they have questions about what should go into the portfolio. Teachers ask about how often student work should be collected and how many samples should be collected. Should the teacher or the student select the work examples? Should parents be involved in selecting portfolio entries? Can materials from home be contributed?

And then, the obvious question arises about how to use portfolio collections for assessment. Many teachers routinely collect student materials each year without thinking about how to use them to evaluate student progress. The current philosophy holds that assessment should be authentic and based on a contextually meaningful activity. The child's performance is being measured. This casts a new light on the use of such collections, provoking the question: "What do I do with all of this stuff?"

The final question might be, "What do I do with the portfolio at the end of the year? Do I send it all home, or should I keep some or all of it to send to the next teacher?"

Initiating the use of portfolios is a major step that does take time. The teacher not only has to plan for time to keep portfolios organized and up-to-date, but also must continually refine the process. Teachers with several years of experience report that they continue to modify and improve how they implement the process (Jervis, 1996). Nevertheless, children, even very young children, can take responsibility for putting work into their portfolio. Teachers find that the time factor becomes less significant once they have established a scheme for organization and made some decisions about how the portfolio will be used.

In response to the questions about how assessment changes when using portfolios, the answer depends upon the teacher's current assessment practices. If the teacher has been using performance-based assessment, the portfolio adds an element of organization. If, however, the teacher has been skill-oriented in the teaching approach, additional strategies might be needed.

Early childhood teachers usually find that assessment strategies that fit the developmental levels of young children are a natural part of a portfolio system. Observation is a primary method in assessment of young children, as it is in portfolio assessment. Teachers of young children are already accustomed to assessing what young children can do, so that the concept of performance assessment is not new. They are comfortable with checklists and other recordkeeping instruments, and find themselves easily able to use additional recordkeeping forms and strategies.

Teachers who have questions about what should go into a portfolio will learn that some basic decisions should be made before beginning portfolio assessment. They will need to decide if the portfolio will be for all developmental domains or content areas, or only for one area, such as literacy or mathematics. Decisions also will need to be made about what kinds of assessments will be included. Then, they can determine how much material will be collected and how often. They also will be able to determine how much students will be involved in selecting and evaluating their own work.

The major decision that teachers make about portfolio assessment concerns how they will evaluate and report students' progress and performance. The expected evaluation practices set by the school will dictate whether profiles of progress will be used for reporting, rather than report cards. Letter grades might be replaced by progress reports, parent conferences, and other systems that reflect performance assessments.

There is no set formula for establishing portfolios. Many possibilities for purposes, formats, recordkeeping, etc. exist. One reason that portfolio assessment initially seems so complex is because there is no prescribed process to follow. In fact, portfolios can be designed and used in many different ways. The next section explores some of the current trends and issues concerning portfolio assessment.

CURRENT TRENDS AND ISSUES IN PORTFOLIO ASSESSMENT

Nationally, portfolio talk is in the air. To some audiences, portfolios are simple folders that hold completed work, including skill sheets; in other venues, portfolios are an elaborately refined collection of a student's best work or an extensive compilation of drafts produced along the way toward a final product. Some portfolios aim to replace standardized tests; others are designed to provoke teacher reflection, aid college admissions, or evaluate programs. Some teachers use them to provide parents, teachers, and students themselves with evidence that students have mastered essential skills. (Jervis, 1996, p. 23)

As described in Kathe Jervis's statement about portfolios, support for the use of portfolios is widespread, but few educators agree on what they are and what their purposes should be. While portfolios are currently a popular form of assessment (Hebert, 1992; Lescher, 1995; Wiener & Cohen, 1997), at least in the United States, the trend still has a short history and certain issues remain that need to be resolved.

One issue is the conflict between performance assessment and ongoing pressures for accountability for student achievement, as reported through standardized tests. Although educators may embrace the intent and benefits of performance assessment on a philosophical level, local and state mandates still require standardized testing and teacher assessments that support accountability.

A related concern is validity and reliability of performance assessments. Goodwin and Goodwin (1993) propose that performance assessments must provide evidence of validity, reliability, objectivity, and freedom of bias if they are to be considered feasible. This element is not easily accomplished by classroom teachers; nevertheless, information is becoming available on how to design quality assessments (Herman, 1996; Herman, Aschbacher, & Winters, 1992; Marzano, 1996). Educators at all levels will need to develop their performance assessment skills to resolve this issue.

The role of parents in the use of performance assessment and portfolios also is a concern. How much to include parents and how to elicit their support can be problematic. Parents are familiar with traditional evaluation and reporting practices. They need to become equally knowledgeable about performance assessment processes if they are to understand and involve themselves in evaluation conferences with their child and teacher. Some parents are reluctant to give up the "sorting" types of assessment, through which their child can be compared with other children. ("My child made all As.") They need to have confidence that alternative assessment methods accurately reflect their child's accomplishments.

Another issue is whether teachers should have a choice in using portfolios. Should portfolios be mandated (Case, 1994)? If so, will the purposes, format, and procedures be centrally mandated, as well? On the other hand, can a teacher use portfolio assessment in a school where other teachers and administrators are opposed to its use?

An inherent problem is lack of preparation and training before implementation of portfolio assessment. Many schools and preschool centers have jumped into portfolio assessment, only to become discouraged when problems arise that they cannot resolve. Until recently, there has been little coherent guidance for portfolio assessment. It is as difficult for teachers to move into a new system of assessment as it is to embrace a totally new system of instruction (Roe & Vukelich, 1997).

A Look at the Contents of the Book

The purpose of this book is to help you get started in the use of portfolios, or gain some new insights or strategies if you are already using them. In this first chapter, the authors introduced performance assessments, portfolios, and the current thinking about their use. The following chapters will include a discussion of the elements of portfolio assessment and examples of how they can be designed and implemented in a variety of settings and contexts. The chapters follow a set of themes or steps in portfolio assessment that were established in a graduate class on assessment. When several of the class participants, most of whom were teachers, expressed interest in starting portfolio assessment, dialogues began that focused on the essential components of portfolio assessment. (Three of those class members, Peggy Apple, Sandy Enders, and Karen Storc, contributed to this book.) They generated the following sequence of steps:

- Establishing a program philosophy
- Developing teaching and learning strategies

- Establishing class organization and the environment
- Organizing the classroom environment
- Establishing the curriculum
- Designing assessment
- Initiating and refining portfolio assessment
- Determining assessment strategies to be used
- Establishing procedures for data collection and interpretation.

The three primary authors later reaffirmed the themes as chapter frameworks. Because assessment should not be separated from how children learn and how teachers should teach, the steps incorporate more than the process of assembling and interpreting portfolio assessment. How children develop and learn should be reflected in how teachers assess through a portfolio.

Chapter 2, "The Basics of Portfolio Assessment," authored by Ann Barbour and Blanche Desjean-Perrotta, discusses the framework for initiating portfolio assessment. It includes the primary decisions that must be made when moving into portfolio assessment. Among the topics discussed are: portfolio components, storage considerations, organization of contents, and examples of forms that can be used for assessment and recordkeeping. This chapter serves as the structure upon which other chapters are organized. Chapters 3 through 7 are case studies of both individual and groups of teachers, and the process they used to begin using portfolio assessment in their individual teaching settings.

Chapter 3, "Portfolio Assessment for Infants, Toddlers, and Preschoolers: Bridging the Gap Between Data Collection and Individualized Planning," reflects the utilization of portfolios in a model child development center serving infants through 4-year-olds. The authors, Peggy Apple and Sandy Enders, are experienced directors of a preschool program who designed a model for portfolios to use in preschool programs. They approached assessment and instruction on an individualized basis for very young children and organized the assessment-learning connection with portfolios based on the development and needs of the individual child.

Chapter 4, "A Model of Portfolio Assessment in Prekindergarten Through Primary Grades," reports the experience of a group of teachers who restructured their school to improve the achievement of children from poverty families, who have not reached their learning potential in public schools. Within the process of moving from self-contained, grade-level classrooms to multiage classrooms, the teachers embraced multicultural education, developmental instruction, learning centers, thematic curriculum, and portfolio assessment for their team approach to guiding children's learning. They describe the restructuring process and how portfolio assessment best reflects how they maximize their students' learning potential in multiage settings.

Chapter 5, "Portfolio Assessment in Elementary Mathematics and Science," reviews the experiences of teachers in the intermediate grades in implementing portfolio assessment. Similar decisions to those used in earlier grades are made in terms of initiating portfolio assessment, but the description of the process and examples of assessment tools and recordkeeping are specific to mathematics and science.

A project approach to curriculum development is described in Chapter 6, "Project Portfolio Assessment in Multiage After-School Programs." The process is used in an after-school program that serves children of all ages in an elementary school. The curriculum-portfolio connection reflects the unique requirements of children in a mixed-age group who attend an after-school program. The program and portfolio purposes are different for this type of program, which emphasizes a child-centered approach to project design.

Each of the case studies describes a different type of setting, two of them beyond the confines of an elementary school. The processes used and decisions made are similar, however. Each chapter demonstrates how portfolios become the vehicle of assessment and reporting, with examples of evaluation forms that can be used by educators in other settings and with other age groups. All of the case studies report how teachers got started in the process and how they addressed the decisions that have to be made in each unique setting.

REFERENCES

Amspaugh, L. B. (1990). How I learned to hate standardized testing. *Principal, 69*, 28-31.

Arter, J. A., & Bond, L. (1993). *Why is assessment changing?* Portland, OR: Northwest Regional Educational Laboratory.

Bergen, D. (1993/1994). Authentic performance assessments. *Childhood Education, 70*, 99-102.

Blum, R. E., & Arter, J. A. (1996). Setting the stage. In R. E. Blum & J. A. Arter (Eds.), *Student performance assessment in an era of restructuring* (pp. 1:1-1:2). Alexandria, VA: Association for Supervision and Curriculum Development.

Case, S. H. (1994). Will mandating portfolios undermine their value? *Educational Leadership, 52*, 46-47.

Conley, D. T. (1993). *Assessment. Roadmap to restructuring: Policies, practices, and the emerging visions of schooling.* Eugene, OR: ERIC Clearinghouse on Educational Management, University of Oregon.

Darling-Hammond, L., & Wise, A. E. (1985). Beyond standardization: State standards and school improvement. *The Elementary School Journal, 85*, 315-316.

Goodwin, W. L., & Goodwin, L. D. (1993). Young children and measurement: Standardized and nonstandardized instruments in early childhood education. In B. Spodek (Ed.), *Handbook of research on the education of young children* (pp. 441-464). New York: Macmillan.

Guskey, T. R. (1994). Making the grade: What benefits students? *Educational Leadership, 52*, 14-20.

Hebert, E. A. (1992). Portfolios invite reflection—from students and staff. *Educational Leadership, 50*, 58-61.

Herman, J. L. (1996). Technical quality matters. In R. E. Blum & J. A. Arter (Eds.), *Student performance assessment in an era of restructuring* (pp. 1-7:1-1-7: 6). Alexandria, VA: Association for Supervision and Curriculum Development.

Herman, J. L., Aschbacher, P. R., & Winters, L. (1992). *A practical guide to alternative assessment.* Alexandria, VA: Association for Supervision and Curriculum Development.

Jervis, K. (1996). *Eyes of the child. Three portfolio stories.* New York: Teachers College Press.

Lescher, M. L. (1995). *Portfolios: Assessing learning in the primary grades.* Washington, DC: National Education Association.

Maeroff, G. I. (1991, December). Assessing alternative assessment. *Phi Delta Kappan*, 272-281.

Marzano, R. J. (1996). Understanding the complexities of setting performance standards. In R. E. Blum & J. A. Arter (Eds.), *Student performance assessment in an era of restructuring* (pp. 1-6:1-1-6:8). Alexandria, VA: Association for Supervision and Curriculum Development.

McNeill, L. M. (1988). Contradictions of control, Part 3: Contradictions of reform. *Phi Delta Kappan, 69*, 478-485.

National Association for the Education of Young Children. (1986). Position statement on developmentally appropriate practice in early childhood programs serving children from birth through age 8. *Young Children, 41*, 3-19.

Pierson, C. A., & Beck, S. S. (1993). Performance assessment: The realities that will influence the rewards. *Childhood Education, 70*, 29-32.

Roe, M. F., & Vukelich, C. (1998). That was then and this is now: A longitudinal study of teachers' portfolio practices. *Journal of Research in Childhood Education, 12*, 16-26.

Shepard, L. A. (1989). Why we need better assessments. *Educational Leadership, 46*, 4-9.

Shepard, L. A. (1995). Using assessment to improve learning. *Educational Leadership, 52*, 38-45.

Stone, S. J. (1995). Portfolios: Interactive and dynamic instructional tool. *Childhood Education, 71*, 232-234.

Tierney, R. J. (n.d.). *Portfolios: Turning assessment upside down and inside out.* Glenview, IL: Scott-Foresman Professional Services.

Valencia, S. (1990). A portfolio approach to classroom reading assessment. *Reading Teacher, 43*, 338-340.

Wiener, R. B., & Cohen, J. H. (1997). *Literacy portfolios. Using assessment to guide instruction.* Upper Saddle River, NJ: Merrill.

The Basics of Portfolio Assessment

INTRODUCTION

For many teachers, portfolio assessment represents a departure from usual forms of assessment. As such, it requires a change or modification of practices that are comfortable and familiar to teachers and parents alike. Teachers who are motivated to attempt using portfolio strategies as part of their assessment program should develop a plan for the gradual implementation of this fluid and flexible tool. Developing a plan will help teachers avoid feeling overwhelmed by the many possibilities that portfolio assessment offers. This chapter provides a map for developing portfolios by outlining the different components of portfolios and offering suggestions for their use. It is intended to be used as a reference to facilitate portfolio implementation and innovation.

PURPOSES FOR PORTFOLIOS

Portfolios can be used for a variety of assessment and reporting purposes. Before beginning to use portfolios, it is important to determine what purposes they will serve. The following list of objectives can be used to identify the functions of portfolios.

Portfolios can be used to:

- Provide data on children's main interests, dispositions, and attitudes
- Document children's growth in all developmental areas over time or in one particular area, such as literacy
- Assess children's learning relative to individual benchmarks established for each child
- Highlight children's accomplishments
- Keep track of the processes that children use in learning
- Provide family members with concrete and extensive evidence of children's progress
- Enable children to reflect upon and analyze their own learning processes

Ann C. Barbour and Blanche Desjean-Perrotta

- Keep records that will accompany children as they move from one grade to the next
- Provide information that may be useful in determining children's special needs
- Furnish data for use by teachers, administrators, and family members to evaluate program effectiveness.

While portfolios can be used for all of these purposes, the primary purpose should be to help teachers and others concerned with children's progress make short- and long-term decisions about instruction that are appropriate for both individual children and the class as a whole. Decisions about portfolio components and methods of assessment can be determined by one or more of the aforementioned objectives. The children's developmental levels and ages also will influence choices teachers make about portfolio objectives. The purpose of a portfolio for a kindergartner will differ in emphasis from that for a 4th-grader. A portfolio for a preprimary- or primary-age child, for example, may emphasize growth relative to developmental milestones, whereas a portfolio for an elementary-age child may highlight the child's progress relative to specific curriculum goals.

Because portfolios are multidimensional and complex, teachers who are beginning to use them as a means to document and assess children's learning may wish to begin gradually and in small increments, initially focusing on one or two of these objectives. It is important to keep in mind that portfolio implementation is an evolving process (Daws, 1993) that may best be accomplished in stages.

TYPES OF PORTFOLIOS

The purpose of the portfolio determines its content and influences its organization. The different types of portfolios can overlap conceptually; components from one may be included in another. All types of portfolios focus on children's strengths (what children know and are able to do), and are used to benefit children. The four commonly used types are:

Evaluative. The purpose of an evaluative portfolio is to enable the classroom teacher, in collaboration with school personnel and family members, to evaluate a child's progress relative to program goals, objectives, or standards. Teachers select various items for each child's portfolio. These may include, but are not limited to, samples of a child's work (either in-progress or finished products), anecdotal records, reading/writing logs, checklists, rating scales, test data, conference notes, and parent surveys or comments. The portfolio will be full of items documenting progress, providing a basis for determining individual children's strengths and areas of need, and will be used for reporting to parents and administrators and for ongoing curriculum development. Evaluative portfolios can be used for either formative or summative evaluation.

Working. The purpose of a working portfolio is to enable the teacher and the child to assess and evaluate progress together. Both the child and the teacher select samples to demonstrate growth and learning. Family members may also contribute related products resulting from the child's endeavors outside of school. Items highlight the ongoing process of learning, not just finished products. Included in this portfolio are samples of the child's work, teacher and child comments and evaluations, collaboratively prepared progress notes, and plans for future work. Parents also contribute comments about their child's work. This portfolio is an evolving repository of a student's thoughts, ideas, growth, and accomplishments. Working portfolios provide a method for formative evaluation.

Showcase. A showcase portfolio shows only the child's best work. Work in progress is not included. It is intended to motivate the child to develop completed projects that show best or favorite work. Both child and teacher can participate in selecting, over a period of time, the contents for this type of portfolio. Children may share their portfolios with parents or participate in parent-teacher conferences that focus on their portfolios. This portfolio does not, however, give enough information to guide instruction, because it lacks evidence of daily performance. Rather, it is a form of summative evaluation.

Archival. The purpose of an archival portfolio is to give the child's next teacher a comprehensive "snapshot" of the student's developing abilities (Puckett & Black, 1989). Items for this portfolio are selected because they provide a summative data record of the child's accomplishment during the year. Items may include both in-process or finished pieces of a child's work, checklists, rating scales, and anecdotal records. Informal evaluations, teacher analyses or comments about a child's work, and parent conference reports should be included, as well. This portfolio is forwarded to the child's next teacher so that appropriate instruction can be planned for the coming year.

SELECTION CRITERIA FOR PORTFOLIO COMPONENTS

Once the objectives have been determined, and a decision has been made about the type(s) of portfolio that will be used, teachers, children, and parents then must determine which items to include in the portfolio. Contents will vary according to purpose. A portfolio that assesses progress in mastering skills and concepts in a particular curricular area will look different from one documenting interests or growth in developmental domains (social/emotional, physical, cognitive, language). If the goal is to assess a kindergartner's motor skills, for example, a portfolio may include a developmental checklist. If the goal is to document and assess the writing progress of a 4th-grader, the portfolio should include all drafts, revisions, and final copies. If the portfolio will be used as a basis for selection into a particular program, samples of the child's best work should be included (Puckett & Black, 1989).

Within the framework of the particular portfolio chosen, many kinds of materials can be included, but selection should be made based on the developmental level and age of the children, the ease with which items can be collected, and the information they will provide. It is important that the items selected for inclusion in the portfolio provide a balanced picture of the child's accomplishments and meet the goals for assessment.

Portfolios are dynamic and fluid assessment tools. Contributions from teachers, students, and parents are necessary if the portfolio is to reflect the broad range of children's development. In selecting portfolio components, teachers can be guided by their instructional goals and objectives and by the kinds of records they have found to be valuable in the past.

Teacher Contributions. Teachers can document children's characteristics and progress through a variety of informal and formal means. A multifaceted approach to collecting information provides a better and more complete picture of the child's rapid growth and development than any single source of information. Teachers can include documentation of observed behaviors, in the forms of anecdotal records, checklists, or rating scales. They also can include interpretations of behavior, narrative reports on a child's progress and needs, and notes made during conferences with the child or her parents. Finally, they can include results from various types of tests.

Teachers decide, with each child's involvement, the type of portfolio to use and which samples best document and demonstrate development. Samples might be chosen because they represent: 1) a child's typical work, 2) the beginning of new skills or concepts, or 3) how specific curricular objectives and goals are being met (Genishi, 1996). See "Child Contributions" (p. 19) for descriptions of various samples of children's work.

- **Anecdotal Records.** An anecdotal record is a written description of a child's behavior resulting from direct observation. It is a factual, nonjudgmental account of a specific event or incident that tells what happened and the context in which it occurred. Anecdotes may include direct quotations and descriptions of children's facial expressions or body language (Grace & Shores, 1994). The behavior described may be typical or unusual for the child observed. Interpretations of the child's behavior are not included in an anecdotal record; they are recorded separately (Goodwin & Driscoll, 1980).

  Some teachers find that carrying notecards or keeping a clipboard handy helps them promptly record specific behaviors. Sticky notes, computer-generated labels, or flip charts of index cards printed with the names of each child also can be helpful. Other teachers routinely write anecdotes during planning time or soon after the children have left for the day. These anecdotes can be directly transferred to a portfolio. An example of an anecdotal entry for a 4-year-old might look like the following:

> 3/4/98
>
> Hooray! Maria ventured into the dramatic play area today after watching Tanya and LaKeesha trying on lab coats. She put a stethoscope in her ears, quietly sat down beside them, and pretended to listen for a stuffed dog's heartbeat.

- **Checklists.** A checklist is a list of sequential behaviors arranged categorically (Wortham, 1995). Teachers can use checklists to determine whether or not a child exhibits the behaviors or skills listed. Each skill or target behavior listed on the checklist can be checked off (indicating mastery), and the dates when the concept or skill was introduced and then mastered can be recorded. A checklist is useful when it is necessary to determine the presence or absence of specific behaviors, or when it is necessary to observe many behaviors at once. Chapter 5 includes an example of a checklist for assessing concepts and skills in measurement.

- **Rating Scales.** Rating scales can be used to determine the degree to which a child exhibits a particular behavior or the quality of that behavior. Instead of simply indicating whether or not a behavior is present, rating scales enable the teacher to qualitatively judge the extent to which the behavior is present. Each trait or desired behavior is rated on a continuum, either numeric or graphic. A numeric rating scale would include a sequence of numbers assigned to descriptive categories (e.g., 1-unsatisfactory to 5-outstanding). A graphic rating scale includes a set of characteristics that can be used to describe behavior along a continuum (e.g., never, seldom, occasionally, frequently). See Chapter 6 for an example of a numeric rating scale.

- **Teacher's Notes.** While anecdotal records are objective accounts of behaviors children demonstrate, they do not include a teacher's interpretation of behaviors, reflections, or insights. Notes that teachers write on a regular or periodic basis can summarize behavior patterns, and may describe changes in children's behavior, thinking processes, developmental milestones and problems (Waters, Frantz, Rottmayer, Trickett, & Genishi, 1992). For example, teachers' notes may summarize children's general interactions with peers in the classroom.

  Teachers also contribute notes about individual pieces of children's work in order to interpret them or describe the context in which they were done. These notes are especially helpful for audiences from outside the classroom. For example, a teacher may caption a photograph of a child's block construction or project work, or she may interpret a child's drawing or emergent writing sample based upon what the child has told her.

- **Conference Notes.** Notes written in conjunction with, or at the conclusion of, conferences with children or with parents can highlight children's progress to date and include plans to advance a child's progress or address a particular concern. Conferences with children about their portfolios provide the opportunity to thoughtfully review portfolio contents together; to discuss children's interests, developing skills and competencies; to celebrate and reinforce progress; and to model means through which children can learn self-assessment. In addition, portfolio conferences with children underscore the importance of the portfolio itself as a means of assessment and often reveal additional information about children that is relevant to successful instruction (Farr & Tone, 1994). During the conference and immediately afterward, the teacher (and the child, if able) makes notes about the child's interests, plans, and needs. These can be reviewed with the child, and compared with notes taken during subsequent conferences.

  Conferences with parents also can furnish information that is useful in providing a unique picture of each child. Notes can be written during the conference (duplicated for parents), or at its conclusion. Information about mutually agreed-upon goals for the child and plans for collaboratively implementing strategies to advance the child's learning and development can be included.

- **Tests.** Results from various types of tests can be included in portfolios, with the caveat that the assessment information these instruments reveal is not appropriate for grading, labeling, grouping, or retaining children (Grace & Shores, 1994). Rather, this information should be used in conjunction with children's work samples and other measures described herein. While screening tests, developmental scales, standardized tests, and achievement tests are not considered appropriate forms of assessment for young children, they may be required by state agencies or school administrators. They should be used to identify the strengths and skills children already possess, and to plan meaningful learning experiences for them. Results from teacher-designed measures that require verbal, nonverbal (e.g., motor), or written responses, or that originate from tests found in teacher resource books or manuals, also can become portfolio components.

- **Program Goals, Objectives, or Standards.** Reporting expectations of school boards, regulatory agencies, and administrators (as well as teachers and parents) may require a variety of records and summaries on standard forms. These forms can be transferred easily to a portfolio. Copies of these program goals, objectives, or standards can be included in portfolios to help adults evaluate children's progress accordingly.

Child Contributions. The saying "A picture is worth a thousand words" is never more appropriate than as it applies to the products of children's work. Children's work products capture information that is often difficult to put into words. Such products provide insight into each child's learning processes, unique approaches and strategies in problem solving, and progress toward a goal. They also provide concrete illustrations of written assessments. Various samples of children's work across the curriculum should be chosen for their ability to represent children's knowledge, skills, attitudes, and dispositions. These may include work samples in two- or three-dimensional form, or documentation using technology.

In addition to work products, children also can provide valuable information about their growth in learning through self-assessment and reflection tools provided by the teacher.

These important items document children's unique interests, knowledge, and preferences in learning. Following are several examples of contributions children can make to their own portfolios:

- **Attitudinal Surveys or Interest Inventories.** Through the use of simple survey-type questions, children can indicate their likes and dislikes, or feelings about topics related to their home or school experiences. Such surveys or inventories provide potentially useful information for planning learning experiences or thematic units of study. It is also likely that children's responses may provide answers to questions related to their performance.

- **Logs and Journals.** No matter what the age level, children can be encouraged to self-monitor and reflect on their learning by periodically recording their feelings, insights, and judgments about their work. Younger children can dictate the contents of their logs and journals to their teacher, and older children can use teacher-initiated prompts to help them get started. Logs and journals may take many forms and can include such things as children's comments about books they have read; responses to classroom activities, projects, and lessons; or reflections on their progress using writing strategies or about themselves as learners. Journals may be interactive, including dialogues between a child and a parent, and a child and the teacher. The possible uses of logs and journals are limited only by the teacher's imagination.

- **Literacy Development Samples.** Children can monitor their progress through the developmental stages in reading and writing by keeping a collection of materials, both finished and in progress. Possibilities for portfolio entries in this area may include writing, spelling, or handwriting samples; audio and video recordings of readings or story retellings; child-authored books; self-reports of favorite books; evidence of time spent reading; and self-evaluation checklists.

- **Project Work Documentation.** The process of children's learning should be re-corded, remembered, revisited, and communicated. Documentation is a practice intrinsic to the development and refinement of education. Documentation helps children to integrate thoughts, hypotheses, and theories into a new system of knowl-edge. It permits all interested parties to follow the pedagogical road traveled by educator and child (Tarini, 1993). Evidence of children's growth in the attainment of new concepts through project or theme work may be documented in a variety of ways, including drawings or paintings done by the child, photographs of a child at work or of a child's work or display, diagrams or sketches of a child's work made by the child, charts and graphs, compositions, research, poetry, artifacts, videotapes, printouts of computer-generated projects, and awards or certificates.

- **Written Justifications for Selections of Products.** Students should be provided the opportunity to select the pieces they feel best represent their progress in learning, and to reflect on why they have chosen these pieces. In doing so, students compose a brief paragraph explaining their reason for choosing a particular piece of work, and then attach this piece of paper to the work itself. Sticky notes work well for this purpose. This kind of self-assessment provides invaluable insight into a child's thinking, encourages ownership of the learning process, and serves as a tool for collaborative goal setting.

- **Videos and Audiotapes.** In some instances, the complexity of a learning situation can be captured best on tape. Audiotapes and videotapes preserve both speech and action in any given situation. These can be viewed and listened to later by any number of people to evaluate performance and/or analyze problems. A taped record provides authentic and accurate evidence of a child's abilities and learning activities, and can be used by the child and the teacher as a self-evaluation tool or as a communication tool for parents.

- **Self-Reports.** Children can keep their own records of participation in classroom activities using appropriate forms provided by the teacher. These forms can serve many purposes, such as tracking a child's use of learning centers, the number of books read, assignments completed, preferred choice of activities or projects, and skills mastered, as well as the child's ability to self-organize.
- **Computer Diskettes.** Some computer software programs on the market today allow children to monitor their own progress in learning various content areas. Children can enter work samples and reflections about the work directly into files stored on a diskette. In some cases, the program is also capable of analyzing and evaluating progress, providing children with instant feedback about their work.

Parent Contributions. Collaboration with families is an important component of authentic assessment. Information and insight that a parent shares about his or her child provide a more complete picture of the child's emerging development and capabilities, and it augments the teacher's ability to individually assess and plan curriculum. Various means can be used to elicit information from parents:

- **Questionnaires and Forms.** Forms that request information about the child's health, previous school experiences, family composition, custody arrangements, or family history can be included in the portfolio. Questionnaires can ask for written responses to open-ended questions such as, "What goals do you have for your child this year?" or "What do you wish me to know about your child?" Questions also can solicit specific information about the child's home environment: "How often do you and your child read together?" Questionnaires may be included in enrollment packets or given to parents periodically throughout the year via newsletters, communication folders, or parent meetings.
- **Work Samples from Home.** Family members can be encouraged to contribute items a child has created outside of school. These may include samples of writing or drawing, photographs, or other representations of the child's conceptual understandings or skills. Products from home related to or extending topics of study within the classroom can provide an added dimension to portfolio contents.
- **Comments on Portfolios.** After examining the portfolio contents, parents can write comments about the portfolio as a whole or about individual pieces included in the portfolio. Sticky notes are a good way to attach parent comments to particular pieces of children's work.
- **Teacher-Parent Dialogue Journals.** Parents who have difficulty meeting face-to-face with teachers find dialogue journals to be an attractive alternate means of sharing information and responding to teacher comments. Writing to teachers requires that parents examine issues and their own thoughts and express them clearly. This process often draws on parents' well-practiced observational skills and their in-depth knowledge of their children (Baskwill, 1996).
- **Notes from Informal Conversations.** The teacher can include notes with information communicated by parents through telephone conversations, messages left at school, or comments made during home visits. These notes may pertain to situations or events that affect a child's development, behavior, or performance within the classroom.
- **Parent-Teacher Conference Notes.** Conference notes may be of two types: notes that teachers write at the conclusion of a conference to document what has transpired, and notes written during the conference (carbon-copied or otherwise duplicated for parents) that include collaborative teacher-parent goal setting strategies and plans for following up on particular strategies to address a problem or concern.

CONTAINERS AND STORAGE

Teachers can use various kinds of containers for portfolios. The main considerations when choosing suitable containers are size, durability, and ease of storage. The containers should have the capacity to hold the anticipated components. If large or three-dimensional items will be included, the containers should be able to accommodate them. Also, containers should be sturdy enough to withstand continual handling. Uniformity of containers for all children within a class can save space and make storage easier. Some prefer, however, to have children participate in the selection of containers, believing this action will encourage their sense of ownership and individuality (Farr & Tone, 1994).

Any of the following can be used to store portfolio entries and can be easily personalized:

```
expandable file folders
x-ray folders
pizza boxes
grocery bags stapled inside each other
large mailing envelopes
magazine holders
office supply boxes
paper briefcases
tag boards folded in half and stapled
shoe boxes containing file folders
plastic crates
```

Regardless of the type of container chosen to house portfolio entries, it is most important that they be easily accessible, both to the teacher and to the children. Accessibility enables working portfolios to be examined, thought about, added to, and reorganized as the teacher requires and whenever children have free time or when they are encouraged to set their own priorities. Accessibility encourages children to work with their portfolios and makes portfolio work a part of the ongoing curriculum.

Limited storage space may influence the type of container that is used and may require that portfolio entries be stored in two places. For example, children's most recent work can be kept in accessible folders housed in a hanging file box, while older work can be stored in another place. Another approach to dealing with lack of space is technological storage. With the proper technological equipment, almost any portfolio entry can be stored on computer diskette. Actual computer productions (e.g., writing with word processing software, multimedia creations) and photographs of children's two- or three-dimensional work that have been scanned can be stored on a diskette or CD-ROM.

ORGANIZING PORTFOLIOS

Approaches to organizing portfolio contents depend upon the ages and developmental levels of the children, the type of portfolio used, and whether documents and work samples provide a complete picture of the child or whether specific subject areas have been targeted. Also, it is important to consider the audiences.

Two logical ways to organize portfolio contents are by traditional developmental domains (social/emotional, physical, cognitive, language) or by subject areas (reading/writing, mathematical thinking, fine arts). Or, contents may be organized by developmental domains and then specific content areas can be targeted. This is a sensible approach to use with preschool and primary grade children (Wortham, 1995).

Meisels and Steele (1991) suggest the following system for organizing portfolios using a developmental approach.

Art Activities (Fine Motor Development)

- Drawings of events, persons, and animals; the child might dictate descriptions or explanations of the drawings to the teacher or a parent or classroom volunteer, or the child might write such explanations (the teacher may need to make explanatory notes if the child writes his own picture caption)
- Photos of unusual block constructions or projects, labeled and dated
- Collages and other examples of the child's use of various media when designing a picture
- Samples of the child's manuscript printing (the appearance and placement of the letters on the page are evaluated in the context of a developmental continuum).

Movement (Gross Motor Development)

- Notes recorded by the teacher or videotapes of the child's movement activities in the classroom or on the playground that reflect the child's developing skills
- Notes, photographs, videotapes, and anecdotal records that demonstrate the child's skills and progress in music activities and fingerplays
- Notes from teacher interviews with the child about his favorite active games at school.

Math and Science Activities (Concept Development)

- Photographs of the child measuring or counting specific ingredients as part of a cooking activity
- Charts on which the child has recorded the planting, care, watering schedule, periods of sunlight, etc., of plants in the classroom or on the school grounds
- Work samples demonstrating the child's understanding of number concepts (e.g., the numeral 4 formed with beans glued to a sheet of paper and the appropriate number of beans glued beside the numeral)
- Work samples, teacher notes, or taped pupil interviews illustrating, in a progressive fashion, the child's understanding of mathematical concepts
- Photographs and data gathered from checklists and taped pupil interviews that document the child's conceptual understanding, explorations, hypothesizing, and problem solving (the documentation will depend upon the child's developmental states during the life of the portfolio).

Language and Literacy

- Tape recordings of a child re-reading stories that she "wrote" or dictated to a parent, teacher, or classroom volunteer
- Examples of the child's journal entries
- Copies of signs or labels the child constructed
- A log of book titles actually read by the child or read to the child by a teacher, parent, or other adult
- Copies of stories, poems, or songs the child wrote or dictated
- Taped pupil interviews that reveal the child's growth, over time, in vocabulary and skill in language use.

Personal and Social Development

- Teacher notes and anecdotal records that document interactions between the child and her peers (such interactions can indicate the child's ability to make choices, solve problems, and cooperate with others)
- Teacher notes, anecdotal records, and video recordings that document events from field trips (such incidents may illustrate the child's social awareness)
- Notes from teacher-parent conferences.

If a teacher prefers a subject-area approach to portfolio organization, a decision must be made whether to include all subject areas or whether to target one area, such as language and literacy. Teachers also may wish to focus on only one aspect of a content area, such as emergent writing (McAfee & Leong, 1997). Batzle (1992) recommends the following organization system for teachers who want to use a comprehensive approach that includes content areas:

I. **Required Tests and Accountability Measures**
Standardized Tests
Minimum Competence Tests
Criterion-referenced Tests
Chapter or Unit Tests

II. **Samples Across the Curriculum**
Language Arts
Reading Responses
Reading Logs
Home Reading Logs
Oral Reading Tapes
Writing Folders
Writing Samples
Spelling Work
Math
Fine Arts
Other Content Areas

III. **Teacher Observations and Measures**
Kid Watching and Anecdotal Records
Running Records
Retellings
Progress Checks
Teacher-made Tests
Rubrics
Conference Records
Summary of Findings

IV. **Inventories and Other Forms**
Reading Inventory
Informal Reading Inventory
Writing Inventory
Parent Surveys, Comments, and Evaluations

V. **Additional Items**
Cassette or Photo of Drama Presentations
Oral Presentation, Booktalk
Oral Language Inventory
Oral "Publishing"

Batzle's organizational system can be adapted for use by teachers who prefer to focus on one content area. An example of a system for organizing a mathematics portfolio is as follows:

I. **Required Tests and Accountability Measures**
   Standardized Tests
   Minimum Competence Tests
   Criterion-referenced Tests
   Chapter or Unit Tests
II. **Samples of Mathematical Work**
   Drawings, Tables, Graphs, Diagrams
   Computer Printouts
   Textbook Assignments
   Written Explanations of Mathematical Thinking
   Math Journals
III. **Teacher Observations and Measures**
   Checklists and Rating Scales
   Progress Reports
   Teacher-made Tests
   Conference Records
   Rubrics
   Notes and Summaries
IV. **Inventories and Other Forms**
   Attitudes and Preference Inventory
   Self-reports
   Parent Surveys, Comments, Evaluations
V. **Additional Items**
   Photographs
   Video or CD-ROM Recordings
   Copies of Awards or Prizes

Keys to Organization. Regardless of the type of portfolio chosen and whether a teacher chooses an integrated or specific content approach, the systematic arrangement of the information contained within the portfolio should be logical, and one that makes the portfolio user-friendly. Teacher and child should work together to create a system of organization that can be utilized by both the child and the adult. Keeping track of portfolio components, the contexts in which they were produced, and other related information can greatly enhance the significance of portfolios and the ease with which contents can be analyzed and interpreted.

- **Balancing.** In order to ensure that the data collected in the portfolio includes evidence of both process and product, some type of profile or checklist should be attached to, or included with, each portfolio. For example, Routman (1991) suggests using a data gathering profile sheet divided into quadrants that indicate whether contents come from traditional assessment measures, observations of children's thinking and learning processes, or performance samples and work products. Placing a check mark in the appropriate quadrant as pieces are added to the portfolio provides a quick visual system to determine what pieces need to be added to maintain a balanced profile. Required items also should be included in the checklist.
- **Dating.** Every item in the portfolio should be dated to facilitate the sequencing of work samples. An ink pad and date stamp simplify this process and enable children to handle this task on their own. Children also may write in names and

dates to practice letter and number formation.

- **Annotating.** An annotation may be a comment or reflection attached to a piece of work that helps to clarify the significance of an item and provides information about the context within which the particular piece was developed. McAffee and Leong (1997, p. 109) recommend including the following annotations in a portfolio:

> - Reason the item was selected
> - Task variables: setting, assigned or voluntary, assisted or independent, type of assistance, directions, materials available, time and effort expended
> - Written or dictated reflections, descriptions, remarks, and assessments
> - Responses to questions or prompts
> - Analysis of what the work shows about the child's learning, and comparisons with previous work
> - Explanation of why the item is significant as an example of the child's work
> - Child's personal responses or observations, such as making a connection to prior knowledge and experience, pride, interest, or preference

Annotations may be spontaneous and written on sticky notes attached to a work sample, or they may be written on a form included in the portfolio. Annotations may be written by the teacher, child, or parent.

- **Table of Contents.** The Table of Contents provides a guide to the organizational scheme developed by the child with the assistance of the teacher. The Table of Contents should list the items included in the portfolio and the order in which they appear. The amount of teacher assistance a child may need to organize the Table of Contents depends on the child's developmental level. The Table of Contents may list content areas or delineate categories within a specific content area. For example, a Table of Contents may list Writing as a category. Various genres of writing may appear under this category, such as stories, poetry, and reading responses. Students also can include a written explanation of the organizational system along with the Table of Contents (Farr & Tone, 1994). Numbering the pages may prove useful.
- **Color Coding.** Color coding provides a quick and easy way to file and find information. File folders or dividers of different colors can be used and their contents color coded with matching stickers. The color coding scheme can be included either in the Table of Contents or in the written explanation.

USING CONTENTS FOR ASSESSMENT

Portfolios provide concrete evidence of children's growth over time that is readily understood by all stakeholders—teachers, children, family members, and administrators. The multifaceted portrait of children's strengths and challenges encompassed in portfolio contents can establish a basis for collaborative decision-making. As Hebert (1998) reminds us, however, portfolios function best when they tell a story that is created by the child with support from adults. Emphasis should be on representing the variances in learning among children as evidenced by their individual choices of artifacts and other documentation, rather than on ensuring that every child's portfolio contains the same teacher-selected items. It is not as important to adhere rigidly to a predetermined list of portfolio contents as it is to include evidence that helps to tell each child's individual story.

Portfolio content is analogous to a child's self-portrait. The story the contents tell provides a unique portrayal of a child's efforts, progress, and achievement in one or more areas. If the contents are unique, each reviewer then has clear evidence of how to plan instruction that addresses individual needs. Rather than collecting writing samples from every child on a teacher-selected topic, it would be more valuable in terms of portfolio content to have the child select a written description of a personally meaningful event. The second sample not only is a more authentic example of a child's writing skills, but also is likely to contain valuable personal information. The second sample provides a direction for planning instruction of discrete skills, as well as information useful in understanding a child's interests and ability to use these skills in context.

The important thing to keep in mind regarding portfolio content is that the content should not become an end in itself, but rather a means to an end. That end is assessment that not only provides a true and well-rounded picture of each child's abilities, but also serves as a guide for improving those abilities. Whatever the path chosen to document and represent the child's learning, it is extremely important that the content reflects variations in learning among students. The ultimate goal of a portfolio system is to intertwine teaching, learning, and evaluation so that each is indiscernible from the other.

CONCLUSION

Teachers who use portfolios as a means of assessment will need to find strategies that meet the needs of their particular student population and that complement their individual teaching styles. Having first determined the purposes for using portfolios, teachers can find what works best for them by experimenting with a variety of portfolio components and organizational systems. It is important to keep in mind that implementing portfolio assessment is a gradual process, one that need not be accomplished overnight. The strategies described in this chapter can serve as guideposts for teachers as they determine goals and procedures and take steps to design practical and authentic portfolio systems. A portfolio design worksheet similar to the one on pages 28-29 can be used as a planning tool for implementing portfolio assessment.

REFERENCES

Baskwill, J. (1996). Conversing with parents through dialogue journals. *Teaching PreK-8, 26*(5), 49-51.

Batzle, J. (1992). *Portfolio assessment and evaluation. Developing and using portfolios in the K-6 classroom.* Cypress, CA: Creative Teaching.

Daws, D. (1993). Schoolwide portfolios. In *Student portfolios* (pp. 33-46). Washington, DC: National Education Association.

Farr, R., & Tone, B. (1994). *Portfolio and performance assessment: Helping students evaluate their progress as readers and writers.* Fort Worth, TX: Harcourt Brace.

Genishi, C. (1996). Portfolios: Collecting children's work. *Scholastic Early Childhood Today, 11*(1), 60-61.

Goodwin, W. L., & Driscoll, L. A. (1980). *Handbook for measurement and evaluation in early childhood education.* San Francisco: Jossey-Bass.

Grace, C., & Shores, E. (1994). *The portfolio and its use: Developmentally appropriate assessment for young children.* Washington, DC: National Association for the Education of Young Children.

Hebert, E. A. (1998). Lessons learned about student portfolios. *Phi Delta Kappan, 79*(8), 583-585.

McAfee, O., & Leong, D. J. (1997). *Assessing and guiding young children's development and learning.* Boston: Allyn & Bacon.

Meisels, S. J., & Steele, D. (1991). *The early childhood portfolio collection process.* Ann Arbor, MI: University of Michigan Center for Human Growth and Development.

Puckett, M. B., & Black, J. K. (1989). *Authentic assessment of the young child.* New York: Merrill.

Routman, R. (1991). *Invitations.* Portsmouth, NH: Heinemann.

Tarini, E. (1993). What is documentation? *Innovations, 1*(4), 4.

Waters, J., Frantz, J. F., Rottmayer, S., Trickett, M., & Genishi, C. (1992). Learning to see the learning of preschool children. In C. Genishi (Ed.), *Ways of assessing children and curriculum* (pp. 25-57). New York: Teachers College Press.

Wortham, S. C. (1995). *Measurement and evaluation in early childhood education.* Englewood Cliffs, NJ: Merrill.

GETTING STARTED
PORTFOLIO DESIGN WORKSHEET

1. What are your objectives for assessment?

    _____

    _____

    _____

    _____

    _____

2. Which type(s) of portfolio best meets the above objectives?

    _____

    _____

3. Will the portfolio be organized by developmental areas or content areas?

    _____

4. Who will make contributions to this portfolio?

    _____

    _____

    _____

Teacher	Child	Parent
( ) Anecdotal records	( ) Attitudinal surveys	( ) Questionnaires
( ) Checklists	( ) Interest inventories	( ) Forms
( ) Rating scales	( ) Logs	( ) Work samples
( ) Rubrics	( ) Journals	( ) Comments
( ) Notes	( ) Literacy development	( ) Dialogue journals
( ) Conference notes	samples	( ) Notes
( ) Tests	( ) Project work	( ) Conference notes
( ) Required materials	( ) Written justifications	( ) Telephone logs
( ) Other	( ) Video/audio tapes	( ) Other
	( ) Self-reports	
	( ) Computer disks	
	( ) Other	

5. What type of container will be used for storage?

expandable file folders   magazine holders
x-ray folders   office supply boxes
pizza boxes   paper briefcases
grocery bags   tag board folded in half
large mailing envelopes   shoe boxes containing file folders
           plastic crates

7. What methods will be used for:

Balancing?_____

Dating? _____

Annotating?_____

8. How often will data be collected? _____

9. Other notes

_____
_____
_____
_____
_____
_____
_____
_____
_____
_____
_____

Portfolio Assessment for Infants, Toddlers, and Preschoolers:
Bridging the Gap Between Data Collection and Individualized Planning

This chapter reflects the development of an assessment system for child care providers. The authors, professors at San Antonio College (SAC), both have headed the Child Development Center at SAC. They wanted to develop a system that could be used by the teachers in their center, which serves infants through 5-year-olds. Moreover, they wanted to design a holistic system that would evolve from the philosophy and goals of the center and that would include parents. The system needed to be clear enough for all staff members to use without extensive training. In addition, they desired strategies that would be consistent across the developmental and age levels represented in their program. They planned to use the portfolio longitudinally as the child progressed from one classroom to another; consequently, they wanted their portfolio process to be continuous from one teacher to another. As described in the following narrative, they started by defining their own understanding of the role of portfolio assessment with very young children.—SW

Introduction

Children from birth through age 5 grow in stages that encompass emotional, social, physical, creative, cognitive, and language development. While infants', toddlers', and preschooler's growth in these domains can be smooth, jags and spurts often appear that place children at different levels on the developmental continuum. Recognizing this uneven span of development, how do we use portfolio assessment to plan for age-appropriate,

Peggy Apple and Sandy Enders, with Sue Wortham

individually appropriate, and culturally appropriate curricula? How do we know we are planning activities to meet the needs of the whole child, without using personal bias as a basis for curriculum decisions? How can the collection of data in the portfolio be planned, rather than haphazard? How do we involve parents in setting goals for their children?

While abundant resources are available on data collection methods and design of portfolios for preschool children, teachers lack the information to help them make the connection between data collection and individualized planning. Furthermore, little information exists regarding portfolio assessment for infants and toddlers. This chapter outlines the steps for planning and implementing a method of individualized instruction based on portfolio assessment in infant, toddler, and preschool classrooms. While dramatic differences in development are found in this broad age range, portfolios can help teachers plan instruction and look for growth over a long period of time as the portfolios move with children when they change classrooms or programs. Also, this method allows the teacher to look for growth and progress in individual children, rather than comparing a child to other children in the group. A child's strengths and progress over time become the focus, rather than concern about rate of development.

Another purpose for portfolios is to foster the growth of the whole child based on the philosophy and goals of the program. The system described in this chapter is designed to help set individual goals and to incorporate age- and individually appropriate activities into lesson plans. Portfolios, when used in this manner, are not intended to serve as a screening tool to identify children with special needs, but rather to highlight growth in the individual child.

PORTFOLIO ASSESSMENT

The Southern Early Childhood Association established five criteria to follow in developing appropriate assessment for young children. Grace and Shores (1992, pp. xi-xii) state these criteria as follows:

- *Assessment must be valid.* It must provide information related to the goals and objectives of a program.
- *Assessment must encompass the whole child.* Programs must have goals and assessment procedures [that] relate to children's physical, social, emotional, and cognitive development.
- *Assessment must involve repeated observations.* Each child should be compared to his or her own individual course of development over time, rather than being compared to average behavior for a group.
- *Assessment must use a variety of methods.* Gathering a wide variety of information from different sources permits informed and professional decision-making.

In order to meet the above criteria, proponents for appropriate assessment of young children advocate using portfolios as the method for data collection and for individualized planning.

Establishing the Portfolio. Meisels and Steele (1991) define an assessment portfolio as "a collection of a child's work [that] demonstrates the child's efforts, progress and achievements over time. Accumulation of a portfolio involves the child and the teacher as they compile the materials, discuss them, and make instructional decisions" (p. 5).

Materials collected depend on the age of the child and the program focus. For instance, data collection for infants will differ from that for preschoolers, while data collection for a full-day program will differ from that for a half-day program. Some suggested items to include in the portfolio are teacher observations such as anecdotal records, checklists, rating scales, and/or narratives. Health records, photographs, audiotapes, videotapes, child work samples with interpretive forms, summaries of parent/teacher conferences, and parental input also could be included (Martin, 1994). In order to document a child's growth, documents must be collected over a period of time and evaluated at regularly scheduled intervals during the learning process. It is vital to collect data in the course of a child's normal activities, rather than creating artificial situations for collection. "To be meaningful, the samples must be preserved in the portfolio over the entire period that the child is enrolled in the program. A collection of work samples gathered over a few weeks will reveal little about a child's development" (Grace & Shores, 1992, p. 25). Data collected should reflect the whole child by representing all domains of learning. These might include documentation of social, emotional, physical, cognitive, creative, and language development.

An early childhood classroom portfolio can be organized in many ways. Grace and Shores (1992) suggest a variety of methods for storing data collection, including accordion folders, pizza boxes, x-ray folders, or manila folders (p. 21). Wortham (1995) suggests that the method of collection selected must be easily accessible to parents, teachers, and children.

> As the authors planned for the process they wanted to use, they were mindful that many teachers are uncertain how to proceed when they first engage in portfolio assessment. Teachers often gather a collection of materials for each child and then hesitate in just how to evaluate development and learning using those materials. In this setting, the authors wanted to be able to guide teachers through the data collection process into appropriate assessment. Furthermore, they wanted their teachers to be able to plan curriculum experiences based on individual development. As they described the process for portfolio use, they considered each step of the process so that the materials they developed could be used for training their staff.—SW

The Process. As previously stated, much has been written about the portfolio collection process, but teachers have little information to help them make the connection from data collection to individualized planning. For portfolios to be beneficial for planning, several steps must precede and follow data collection. Merely collecting data does not provide a framework for individually and culturally appropriate curriculum. Meisels's Work Sampling System (1993) and Schweinhart's High Scope Child Observation Record (1993) are detailed methods of data collection and assessment. Grace and Shores (1992) also discuss methods of authentic assessment, but no one has yet provided the detailed steps needed to assist the teacher in moving from data collection to individualized planning.

The *program planning process* (philosophy, program goals, performance objectives) provides the strong foundation necessary for individualized planning. During the *individualized planning process,* data for portfolios are collected, interpreted, and analyzed. Parental input is sought and individualized activities are planned. Finally, activities from the individualized planning profiles are included in the lesson plan during the integration process (Figure 3.1).

The process for individualized planning based on portfolio assessment is consistent for children birth to age 5. What will differ for children at different ages are the methods of data collection. For instance, a portfolio for a 3-month-old child might include checklists, anecdotal records, audiotapes, photographs, and/or videotapes. The portfolio will expand to include work samples as the child grows and gains new skills.

THE PROCESS

STAGE I   PROGRAM PLANNING PROCESS

1. Develop a **program philosophy** that reflects how children learn, the program's developmental focus, the role of the teacher, and the role of the family.
2. Develop **program goals** that support the program philosophy.
3. Develop **performance objectives** for the program goals.

STAGE II   INDIVIDUALIZED PLANNING PROCESS

4. Determine the data to be collected (based on the performance objectives), develop a timeline and the method of portfolio organization. Begin the collection process for each child.
5. Based on an informal observation period, complete an **individualized planning profile** for each child. The profiles at this stage will indicate what additional information the teacher needs to collect.
6. At least three times a year, evaluate each portfolio. Check each domain for an over- or underabundance of collected data. As needed, update the **individualized planning profiles**.
7. Share each child's **individualized planning profile** with parent(s) at least twice a year. Hold dialogues with parents to gain an awareness and understanding of the home culture, including their expectations for the child. Update each child's profile to reflect parent input and observations.

STAGE III   INTEGRATION PROCESS

8. Each time lesson plans are developed, review **individualized planning profiles**. From each profile, prioritize areas needing improvement and select activities to include in the lesson plan.

Figure 3.1

Steps for Individualized Planning Based on Portfolio Assessment

Stage 1: The Program Planning Process. Meisels (1993) describes a portfolio as "a purposeful collection of children's work that illustrates their efforts, progress, and achievements . . ." (p. 34). This collection of work becomes purposeful, as opposed to haphazard, when it is based on a planned method that demonstrates to the teacher and parents that work is collected for a reason. The purpose of the collection is to support those established program goals and objectives that are age- and individually appropriate for furthering a child's growth. In order to support this planning process, teachers must collect work that reflects established performance objectives based on program goals dictated by a clearly defined philosophy. A detailed description of the steps in this process follows:

1. Develop a program philosophy *that reflects how children learn, the program's developmental focus, the role of the teacher, and the role of the family.*

The program philosophy is a very broad set of beliefs, based on theory that guides the program. Generally, a philosophy reflects a program's beliefs regarding four important areas. First, a program must define assumptions about how children learn. Child development theory on learning falls into three major categories: environmental, maturational, and interactional. Program developers must decide which approach or combination of approaches best reflects their beliefs.

Second, the philosophy must accurately describe the developmental focus of the program. If a philosophy states that it reflects the whole child, then the curriculum must include activities that meet the needs of the whole child. For example, a program that truly supports the whole child must include outdoor play in its daily schedule.

> When questioned, most administrators would state that they value the optimum development of the whole child—the social, emotional, physical, creative, and cognitive development of the child. Concern for the development of the whole child may be stated, but careful analysis reveals that cognitive outcomes are given priority over social/emotional goals or vice versa. (Sciarra & Dorsey, 1995, p. 17)

Finally, it is important that the philosophy reflect the role of both the teacher and the family. Is the teacher's job one of a facilitator, observer, or planner, or of a powerful figure that imparts knowledge? Does the family enter into curriculum planning or is this the sole responsibility of the teacher? The philosophy that forms the foundation for the program at San Antonio College is found in Figure 3.2.

2. *Develop* program goals *that support the program philosophy.*

Program goals can be defined as broad outcomes that children will achieve over a period of time. An example of a goal would be, "The child acquires fine motor skills." As stated earlier, program goals must support the center's philosophy. Programs may either establish

---

San Antonio College Child Development Center

PROGRAM PHILOSOPHY

The San Antonio College Child Development Center is designed to meet the needs of the whole child, including the areas of social, emotional, creative, physical, cognitive, and language development. The curriculum emphasizes developmentally appropriate play experiences. The environment is carefully planned to provide quality care and education for young children. This approach recognizes the uniqueness of each child and their family. Adults involved in the child's life actively participate in decisions affecting the care of the child. To help children reach their maximum potential, our program solicits parental input and utilizes authentic assessment in the planning of individualized experiences. The daily schedule is organized to meet the children's needs for a balance of active and quiet play, large- and small-group interactions, and indoor and outdoor activities. The role of the teacher is to:

- respect and respond to family culture
- schedule the days' activities
- provide a variety of activities, materials, and equipment
- observe, assess, and provide for individual needs
- stimulate children's learning by listening, questioning, giving choices, making suggestions, and allowing for a balance between child-centered and teacher-initiated activities
- foster creativity
- reinforce and enhance curiosity
- serve as a role model.

Figure 3.2

their own goals or adopt goals that reflect their philosophy. It is important to modify goals on individual bases, in order to respect and incorporate family culture. The goals for the Child Development Center at San Antonio College are shown in Figure 3.3.

3. *Develop* performance objectives *for the program goals.*

Performance objectives are specific, observable behaviors that are age appropriate for a classroom. These are "the paths or steps that lead to the goals" (Click, 1995, p. 82). "Child snips paper held by another person" is an example of a performance objective that addresses a fine motor development goal. When used at the classroom level, these performance objectives measure a child's growth. Data in the portfolio is visual proof that supports the child's level of performance. Like goals, performance objectives can be written specifically for the individual program. Because of the detailed nature of this work,

---

PROGRAM GOALS

The goals of the SAC Child Development Center support development of the whole child, including the areas of social, emotional, creative, physical, cognitive, and language development.

Our program encourages children to:

- develop a positive self-concept and attitude toward learning, self-control, and a sense of belonging
- develop relationships of mutual trust and respect with adults and peers, understand perspectives of other people, and negotiate and apply rules of group living
- understand and respect social and cultural diversity
- know about the community and social roles
- develop curiosity about the world, confidence as a learner, creativity and imagination, and personal initiative
- represent ideas and feelings through pretend play, drama, dance and movement, music, art, and construction
- become competent in the management of their bodies and acquire basic physical skills, both gross motor and fine motor
- gain knowledge about the care of their bodies and maintain a desirable level of health and fitness
- think critically, reason, and solve problems
- construct understanding of relationships among objects, people, and events, such as classifying, ordering, numbers, space, and time
- construct knowledge of the physical world, manipulate objects for desired effects, and understand cause-and-effect relationships
- acquire knowledge of and appreciation for the fine arts, humanities, and sciences
- use language to communicate effectively and to facilitate thinking and learning
- become literate individuals who gain satisfaction, as well as information, from reading and writing.

Goals taken from: National Association for the Education of Young Children, & National Association of Early Childhood Specialists in State Department of Education. (1991). Guidelines for appropriate curriculum content and assessment in programs serving 3 through 8. *Young Children, 46.*

Figure 3.3

however, a program may find it easier to adapt performance objectives from a checklist that reflects the goals of the program. The performance objectives in Figure 3.4 support the program goal: "The children will become competent in management of their bodies and acquire basic physical skills, both gross and fine motor."

Stage 2: The Individualized Planning Process. The individualized planning process involves collecting appropriate data, based on a timeline. This collection is used to analyze the growth of each child in a classroom and to plan beneficial activities that will help each child's growth in all domains.

San Antonio College Child Development Center

PERFORMANCE OBJECTIVES PHYSICAL DOMAIN
Classroom for 3-year-olds

The following performance objectives support the program goal:

**"The children will become competent in management
of their bodies and acquire basic physical skills,
both gross motor and fine motor."**

	Introduced	Progress	Mastery
MOTOR DEVELOPMENT			
Gross Movement			
1. Catches a ball with both hands against the chest			
2. Rides a tricycle			
3. Hops on both feet several times without assistance			
4. Throws a ball five feet with accuracy			
5. Climbs up a slide and comes down			
6. Climbs by alternating feet and holding onto a handrail			
7. Stands on one foot and balances briefly			
8. Pushes a loaded wheelbarrow			
9. Runs freely with little stumbling or falling			
10. Builds a tower with nine or ten blocks			
Fine Movement			
1. Places small pegs in pegboards			
2. Holds a paintbrush or pencil with the whole hand			
3. Eats with a spoon			
4. Buttons large buttons on his or her own clothes			
5. Puts on coat unassisted			
6. Strings beads with ease			
7. Hammers a pound toy with accuracy			
8. Works a three- or four-piece puzzle			

Frost-Wortham Developmental Checklist: Level II. Used by permission of J. L. Frost.

Figure 3.4

4. Determine the data to be collected (based on the performance objectives), develop a timeline and the method of portfolio organization. Begin the collection process for each child.

For each performance objective, determine how to collect data throughout the year. For instance, anecdotal records might serve as a method of data collection to document a child's ability to separate from a parent, while an interpretive data form, listing the stages of block building, might be used to help determine the child's stage of cognitive development. A variety of data collection methods should be used so that the teacher can choose what will best document the growth of children in the classroom. Care should be taken to ensure that data is collected that will document growth for each performance objective. An example of an interpretive data form is shown in Figure 3.5. Additional interpretive forms can be found in Appendix B.

Data may be collected in many different ways. Checklists, narrative reports, anecdotal records, photographs, videotapes, audiotapes, and/or work samples (with or without interpretive forms) may be used.

Develop a timeline to indicate when data will be collected for each performance objective. It is unrealistic and unnecessary to collect data in each domain on a weekly basis.

Name_____ Date_____

LANGUAGE DEVELOPMENT

DIRECTIONS: Circle the stage of development that the child exhibits. Attach an Anecdotal Record or audiotape.

1. **SOUNDS**
   Crying, gurgling, and cooing are important first steps in the language learning process.
2. **BABBLING**
   Babbling encompasses all of the sounds found in all languages. Gradually, it becomes more specific with the syllables of the native language.
3. **HOLOPHRASES**
   Single words that reflect much meaning (e.g., "car" may mean "I want my toy car" or "Look at the car outside").
4. **TWO-WORD SENTENCES**
   Sentences of two words that often express ideas concerning relationships (e.g., "Mommy-sock" or "cat-sleeping").
5. **TELEGRAPHIC SENTENCES**
   Short and simple sentences that omit function words and endings that contribute little to meaning (e.g., "Where Daddy go?" or "Me push truck").
6. **JOINED SENTENCES**
   Child joins related sentences logically and expresses ideas.
7. **OVERGENERALIZATIONS**
   As children become more sophisticated in their language, they overgeneralize rules in ways that are inconsistent with common usage (e.g., "I comed home").

Source: Feeney, S., Christensen, D., & Moravcik, E. (1991). *Who am I in the lives of children?* New York: Macmillan.

Figure 3.5

Although data collection is time-consuming, the timeline will help set realistic expectations for the classroom teacher. The timeline should be structured to give a picture of the child's development over time in each domain, not a comparison of one child's development to other children in the classroom. For instance, data to document the child's stage of block building might be collected in September and then again in March, giving teachers and parents insight into the growth of the child and data for individualized planning.

Perrone (1991, p. 141) states that ". . . performance-based assessment guarantees a greater understanding of the growth of individual children, which should reduce the need for any of the testing programs that currently exist." Portfolios are not designed to be a developmental screening test to identify a child's special needs or need for intervention. If an educator suspects that child might have a developmental delay or might require special services, an early intervention program should be contacted to conduct developmental screening tests.

The timeline should also indicate when the portfolios will be evaluated throughout the year. In the "Work Sampling System," Meisels (1993) recommends that data in the portfolio be evaluated at least three times a year. In addition to eliciting parent input and sharing the contents of the portfolio, the timeline should include parent conferences. A sample timeline follows in Figure 3.6.

The method for portfolio organization should meet the program's needs. It is important to consider the amount of space available, amount and size of data to be collected, children's and parents' ability to access the portfolio, and a format that will facilitate portfolio evaluation. *Week by Week: Plans for Observing and Recording Young Children* (Nilsen, 1997), *Take a Look* (Martin, 1994), and *The Portfolio and Its Use* (Grace & Shores, 1992) offer many suggestions for portfolio organization.

Collect data throughout the year as children interact with the environment and engage in typical classroom activities. Data collection for the portfolio should document interactions in the natural classroom environment, not in an artificial testing environment where young children are disconnected from classrooms and peers. Children may react adversely in an artificial setting and the results may not give a true picture of the child's growth.

In addition, parents should be encouraged to provide documentation for the portfolio, including such items as photographs, written accounts of events at home, enrollment forms, health records, information on the family tree, and/or biographical information about the child. Teachers must actively seek ways to obtain information about the child's family culture and about family goals for the child. Parental input helps ensure that individualized activities are culturally appropriate.

5. *Based on an informal observation period, complete an* individualized planning profile *for each child. The profiles at this stage will indicate what additional information the teacher needs to collect.*

Teachers' informal observations and parents' knowledge of their child provide an excellent starting point for completing the profile. After approximately two weeks of informal observation and eliciting information from parents, teachers will record known information on the profile. Those areas lacking information will be targeted for further observation and data collection. Figure 3.7 shows an individualized planning profile for Ricky, while Figure 3.8 provides an individualized plan for Victoria.

6. *At least three times a year, evaluate each portfolio. Check each domain for an over- or underabundance of collected data. As needed, update the* individualized planning profiles.

The child's strengths and areas that need work are determined by analyzing the portfolio. By focusing on weaker areas, teachers can plan classroom activities to enhance the environment and maximize the child's learning experiences.

San Antonio College Child Development Center

TIMELINE
for
Portfolio Data Collection
Parent Conferences
Portfolio Evaluation

Months

Tasks	J	F	M	A	M	J	J	A	S	O	N	D
Collect gross motor physical domain data												
Collect fine motor physical domain data												
Collect emotional domain data												
Collect social domain data												
Collect language domain data												
Collect cognitive domain data												
Parent conferences												
Portfolio evaluation (at least 3 times a year)												
Notes:												

Figure 3.6

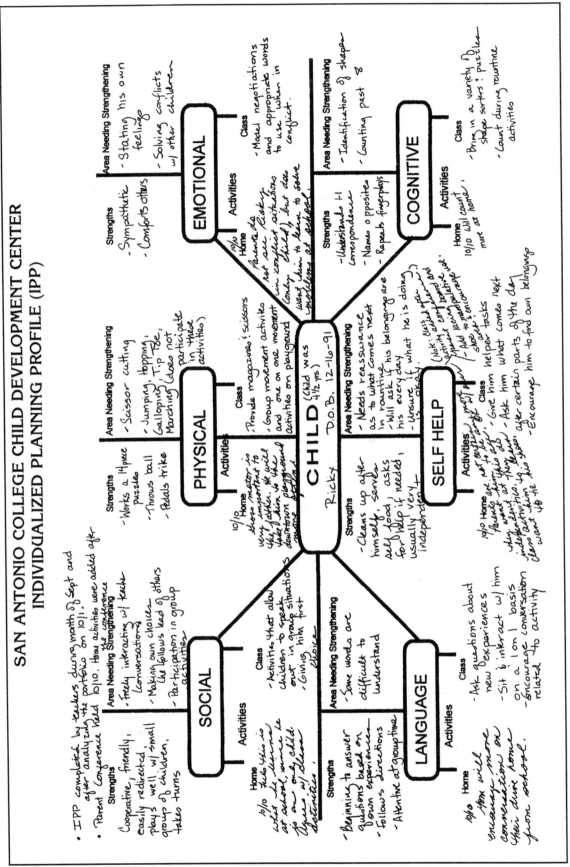

SAN ANTONIO COLLEGE CHILD DEVELOPMENT CENTER
INDIVIDUALIZED PLANNING PROFILE (IPP)

CHILD (Child was 4½ yrs)
Ricky   D.o.B. 12-16-91

- IPP completed by teachers during month of Sept and after analyzing the portfolio on 10/1.
- Parent Conference held 10/10. Home activities were added after the conference.

EMOTIONAL

Area Needing Strengthening
- Stating his own feelings
- Solving conflicts w/ other children

Strengths
- Sympathetic
- Comforts others

Class
- Model negotiations and appropriate words to use when in conflict.

Activities

Home 10/10
Parents do not see Ricky in conflict situations (only child), but are working to learn to solve problems at school.

COGNITIVE

Area Needing Strengthening
- Identification of shapes
- Counting past 8

Strengths
- Understands 1-1 correspondence
- Names opposites
- Repeats fingerplays

Class
- Bring in a variety of puzzles, shape sorters; puzzles
- Count during routine activities

Home 10/10 Will count more at home

PHYSICAL

Area Needing Strengthening
- Scissor cutting
- Jumping, Hopping, Galloping, Tip Toe, Marching (does not participate in these activities)

Strengths
- Works a 14 piece puzzle
- Throws ball
- Pedals trike

Class
- Provide magazines; scissors
- Group movement activities and one on one movement activities on playground

Activities

Home 10/10
these motor is very important to they father who will take him to the downtown playground more often

SELF HELP

Area Needing Strengthening
- Needs reassurance as to what comes next in routine
- Will ask if his belongings are his every day
- Unsure if what he is doing is okay.

Strengths
- Cleans up after himself, serves self food, asks for help if needed, usually very independent

Class
(Note: class activities spread accross curriculum)
- Add more reassurance to maintain use
- Give him helper tasks
- Give him what come next
- Ask him

Activities

Home 10/10 Home
Parents are not willing to let him want him at home do independent activities (clean up shoes dressing beyond) Ask him clean him his shoes after certain parts of the day
- Encourage him to find own belongings
- want him to

SOCIAL

Area Needing Strengthening
- Freely interacting w/ teacher conversations
- Making own choices (he follows lead of others)
- Participation in group activities

Strengths
- Cooperative, friendly, easily redirected, plays well w/ small group of children, takes turns

Class
- Activities that allow children to speak out in group situations
- Giving him first choice

Activities

Home 10/10
what he wants to at school, wants to an only child plays w/ older activities.

LANGUAGE

Area Needing Strengthening
- Some words are difficult to understand

Strengths
- Beginning to answer questions based on own experience
- Follows directions
- Attentive at grouptime

Class
- Ask questions about new experiences
- Sit & interact w/ him on a 1 on 1 basis
- Encourage conversation related to activity

Activities

Home 10/10 Home
Mom will encourage more conversation on their drive home from school.

Figure 3.7

Case Study: Chris's teacher reviews the data collected in the physical domain. She notes that Chris is able to string beads, but that he has difficulty cutting with scissors. She marks "strings beads" as a strength on his individualized planning profile, but indicates that he needs work on "cutting with scissors." She reviews the data and records pertinent information for each domain in the same manner.

This step is vital, as it provides the information necessary to plan appropriate individualized activities. Grace and Shores (1992) emphasize ". . . that teachers should use a comprehensive compilation of developmental stages and characteristics when evaluating the entire portfolio" (p. 26). After identifying the child's strengths and areas needing strengthening in each domain, educators can plan classroom activities accordingly.

Each child's portfolio should be analyzed at least three times a year to look for growth and to reevaluate which areas need strengthening and supplemental activities. This process may occur more often if a child acquires a certain skill or if circumstances dictate extra attention. For example, if a child is coping with a recent move or with the birth of a sibling, teachers should change activities in the emotional domain to help the child adapt to the situation.

As portfolios are evaluated, check the adequacy of data collected in each domain. The teacher may find a great deal of documentation on the physical development of a child, very little documentation about the child's social development, and adequate documentation regarding emotional, language, and cognitive skills. The teacher then can try to collect data in the area of social development. Another child's portfolio may indicate that more physical development data needs to be collected. Collection patterns can be adjusted as needed throughout the year.

7. Share each child's individualized planning profile *with parents at least twice a year. Hold dialogues with parents to gain an awareness and understanding of the home culture, including their expectations for the child. Update each child's profile to reflect parent input and observations.*

Parent conferences provide an avenue for formal review of the profiles. At this time, parents can share home activities, which are recorded on the profile. While informal dialogue occurs throughout the year, formal conferences allow for in-depth dialogue regarding family and classroom goals for the child. It is important to continually realign goals so that they reflect family expectations.

Case Study: Chris's teacher knows he frequently chooses the art center, so she provides colorful paper scraps and encourages him to snip scraps for collages. During a parent conference, the parent agrees that this is an area to target, and so decides that she will have her child use safety scissors to cut coupons at home. The teacher records this as a home activity on the profile.

Stage 3: The Integration Process. The integration process incorporates individualized activities into the lesson plan. This process, which occurs throughout the year, is a compilation of ongoing data collection, analysis, and dialogue between parents and teachers.

8. Each time lesson plans are developed, review individualized planning profiles. *From each profile, prioritize areas needing improvement and select activities to include in the lesson plan.*

This step is critical in order to bridge the gap between data collection and individualized planning. After reviewing the profiles, the teacher must decide which activities to select for inclusion in the lesson plan. It would be unrealistic to believe that *all* activities for all children can be included in each lesson plan. Guidelines for activity selection are deter-

INDIVIDUALIZED PLANNING PROFILE: INFANTS AND TODDLERS

Child
Victoria (10 mts)

Physical

Emerging skills
Stand on her own

Activities
encourage her to use
cruise bar & coax her
to "let go" & fingers
of adult

Emotional

Emerging skills
dealing w/ separation

Activities
Label feelings & promote
interest in other things
in environment.
Encourage her to wave bye-bye
to mom

Cognitive

Emerging skills
find hidden objects

Activities
play "Where is it?"
with object & mommy.
Containers, cloth etc.

Social

Emerging skills
imitation –

Activities
Model imitation skills by
mimicing her actions - ex)
She shakes toy/adult will shake toy.
encourage behavior by
reinforcement

Language

Emerging skills
imitate voice intonation
patterns

Activities
Simple holophrases)
with variety & intonation.
Mirror back her intonation encourage her to hold cup with 2 hands
and drink from it.

Self-Help

Emerging skills
holding sippy cup

Activities
encourage her to hold cup with 2 hands
and drink from it.

Figure 3.8

mined in response to parent/teacher dialogue. Throughout the year, in various lesson plans, the teacher strives to include individualized activities from each domain. Unplanned, individualized activities that occur in a child's typical day can be noted on the profile. For example, a child's profile indicated that conflict resolution was an area that needed strengthening. While the activity of "negotiation" was not included on a particular lesson plan, the teacher implemented this strategy in a conflict situation. The teacher noted this event on the child's profile.

CONCLUSION

A program foundation is built with clear philosophy, goals, and objectives. With this foundation, portfolio assessment and a strong interpretive element provide the basis for individualized planning. There is no guarantee that age-appropriate curriculum will meet the needs of individual children. To ensure individually and culturally appropriate curriculum, it is critical that early childhood teachers adopt a planned, structured approach.

This process can be overwhelming! To become familiar with the individualized planning process, begin slowly by planning for one or two domains. Gradually include the remaining domains in the planning process. It may take several years for this process to be fully integrated into your program. The time investment in appropriate assessment and individualized planning cannot be underestimated. It is as critical as time spent interacting with children, and should be given adequate attention in a teacher's day.

Peggy and Sandy have implemented the portfolio process at San Antonio College for three years. They have modified some of their process to meet the time constraints of their teachers. Their portfolio system continues to evolve as they and their staff gain more experience with the young children they serve. —SW

REFERENCES

Click, P. (1995). *Administration of schools for young children* (4th ed.). Albany, NY: Delmar.

Grace, C., & Shores, E. (1992). *The portfolio and its use.* Little Rock, AR: Southern Association on Children Under Six.

Martin, S. (1994). *Take a look: Observation and portfolio assessment in early childhood.* Don Mills, Ontario: Addison-Wesley.

Meisels, S. (1993). Remaking classroom assessment with the work sampling system. *Young Children, 48*, 34-40.

Meisels, S., & Steele, D. (1991). *The early childhood portfolio process.* Ann Arbor, MI: University of Michigan Center for Human Growth and Development.

National Association for the Education of Young Children, & National Association of Early Childhood Specialists in State Department of Education. (1991). Guidelines for appropriate curriculum content and assessment in programs serving 3 through 8. *Young Children, 46*.

Nilsen, B. (1997). *Week by week: Plans for observing and recording young children.* Albany, NY: Delmar Publishers.

Perrone, V. (1991). On standardized testing. *Childhood Education, 67*, 132-142.

Schweinhart, L. (1993). Observing young children in action: The key to early childhood assessment. *Young Children, 48*, 29-33.

Sciarra, D., & Dorsey, A. (1995). *Developing and administering a child care center.* Albany, NY: Delmar.

Wortham, S. (1995). *Measurement and evaluation in early childhood education* (2nd ed.). Englewood Cliffs, NJ: Merrill.

A Model of Portfolio Assessment in Prekindergarten Through Primary Grades

INTRODUCTION

As we approach the 21st century, elementary educators are continuing the effort to improve academic achievement for all young children. In the preschool and primary grades, this effort is linked to the need for educational programs that recognize children's individual developmental levels and cultural backgrounds. This chapter describes how preschool through 2nd-grade educators at one elementary school have engaged in the process of restructuring their schools to better serve their students and families. The model presented here focuses on a multiage setting for students from low-income families, who generally do not meet their potential for learning in public schools. However, the steps in design and implementation, as well as examples of performance strategies and recordkeeping instruments, are useful for any early childhood setting. The sections that follow include discussions of the setting and the process of restructuring curriculum and evaluation for portfolio assessment, the steps in using portfolio assessment, and the experience of teachers learning to use portfolios.

The Setting: Multiage Classrooms in an Inner City Elementary School. Public elementary schools are attended by children of every type. Their parents may be poor, middle-class, or affluent. Their parents may be blue- or white-collar workers, or may be unemployed. Some children in elementary schools find they can manage learning easily. Others, for one reason or another, find their first attempts at successful learning to be difficult. Children who are from a low-income home or whose first language is not English may have difficulty achieving in school. These children may have a limited English vocabulary and limited understanding of concepts necessary for academic learning. School restructuring is considered a way to enhance learning for children who encounter such difficulties.

New strategies and programs are continually being proposed for elementary school. Yet, school

Sue Wortham

restructuring goes beyond these efforts for improvement; major changes are required (Newmann, 1991). Before a school can be reorganized, however, it must be dismantled. Practices and policies that do not support successful learning must be eliminated (Corbett & Blum, 1993).

The model presented in this chapter represents elementary school restructuring for children in the early childhood years from ages 4 to 8, or prekindergarten through 2nd grade. The rationale for restructuring is congruent with current approaches to developmentally appropriate curriculum and instruction (Bredekamp, 1987; Bredekamp & Copple, 1997). This reorganization follows the belief that a developmentally appropriate program uses curriculum and instruction that views the child's development as a continuum, rather than something achieved according to grade level. If curriculum and instruction is continuous and complements the child's development, the goals of enhancing achievement and reducing retention will be reached. Moreover, the program presented in this model is based on the theories of Jean Piaget (1963) and Lev Vygotksy (1978), as well as other constructivist learning theorists, who believe the child reconstructs learning through active interaction with the environment. A child's learning is supported and influenced by home, culture, and social relationships in the school.

A program that is continuous and developmental can be achieved through multiage grouping. Such grouping can be designed with many variations: one teacher can teach the same group of children for multiple years, or children of more than one age can be grouped together in a classroom. Whatever the organization, the goal is to have differentiated curriculum and instruction that maximizes learning for all children. Children benefit from different levels of learning experiences that meet their developmental levels, interests, and learning styles. Whole class instruction is minimized; conversely, small-group and individual instruction are used for a majority of instructional time. In addition, child-initiated and child-directed learning are the focus of curriculum and instruction.

The Decision Process: Selecting Portfolio Assessment. A multiage early childhood classroom that focuses on the child's individual development and learning needs must have an evaluation system that also is appropriate for assessing the child's development and learning. In this model, portfolio assessment is the best choice to reflect each child's developmental progress and learning, because child-initiated and child-directed learning are best evaluated by examples of the child's performance. Portfolio assessments permit the child, the teacher, and the parents to trace the child's progress through examples of the child's work over a period of time.

Teachers who are in the process of school restructuring using this model must evaluate how they have been teaching and assessing children and consider the implications of a multiage classroom. They must understand performance assessment that relies on the child's ability to demonstrate how knowledge is applied, rather than assessment that measures merely what the child understands. Performance assessment indicates that the child must be able to *use* new information in meaningful work. Memorizing or repeating information is not significant. The ability to apply information in a realistic context is most important for lifelong learning. Portfolio assessment reflects such realistic, meaningful learning (Hills, 1992).

Restructuring Curriculum and Instruction for Portfolio Assessment. At the beginning of this chapter, school restructuring was described as dismantling a school and reorganizing it to achieve improved learning for all students. Deciding to use portfolio assessment is a part of the plan for reconstructing the school. Curriculum and instruction also must be dismantled and reconstructed in order to design an instructional approach that meets the needs of at-risk children. Each child's development and learning strengths must be considered in order to facilitate learning and ensure individual success. Curriculum experiences planned for a chronological age are replaced by those that can help children at different chronological ages and developmental levels, regardless of their backgrounds or preparation. In the next part of this chapter, the process of reorganizing curriculum, instruction, and portfolio assessment will be described in more detail to demonstrate how teachers remodel their own philosophy of the teaching-learning process when they design a new model for schooling in the early childhood grades.

STEPS IN USING PORTFOLIO ASSESSMENT

The steps for implementing portfolio assessment as described in the following sections reflect the experiences of a team of prekindergarten, kindergarten, 1st-grade, and 2nd-grade teachers who worked with their principal for three years at Roosevelt Elementary School, in Edgewood Independent School District in San Antonio, Texas, to implement school restructuring and portfolio assessment. During the first year, the team visited schools that had multiage projects in order to study how schools successfully designed curriculum and instruction for traditionally low-achieving children. It was not until the second and third years of observation, however, that the principal and team followed the steps described below.

Establishing a Program Philosophy. Before restructuring, Roosevelt Elementary School had a traditional organization. Teachers at each grade level taught in self-contained classrooms. The curriculum was based upon learning objectives established at the state level for each grade. Letter grades were given based upon weekly tests and teacher evaluations. Preschool children did not receive letter grades; rather, they received progress reports concerning their mastery or nonmastery of learning objectives. The teachers and the principal were not clear about the philosophy that guided their program, other than that the children were expected to perform well on the state-mandated achievement exams that are administered beginning in the 3rd grade.

Curriculum and instruction was teacher-planned and -directed. Preschool teachers used learning centers to support learning themes and used large- and small-group instruction. Primary grade teachers used mostly teacher-directed learning strategies and depended upon basal materials for instruction.

The first step in restructuring the school was to determine a philosophy for the program. The team reviewed theories of learning and determined that they needed to move from a behaviorist and maturational orientation toward a constructivist approach. That is, they needed to change from a teacher-directed program that focused on instruction for a whole class, to a constructivist approach that complemented children's current accomplishments and development.

The multiage program's philosophy was that all children can learn. The theories of Jean Piaget and Lev Vygotsky, emphasizing that children reconstruct knowledge through interactions with the world, served as the foundation for that philosophy. For this reconstruction to happen, children must have the opportunity to encounter new experiences, be provided with additional activities that help them make connections with the new information, and integrate the new information into a broader understanding. Each child brings different past experiences to the newly acquired knowledge and will construct further knowledge within an individual perspective. Furthermore, children will acquire knowledge differently depending upon their thinking style and developmental level.

To achieve this approach or philosophy, the learning process must be child-centered.

Teachers structure the environment and learning activities to permit the child to take the initiative for interacting with, rather than being a passive recipient of, new information. Learning takes place in exchanges among children, and between children and adults (Bodrova & Leong, 1996). Active learning within the social context means that the child learns by active involvement with information and with other children and/or adults. Real-life problem solving places that learning in a meaningful context (New, 1992). Roosevelt teachers further described their philosophy through the following beliefs:

> - All children are lifelong learners
> - All children need to feel successful
> - Learning is a shared experience involving students, family, community, and educators
> - Students succeed in a loving, nurturing environment
> - Children learn to read by reading.

Developing Teaching and Learning Strategies for Multiage Classrooms. To be able to restructure their early childhood program, team teachers needed to examine their current teaching strategies and determine how they would redesign learning experiences to provide the children with cognitive-developmental learning strategies. They determined to use strategies that would focus on their role as curriculum designers rather than as dispensers of knowledge. Instead of depending upon commercial, pre-planned curriculum kits and teacher guides, they would use those resources as sources of information in their design of curriculum and instruction. The teacher's role would be to use the environment and teaching activities to facilitate learning; rather than instruction being primarily teacher-directed, however, it would emphasize possibilities for the child to take the initiative, make selections, and assume active responsibility for their own learning.

Children's learning strategies would be facilitated through opportunities for active learning. The ingredients of active learning described by Hohmann and Weikart (1995) reflected the strategies that multiage teachers wanted to provide for their children:

> - *Materials.* There are abundant, age-appropriate materials that the child can use in a variety of ways. Learning grows out of the child's direct actions on the materials.
> - *Manipulation.* The child has opportunities to explore, manipulate, combine, and transform the materials chosen.
> - *Choice.* The child chooses what to do. Since learning results from the child's attempts to pursue personal interests and goals, the opportunity to choose activities and materials is essential.
> - *Language of the child.* The child describes what he or she is doing. Through language, the child reflects on those actions, integrates new experiences into an existing knowledge base, and seeks the cooperation of others.
> - *Adult support.* Adults recognize and encourage the child's reasoning, problem solving, and creativity. The concept of active learning is used to describe how adults initiate and use a child-centered program that is appropriate for groups and individuals. (p. 38)

Teachers also considered how to adapt their learning strategies for children with disabilities who were included in their program. They also recognized that they needed to reflect the family and community cultures represented in the classroom. Because the students were predominantly Hispanic, an understanding of their own and other cultures would be incorporated into curriculum and teaching/learning strategies.

Establishing Class Organization and the Environment.

- **Class Organization.** A major step in restructuring was to move from self-contained, grade level classrooms to multiage team teaching. After many discussions, the team decided to have two multiage units. The first unit was comprised of prekindergarten and kindergarten. Children would enter the program at the prekindergarten level and remain in that classroom until the end of kindergarten. Each teacher in the preschool team had a group of children who moved to the 1st-2nd grade unit each year, a new group of prekindergarten students, and a group of children who remained as kindergartners. The primary grade unit included 1st- and 2nd-grade students. Team teachers had a balance of 6- and 7-year-old children. In addition, some children were assigned to the district bilingual program, in which designated bilingual teachers taught students whose dominant language was Spanish.

  The two unit teams functioned as a larger team. Although the classrooms remained mostly self-contained, all planning was conducted as a team. In addition, some teachers within the 1st-2nd grade unit exchanged children for some activities during the day. The multiage team described their multiage model as having the following goals:

- Elimination of age and grade levels
- Inclusion of a range of developmental levels in the makeup of the classroom
- A curriculum that is challenging and that provides all children opportunities for success
- Curriculum and instruction guided by a continuum of competencies.

- **Organizing the Classroom Environment.** A major step involved reorganization of the classroom learning environment. The teachers were accustomed to predominantly whole-class instruction; as a result, they had to rethink the classroom organization in order to create a multiage classroom that used a cognitive-developmental approach. Their challenge was to understand how the classroom needed to change. They wanted to move from large-group instruction toward small-group and individual instruction, from teacher-directed instruction to a combination of teacher-directed and child-initiated instruction. After discussion, the multiage team proposed that their learning centers would:

- Be child-centered
- Complement thematic curriculum and content areas
- Provide differentiated curriculum for different developmental levels
- Vary in duration
- Accommodate individual interests.

They developed a Learning Center Guide Sheet to facilitate planning for learning centers and stations. The form provided for the center's objectives, the materials to be used, and the length of time the center would be in operation. In addition, provisions were made for describing three levels of activities to be conducted in the centers and how they would be assessed. Figure 4.1 shows the form used for learning center planning. The example in the figure is for a writing center in a kindergarten-1st grade classroom. The rubric for assessment is included in the boxes for assessment. Rubrics will be discussed later in this chapter.

To enhance teaming within the units, double doors were built between classrooms. This facilitated exchanges of children and enabled teachers and children to move between classrooms for combined activities.

The process for team teaching would include daily team interaction; exchange of students for various activities; weekly unit meetings to exchange ideas, plan, and evaluate strategies through group discussion; and monthly multiage team meetings.

Multiage team teachers described the restructuring process for classroom organization as progressions. They moved from student desks to tables; self-contained classrooms to teams of teachers; teacher-directed strategies to child-centered strategies; and whole-group classroom orientation to small-group orientation, using centers and differentiated activities for different levels.

LEARNING CENTER DEVELOPMENT GUIDE SHEET

Objective(s): The student will use descriptive language

Materials: paper, pencils, markers, pens

Duration: 1 week

Addressing different levels and Assessment:

Level	Activity/Expectation	Assessment
Pre-writer	The student will describe a picture using words	Rubric Uses pictures May copy letters or words Can write some familiar words
Developing Writer	The student will describe a picture using sentences. • upper and lower case letters • Some punctuation	Understands sound-symbol relationship Uses invented spelling Can read own writing
Experienced Writer	The student will describe a picture using sentences in a paragraph • Capitals used correctly • Correct punctuation	Using conventions of print in spelling Demonstrates sentence sense Can use correct punctuation and use of upper and lower case letters

Figure 4.1

Establishing the Curriculum. As was indicated in the discussion on reorganization, the restructured curriculum was divided into two categories. One component of the curriculum was content-specific for language arts and mathematics. The teachers designed the curriculum and instruction for these two content areas using a cognitive-developmental approach, which is based on a continuum of outcomes that range from prekindergarten through 3rd grade. The language arts curriculum focuses on the process of emergent literacy, interfaced with a language arts program model developed by Patricia Cunningham at Wake Forest University. The Cunningham model was organized into four instructional blocks: Basal, Self-Selected Reading, Writing, and Working with Words (Hall, Prevatte, & Cunningham, 1995). Figure 4.2 shows multiage reading strategies for literacy development.

The mathematics curriculum is based on learning objectives, or Essential Elements, established by the Texas Education Agency for the state's public schools. Mathematics instruction combines small-group and individual instruction with independent and self-selected activities within an hour of instructional time. Teachers conduct instruction based on individual and group progress. Students attend a small-group or individual lesson. They complete assigned work to practice or reinforce the skills they are learning, and select additional activities from the mathematics center. They might engage in a mathematics game with other students or work independently on a mathematics activity.

The second component of the curriculum is a thematic-integrated curriculum, which incorporates all developmental domains or content areas within units of study. The thematic units afford teachers the opportunity to be creative in a developing child-centered curriculum that enhances children's developmental levels, learning styles, and interests. Thematic curriculum is planned around a theme that students have identified as a learning topic, or that team teachers have selected based on children's interests or from curriculum objectives. Learning activities selected for the theme reflect how the students want to explore the topic or activities that they have identified as helpful for acquiring unit concepts. The team of teachers usually conducts some initial brainstorming about unit activities, and students also are included in the planning process. The curriculum is integrated, in that the teacher and students use a webbing process to determine how unit activities will incorporate content areas of the curriculum (Wortham, 1998). The integrated-thematic curriculum provides not only for integrated, purposeful learning, but also for developmental differences (Bredekamp & Copple, 1997). The selected activities will be planned to accommodate a range of developmental levels, so that all students will have successful experiences by being actively involved in unit projects (Katz & Chard, 1990).

Multiage teachers established the following guidelines for designing integrated-thematic curriculum:

- The students should have some input into the selection of themes and activities.
- The curriculum should be planned to ensure that the students move from activities that require teacher assistance to activities that promote independence (Bodrova & Leong, 1996).
- The ideas for units should take into consideration the entire team of teachers and the differing needs of students in individual classrooms (bilingual classrooms).
- Selected activities should be meaningful and include problem solving.

Both multiage units used a common form for planning unit activities through webbing, represented in Figure 4.3. The example shown in the web is for a unit on plants and nutrition for prekindergarten, kindergarten, and 1st-grade multiage classrooms.

ROOSEVELT ELEMENTARY SCHOOL
MULTIAGE READING STRATEGIES FOR LITERACY DEVELOPMENT THROUGH INITIAL AND ONGOING STUDENT ASSESSMENT

	Comprehension of Story	Reading	Writing	Oral Language

Pre-Literacy	A. D.L.T.A. Process*
	B. Techniques for Retelling
	  1. Felt Board
	  2. Prop stories/puppets
	  3. Chalk Talk
	  4. Sound Effects
	C. Story Mapping/Elements
	  1. Re-reading
	  2. One-to-One
	  3. Big Books
		A. Read Alouds/Re-reads
		  1. Silent reading/paired readings
		  2. Library/listening centers
		B. Language Experience Activities
		  1. Class books
		  2. Charts/lists
		  3. Word wall
		  4. Songs/poems
		C. Phonics
			A. Language Experience Activities
			B. Print Concepts
			  1. Left-to-Right using finger
			  2. Thought→print→reading
			  3. Letters/sounds (letter of week)
			  4. Identification of words/word wall/writes familiar words
			C. Writing
			  1. Journals
			  2. Pictures/pictures with dictation
			  3. Classbooks/individual
			  4. Penpals
			  5. Centers
				A. Story retelling
				  1. Questions=/ opinion (respond to story)
				  2. Repeating words and phrases
				  3. Retell from memory
				  4. Compares experiences to story
				  5. Language experiences
				  6. Word wall
				B. "Independent" Activities
				  1. Buzz groups**
				  2. Class books
				  3. Centers
				  4. Shared Reading
				  5. Circle sharing
				  6. Songs and chants

Beginning Literacy	Pre-Literacy Strategies and
	(C.) 4. Shared Reading
		Pre-Literacy Strategies and
		D. Reading Groups
		E. Trade Books/Basal Reading
		F. Phonics (letter of the week)
			Pre-Literacy Strategies and
			(B.) Print Concepts
			  1. Identify sentences (naming and action parts)
			  2. Invented spelling
			  3. Capitalization and punctuation
			(C.) Writing
			  1. Story writing
			  2. Descriptive writing
			  3. Process writing
			  4. Graphic organizers	

Primary Literacy	A. Story Readings
	  1. D.L.T.A.* Process
	  2. Pre/Post Reading Activities
		A. Basal Block
		  1. Mini-lessons
		  2. Reading by students
		    a. Guided Reading
		    b. Reading Task Time
		    c. Book Baskets
			A. To and For Students
			  1. Teacher models
			  2. Shared writing working with words
			  3. Structure writing
			  4. Process writing
				A. Buzz Groups**
				B. Poetry/Songs/Chants

These strategies can be used within each block as a mini-lesson as needed.

*D.L.T.A.: Directed Listening-Thinking Activity

**Buzz Groups: In small groups, students talk about something they did the day before; the teacher will call on them to share the information and then use that for sentences on the Daily Oral Language or Writer's Workshop.

Figure 4.2

ROOSEVELT ELEMENTARY SCHOOL PRE K–K THEMATIC WEB

Theme: Plants/Nutrition

Science
- I.D. characteristics of living things
- Name/label parts of plants & seeds
- I.D. the food groups
- I.D. resources of food groups
- I.D. sequence of events
- Observe changes in nature and daily growth

Resources
- Scholastics
- Library resources
- Region XX
- Science Lab
- Windows on Science

Assessments
- Checklists
- Narratives
- Journals
- Sample writings
- T.O. during centre activities
- Centre products

Social Studies:
- I.D. animals that give us food
- I.D. plants that give us food
- Compare and contrast farm life to city life.
- Explore food processing: From farm to Kitchen

Resources
- Scholastics
- Library Resources

Fine Arts:
- Express individual thoughts, ideas, and feelings through picture-making using burlap
- Create Pizza Puppets
- Create veg. & fruit-prints patterns.
- Create art collage, collec. W parts

Resource
- Little Red Hen
- Pumpkin Seed
- Carrot Seed
- Open Court
- Paper came
- Show Stop
- Scholastic

Math
- Count money and change
- Explore concepts of weight, mass, and volume through cooking.
- Estimate number of seeds in fruits
- Collect and graph growth of plants
- Form graphs by sorting and matching objects, size, and one-to-one correspond.
- Match objects in one-to-one correspondence

Resources
- Roswell Wall
- Anytime Math
- Manipulatives
- Scholastic

Language Arts/ Reading
- Draw conclusions and predict outcomes
- I.D. sequence of events
- I.D. main idea
- Recognize letters and sounds
- Create their plant growth book
- Share their feelings and stories through SLA
- Sound and invented spelling
- Predict probable outcomes
- Develop vocabulary in spoken language
- Engage in conversation by sharing ideas with others.
- Dictate ideas and feelings as they are recorded

Resources
- Scholastic

ESL
- Predict probable Outcomes
- Develop vocabulary; Understand the meaning of words in spoken language
- Engage in supportive conversation by sharing ideas with others
- Dictate ideas and feelings as they are recorded

Figure 4.3

Designing Assessment. The final step in restructuring the early childhood program at Roosevelt Elementary School was to design a new assessment system for the multiage organization of classrooms. Again, the old system had to be dismantled and a new approach to assessment planned to complement the goals of the program and the theoretical underpinnings of curriculum and instruction. Multiage team teachers began the process of deconstructing their practice of assessing in order to determine grades and then redesigning assessment to be more authentic and meaningful.

The new approach to assessment was based on the goal of informing teaching and improving learning (Mitchell & Neill, 1992). This meaningful approach to assessment had to be constructed for the multiage units. If assessment was to inform teaching and improve learning within a multiage arrangement, Roosevelt teachers determined that the following processes would be used:

- *Initial assessment at the beginning of the year would determine placement.* Classroom teachers would need to evaluate the current developmental and achievement status of each child at the beginning of the year. Children entering school for the first time would need an extensive initial assessment. For children remaining in a unit for a second year, or moving from the preschool to the primary unit, the initial assessment would be more in the nature of a "checkup."
- *Assessment would be ongoing.* Previously, assessment had been periodic, based on grading periods. Now, teachers were committed to continuous assessment in order to monitor development and learning progress. They would work to obtain information that would help them modify and adjust their teaching practices, in order to achieve their goal of improving student learning.
- *Performance assessments using portfolio assessments would be used to provide authentic information about children's progress.* Teachers studied strategies they could use that would closely link assessment with a constructivist educational program. In addition, they also searched for appropriate strategies to help students at risk for learning difficulties, bilingual students, and students with disabilities who were included in regular classrooms.
- *Improvement and refinement of portfolio assessment would be systematic.* Understanding that using portfolio assessment would require experience and practice, the teachers recognized that they would have to evaluate the process and regularly modify their strategies for using portfolios. This process is discussed in the next section.

Initiating and Refining Portfolio Assessment.
- **Determining the Purposes for the Portfolio.** There are many types of portfolios; some are for the teachers to use for evaluation, while others are for students to showcase their best work for parents. In the case of the multiage units at Roosevelt Elementary School, the portfolios are for both student evaluation and to highlight student work. Some of the entries are selected by teachers. Students also have the opportunity to select examples of their best work. The purposes, then, are to assess student development and achievement, to document student performance, and to share student progress with parents and other teachers. The role of parents is significant. Portfolio assessment is a new process for them. They need to not only understand how portfolio assessment differs from traditional report cards, but also how to appreciate their opportunity to be involved in their children's evaluation.

- **Determining the Format for the Portfolio.** Initially, a simple folder system was selected for storing portfolio contents. Later, boxes were used when teachers began to incorporate cassette tapes. Now, plastic storage boxes are used to organize individual portfolios in alphabetical order. Preschool teachers divide portfolio contents by developmental domain. The dividers for each category of development are color coded, with a different color for physical, cognitive, language, and social development.

    Primary unit teachers decided to keep a portfolio for language arts and mathematics. They, too, use a divider for each content area. Each of the two dividers is a different color.

Determining Assessment Strategies To Be Used. The goal for Roosevelt Elementary School teachers was to use authentic assessment strategies. They did not eliminate teacher-designed tests and worksheets. Rather, they put them into an appropriate context with a variety of other types of strategies. They wanted their assessments to:

> - Be meaningful and relevant to the child
> - Reflect what the child can do
> - Be ongoing
> - Include a variety of strategies.

ANECDOTAL RECORD FORM

Lindsey Salazar _____ Student _____

Date 1/27/97 Listening Station
Lindsey listened to the story.
Then she completed the form
listing the title, author, and
a brief summary.

Date 1/28/97 Writing
Lindsey made posters and
price tags for the dramatic
play pet shop.

Date 1/28/97 Computer Center
Lindsey typed sight words
and made sentences.
Made a printout.
(Kid's Work)

Date

Date

Date

Figure 4.4

To ensure that a variety of assessment strategies would accurately reflect each child's progress, teachers decided to make observation their primary resource. They would supplement observation with interviews, work samples, performance examples, and teacher assessments. The discussion that follows describes these strategies and the types of recordkeeping that are useful with each type of assessment.

- **Observation.** Teacher observation, or "kid watching" (Goodman, 1985), can serve many purposes. By observing, teachers can evaluate developmental progress in all domains. In addition, observations of children working in learning centers or completing assignments can yield valuable information. By observing children on the playground, for example, teachers can gain information on gross motor skills. Observation of children working with puzzles or writing in their journals helps teachers to evaluate each child's fine motor skill development.

Written Language Inventory
Emergent and Early Writer (Side 2)

Key
N-Not observed
B-Beginning
S-Secure

Name _Rogelio Hernandez_

	Grade/Date				Anecdotal Notes
PUNCTUATION/CAPITALIZATION					Rogelio enjoys writing in his journal. In September the length of his entries were very brief. By December the entries were nearly a page in length for a few entries.
Uses periods	N	10/3	B	12/7	
Is aware of question marks, exclamation points, commas, quotation marks	N	10/3	N	12/7	
Uses capitals at the beginning of sentences	B	10/3	B	12/7	
Uses capitals for most proper nouns	B	10/3	B	12/7	
SPELLING					
Random use of symbols, scribbles, letters	S	10/3	S	12/7	
Uses initial consonants	B	10/3	S	12/7	
L to R progression in words	S	10/3	S	12/7	
Spaces between words	S	10/3	S	12/7	
Takes risks in spelling	N	10/3	B	12/7	
Uses initial, final consonants	N	10/3	B	12/7	
Conventional spelling of some words	N	10/3	B	12/7	
Uses incorrect vowel but in correct place					
Conventional spelling of word endings					
Vowel approximations are more accurate					
Recognizes misspellings					
Uses classroom resources to check spelling					

Source: Batzle, J. *Portfolio Assessment and Evaluation.* © 1992, Creative Teaching Press, Inc., Cypress, CA 90630. Used by permission.

Figure 4.5

Teachers at Roosevelt Elementary School use both planned observations and incidental observations to document student progress or to pinpoint difficulties. They use anecdotal records and checklists to record and document their observations. Figure 4.4 shows a form for recording anecdotal information. The student, Lindsey, was observed during work time in three learning centers. Figure 4.5 shows an example of a checklist used to record information about progress in emergent writing. Rojelio, an early writer, was observed in a 1st- and 2nd-grade classroom. The form was filled in after reviewing Rojelio's writing samples in his portfolio.

- **Interviews.** Activities and projects evolving from thematic curriculum represent opportunities to assess through interviews. The teacher can question a child or a group of children about a project or activity. Such interviews also can be incidental.

CAP GENERALIZED RUBRIC
CALIFORNIA STATE DEPARTMENT OF EDUCATION 1989

DEMONSTRATED COMPETENCE

Exemplary Response . . . Rating = 6
Gives a complete response with a clear, coherent, unambiguous, and elegant explanation; includes a clear and simplified diagram; communicates effectively to the identified audience; shows understanding of the open-ended problem's mathematical ideas and processes; identifies all the important elements of the problem; may include examples and counterexamples; presents strong supporting arguments.

Competent Response . . . Rating = 5
Gives a fairly complete response with reasonable, clear explanations; may include an appropriate diagram; communicates effectively to the identified audience; shows understanding of the problem's mathematical ideas and processes; identifies the most important elements of the problem; presents solid supporting arguments.

SATISFACTORY RESPONSE

Minor Flaws But Satisfactory . . . Rating = 4
Completes the problem satisfactorily, but the explanation may be muddled; argumentation may be incomplete; diagram may be inappropriate or unclear; understands the underlying mathematical ideas; uses mathematical ideas effectively.

Serious Flaws But Nearly Satisfactory . . . Rating = 3
Begins the problem appropriately but may fail to complete, or may omit, significant parts of the problem; may fail to show full understanding of mathematical ideas and processes; may make major computational errors; may misuse or fail to use mathematical terms; response may reflect an inappropriate strategy for solving the problem.

INADEQUATE RESPONSE

Begins, But Fails To Complete Problem . . . Rating = 2
Explanation is not understandable; diagram may be unclear; shows no understanding of the problem situation; may make major computational errors.

Unable To Begin Effectively . . . Rating = 1
Words do not reflect the problem; drawings misrepresent the problem situation; copies parts of the problem but without attempting a solution; fails to indicate which information is appropriate to problem.

No Attempt . . . Rating = 0

Source: California Department of Education, 1989. Used by permission.

Figure 4.6

The teacher might engage in an informal interview upon observing an interesting event during student work time or center time. Anecdotal records and checklists are helpful in recording student responses.

- **Work Samples.** More traditional assessment strategies fit into the category of work samples. Roosevelt teachers collect worksheets and written reports to document student progress and mastery of skills. They also use journal entries to document progress. Other resources for work samples are written reports and student artwork. Checklists, such as the one presented in Figure 4.5, might be used to evaluate written work samples and journal entries; rubrics can be developed to grade written reports. Figure 4.6 provides a scale for developing rubrics. An example of a simple rubric developed by Roosevelt teachers can be found in Figure 4.1.
- **Performance Examples.** Student artwork also can be categorized as a sample of student performance—what the student can do. Multiage teachers use photographs and cassette tapes to record what students can do. Photographs accompanied by an anecdotal record document the performance of preschool children. Students in the primary grades might be able to write their own explanation of a project that has been photographed for their portfolio. Cassette tapes might be used to record a child or children reading. The cassette recording then might be analyzed for a child's oral reading assessment. Roosevelt teachers developed a rubric to assess a student's progress in reading literacy. The stages of reading in their rubric are shown in Figure 4.7.
- **Teacher-designed Assessments.** Teacher-designed assessments can take many forms in the multiage units. Preschool teachers design concrete tasks for assessment purposes. Teachers in the primary grades unit use concrete tasks, as well as teacher-designed paper-and-pencil tests. Informal reading inventories and directed assignments are other possibilities that can be used for assessment. Rubrics might be used for directed assignments, while checklists and numerical scoring also are used for teacher-designed assessments.

RUBRIC FOR READING ASSESSMENT

Emergent Reader
    Enjoys hearing stories
    Enjoys looking at picture books
    Shows some understanding of book knowledge (left to right; front and back of book)
    Displays limited attention span to storybook readings
Beginning Reader
    Knows some letters and sounds
    Participates in Big Book readings
    Reads Big Book texts from memory
    Reads own writing
    Reads some words in isolation
Developing Reader
    Reads familiar and predictable books independently
    Is developing a one-to-one correspondence with words
    Is beginning to apply phonics skills
    Uses illustrations for meaning
Experienced Reader
    Chooses to read familiar and new books independently
    Self-corrects for meaning
    Is beginning to make inferences and predictions
    Uses reading to acquire new information

Figure 4.7

- **Portfolio Conferencing.** Periodically, teachers and individual children meet to evaluate portfolio entries. The teacher and child might make final decisions about items that help document the child's learning. Entries will be discussed to provide mutual feedback. If a parent conference is scheduled, the teacher and child will discuss what information might be shared with the parents. When the parent conference is conducted, both teacher and child share the portfolio with the parents. In turn, the parents can contribute their reactions to the child's progress and provide additional assessment information from their own observations.

Establishing Procedures for Data Collection and Interpretation. Once teachers have determined that they will use portfolio assessment, and decided how they plan to select materials for portfolio assessment, the next questions concern how much should be collected and when. These multiage teachers first determined to conduct initial assessments at the beginning of the year, as discussed earlier. They had beginning-of-the-year assessment forms in language arts and mathematics for this purpose. These instruments could also serve as a continuum of objectives for the multiage program. The instruments took the form of checklists, with spaces for information to be recorded at the end of each six-week grading period. They were placed in each child's portfolio in a section designated for recordkeeping. The entire instruments can be found in Appendix C.

The procedures for ongoing assessment and selection of portfolio entries vary for each teacher at Roosevelt Elementary School. Some teachers keep two folders for each child. One is the child's folder, into which the child can put as many examples of work as desired. The teacher keeps a separate folder of significant work and assessment samples. At the end of a six-week period, the teacher and child review the work together and make final selections for the permanent portfolio. Other teachers make selections at the end of each week and keep a single folder. Entries that are not retained are sent home with the child on Fridays.

Unit teachers meet frequently to discuss interpretation of portfolio materials. Teachers sometimes discuss individual children and their progress, and exchange ideas on how to plan for them. They also try to reach a consensus on assessment and evaluation of student progress in order to achieve consistency and reliability in how they use portfolio assessment. Together, they design rubrics for assignments and reports so that grading will be consistent across classrooms. They also exchange ideas on which assessment strategies will be used to demonstrate accountability for student learning.

Each unit of multiage teachers meets during a daily planning, which is scheduled in conjunction with their lunch periods so that teachers can extend their planning while they are eating lunch. Unit teachers also meet after school for unit planning and to complete six-week planning forms that must be filed in the school office. Forms for learning centers, new assessment rubrics, and other assessment forms also might be turned in with the planning information.

Establishing How Results of Portfolio Assessment Will Be Shared. Sharing portfolio assessments with parents was discussed earlier under the topic of using portfolio conferencing as an assessment strategy. Sharing of portfolio results goes beyond informing parents; school personnel also must decide whether the portfolio will follow the child to succeeding grades. Then the questions become, "How much of the portfolio should be shared with the next teacher?" and "Should the portfolio be maintained for the entire elementary school experience?"

Teachers in the multiage project decided to maintain the system they used for the school year. They were expected to send relevant information on to the next teacher. The teaching staff decided to send each child's portfolio forward at the end of the year with the following information:

- Beginning-of-the-year assessment forms, with progress recorded each six-week period
- Two or three different kinds of writing samples, with rubric or checklist for each six-week period
- One math sample for each major objective
- Samples of performance assessments
- Samples of significant teacher observations, with anecdotal notations.

After a review at the beginning of the year, the receiving teacher could retain some of the examples and send the rest home with the child.

The Learning Process in Getting Started. Making the transition to portfolio assessment was the most difficult component of restructuring the instructional program at Roosevelt Elementary School. Although teachers engaged in training before making the change, they were not initially confident that they could implement portfolios fully. At first, they tended to collect materials without using them as assessment tools. Eventually, they learned to correlate the entries with their continuum of learning objectives. Once they made this step, they were able to classify work and performance samples into the correct instructional category. Having learned to evaluate how much documentation to acquire for the learning objectives, they were able to plan for a balance of entries across developmental domains or content areas.

Now, as the teachers begin the second year of portfolio assessment, they are able to evaluate their progress. They realize that they have very little information on social development, and thus are searching for instruments and checklists that will help strengthen their assessment in this area. They also have recognized their overreliance on worksheets and tests, rather than performance assessments. They understand that they still feel more comfortable with familiar assessment strategies; nevertheless, they now have a goal to work on authentic assessment practices and make them the strongest element of their assessment system.

CONCLUSION

The decision to restructure an instructional program is complex. Consequently, it is helpful if it can be accomplished in steps or stages. Portfolio assessment is complex as well; when combined with a total restructuring process, it should be undertaken slowly and carefully. All of the components of restructuring need to be compatible and consistent. Each step must be implemented successfully before the next is attempted. Roosevelt Elementary School teachers recognized that assessment should be the last element of restructuring. After one year, they felt that they had made significant progress in understanding and using portfolio assessment. They also realized, however, that the process is dynamic. They are not ever likely to be satisfied with the system they have developed. As a result, they know that they will be working each year to improve upon and refine their use of portfolios to assess and document student progress. Their biggest remaining hurdle is learning to use time more effectively and make portfolio assessment less time-consuming. They have accepted that it takes more time in the beginning, and they are learning from their mistakes.

References

Batzle, J. (1992). *Portfolio assessment and evaluation.* Cypress, CA: Creative Teaching Press.

Bodrova, E., & Leong, D. J. (1996). *Tools of the mind. The Vygotskian approach to early childhood education.* Englewood Cliffs, NJ: Merrill/Prentice Hall.

Bredekamp, S. (Ed.). (1987). *Developmentally appropriate practice in early childhood programs serving children from birth through age 8.* Washington, DC: National Association for the Education of Young Children.

Bredekamp, S., & Copple, C. (Eds.). (1997). *Developmentally appropriate practice in early childhood programs* (Rev. ed.). Washington, DC: National Association for the Education of Young Children.

Corbett, D., & Blum, R. (1993). Thinking backwards to move forward. *Phi Delta Kappan, 74,* 690-694.

Goodman, Y. M. (1985). Kidwatching: Observing children in the classroom. In A. Jagger & M. T. Smith (Eds.), *Observing the language learner* (pp. 9-18). Newark, DE: International Reading Association and National Council of Teachers of English.

Hall, D. P., Prevatte, C., & Cunningham, P. M. (1995). In R. L. Allington & S. A. Walmsley (Eds.), *No quick fix* (pp. 137-158). New York: Teachers College Press.

Herman, J. L., Aschbacher, P. R., & Winters, L. (1992). *A practical guide to alternative assessment.* Alexandria, VA: Association for Supervision and Curriculum Development.

Hills, T. W. (1992). Reaching potentials through appropriate assessment. In S. Bredekamp & T. Rosegrant (Eds.), *Reaching potentials: Appropriate curriculum and assessment for young children* (Vol. 1) (pp. 43-65). Washington, DC: National Association for the Education of Young Children.

Hohmann, M., & Weikart, D. (1995). *Educating young children: Active learning practices in preschool and child care programs.* Ypsilanti, MI: High/Scope Press.

Katz, L. G., & Chard, S. C. (1990). *Engaging children's minds: The project approach.* Norwood, NJ: Ablex.

Mitchell, R., & Neill, M. (1992). *Criteria for evaluation of student assessment systems.* Washington, DC: National Forum on Assessment.

New, R. (1992). The integrated early childhood curriculum: New interpretations based on research and practice. In C. Seefeldt (Ed.), *The early childhood curriculum: A review of current research* (2nd ed.) (pp. 286-322). New York: Teachers College Press.

Newmann, F. M. (1991). Linking restructuring to authentic student achievement. *Phi Delta Kappan, 72,* 458-463.

Piaget, J. (1963). *The origins of intelligence in children* (M. Cook, Trans.). New York: W. W. Norton.

Vygotsky, L. (1978). *Mind in society: The development of psychological processes.* Cambridge, MA: Harvard University Press.

Wortham, S. C. (1998). *Early childhood curriculum: Developmental bases for learning and teaching* (2nd ed.). Upper Saddle River, NJ: Merrill/ Prentice Hall.

Portfolio Assessment in Elementary Mathematics and Science

INTRODUCTION

Teachers in early childhood and elementary classrooms increasingly use portfolios to assess children's progress in literacy. Many teachers keep writing samples, reading logs, or checklists of literacy skills to track individual growth. Portfolio assessment can be used equally effectively as a strategy to appraise children's mathematic and scientific understandings and skills. In fact, shifts in curricular emphases make alternative forms of assessment, such as portfolios, imperative for mathematics and science. Proficiency in computation and knowledge of science content were once the focal points of these subject areas, and still can be assessed using traditional paper-and-pencil appraisals. Nevertheless, acquisition of science processes, mathematical reasoning, problem solving, and communication skills require alternative measurements.

This chapter briefly describes professional organizations' standards for mathematics and science literacy, and discusses ways to incorporate data from various kinds of assessment tools into portfolios in order to provide a complete picture of a child's mathematic and scientific knowledge and skills. Various examples from classroom teachers and teacher educators illustrate methods for organizing mathematics and science portfolios and assessing their contents.

Curriculum Framework.

- **Program Goals.** Effective assessment begins with clearly stated goals. As in other areas of the curriculum, instructional decisions in mathematics and science are based on broad program goals. These usually are derived from state, district, or school guidelines, and sometimes from composite standardized achievement test results. One such program goal might be to increase the passing rate on the mathematics portion of a standardized test to 90 percent. Program goals targeting specific populations of students provide a framework for curriculum development across grade levels.

Ann C. Barbour

- **Performance Standards.** Within that framework, more specific performance standards or behavioral objectives become the foundation for designing grade level curriculum. In mathematics and science, performance standards usually originate from three sources: 1) state-mandated curricula, 2) professional organizations' standards, and 3) characteristics and needs of both individual and groups of children.

   School district curriculum guidelines may incorporate objectives adapted from mathematic and science textbooks, or they may use unmodified state-mandated performance standards. In Texas, for example, state-mandated performance standards come from two sources: 1) the State Board of Education Rules for Curriculum (Essential Elements), and 2) the Texas Assessment of Academic Skills (TAAS) test. There is a list of Essential Elements for every content area in each grade level. These "elements" are specific in nature. Fourth-graders, for example, should be provided opportunities to "identify and construct models of intersecting lines, parallel lines, perpendicular lines, right angles, and related two- and three-dimensional figures" (Texas Education Agency, 1993). By contrast, the TAAS tests student performance based on broadly stated objectives for mathematics, reading, and writing. One TAAS objective for 4th-grade mathematics states, "The student will recognize two- and three-dimensional figures and their properties" (Texas Education Agency, 1993). The Essential Elements and TAAS objectives can serve to guide school districts and individual teachers in developing curriculum and articulating their own lists of behavioral objectives, as can other well-defined standards.

   While state- or district-mandated performance standards may appear comprehensive, they may not include everything that is important for students to learn in mathematics and science. Some performance standards may not incorporate problem-solving or higher order thinking skills. Others may not require students to develop inquiry skills, to experiment by manipulating variables, or to assess their own learning. In addition, they may not emphasize students' positive dispositions toward mathematics and science.

   In recent years, professional organizations have published mathematics and science standards. The National Council of Teachers of Mathematics' (NCTM) *Curriculum and Evaluation Standards for School Mathematics* (1989) five goals call for students to: 1) learn to value mathematics, 2) become confident in their ability to do mathematics, 3) become mathematical problem solvers, 4) learn to communicate mathematically, and 5) learn to reason mathematically (NCTM, 1989). Teachers who implement the *Standards* help children to:

- Solve problems in meaningful situations
- Use manipulatives
- Work cooperatively with others in small groups
- Develop their own procedures, which they can discuss, explain, modify, write about, and value
- Use thinking strategies to learn basic facts
- Encounter math throughout their curriculum—in language and reading, social studies and science, and even art and physical education (Rowan & Bourne, 1994).

   The National Science Teachers Association's goals for science education (NSTA, 1990-1991) also emphasize a student-centered approach, one focused on student acquisition of science concepts and processes through firsthand experiences, rather than through didactic teaching methods. Science process skills in which students should develop proficiency include:

• Observing	• Predicting
• Comparing	• Hypothesizing
• Measuring	• Defining and controlling variables
• Communicating	• Experimenting
• Inferring	• Relating or applying.

High-quality mathematics and science programs incorporate these standards through planned curriculum, instruction, and assessment.

Instructional decisions based on goals and objectives for groups of students also should be based on the needs of individuals. It is neither realistic nor appropriate to expect that every child within the group will perform at the same level. Accordingly, some objectives will be unique for each child. One child may need to demonstrate place value using concrete materials, while another may be ready to perform operations on paper using two- or three-digit numbers.

Assessing Student Achievement. Traditional forms of measuring student achievement in mathematics and science cannot indicate the degree to which students have met the group or individual objectives derived from the NCTM standards or the NSTA goals. Written tests may succeed only partially in assessing student progress toward meeting district or state curriculum mandates. Students' conceptual understandings, thinking and reasoning skills, use of processes in context, and attitudes toward mathematics and science are difficult to measure using traditional tests. Hands-on, or performance-based, assessment activities are necessary to validate these kinds of learning (Foster & Heiting, 1994).

The most useful assessment strategies provide continuous information. Assessment that is embedded in everyday learning activities, rather than subsequent to or separate from learning activities, helps to guide teachers in making informed instructional decisions (Foster & Heiting, 1994). Embedded assessment involves observing children who are engaged in learning activities, listening to their comments (e.g., "So that's why I feel hotter when I wear a black t-shirt than when I wear a white one!"), and asking open-ended questions (e.g., "How do you know?" or "What might happen if . . . ?"). Embedded assessment provides information about children's strengths and challenges; it furnishes teachers with insight into *how* children learn as well as *what* they are learning. Teachers who observe, question, and interact with students who are engaged in investigations or problem-solving activities learn about their levels of conceptual understanding and abilities to use processes and skills. This information can be recorded in anecdotal comments or on observation checklists that subsequently can be included in portfolios.

Performance tasks also provide additional ways for students to demonstrate and apply their understandings and abilities. Students use concrete materials to carry out investigations or experiments, construct models, collect and interpret data, or solve complex problems. Products from these tasks are indicators of progress. They can be evaluated through checklists, scoring rubrics, and written reports.

Adopting a multidimensional approach to assessment is necessary in light of the goals and objectives of high-quality mathematics and science programs. Diversified assessment systems themselves become tools for improving teaching methods because they supply ongoing and specific information to teachers about students' strengths and weaknesses.

Portfolios are a repository for various kinds of information about student achievement. More important, however, they provide a systematic method to assess student progress and put current mathematics and science standards into practice.

ORGANIZING THE PORTFOLIO

Purposes for the Portfolio. Using portfolios in mathematics and science serves several purposes. First, portfolios provide a systematic way to store, organize, and assess evidence of students' mathematic and scientific literacy. Samples of student work, combined with other data in a portfolio, can give a comprehensive picture of each student's progress in relation both to curriculum mandates and to mathematics and science standards. For example, a student's written explanations of geometric properties, drawings of two-dimensional figures, a model that required application of geometric relationships to construct, and a teacher-completed checklist can indicate the extent to which the student has mastered the Essential Elements and TAAS objectives in geometry.

Second, teachers who use portfolios as a basis for assessing mathematic and scientific literacy report that portfolios make it easier for everyone—teachers, children, parents, and administrators—to track children's progress and growth. Portfolios provide concrete, detailed, and readily understood evidence about children's abilities, strengths, and challenges. They allow portfolio reviewers to compare a student to himself over time, rather than to an artificial standard (Clarkson, 1997). Portfolios also encourage dialogue among students, teachers, and parents (Stenmark, 1991).

Third, the act of keeping and reviewing portfolios emphasizes the value of quality work to children and encourages them to assess their own learning as they look critically at portfolio contents. Portfolios become a source of pride for most children because they document what children are able to do.

Fourth, portfolios enable teachers to narrow the gap between what they try to teach in mathematics and science and what they try to measure (Reichel, 1994). Portfolios furnish a means to make assessment an integral part of instruction.

Selection of Portfolio Format. Formats for mathematics and science portfolios vary greatly. Some teachers require their students to keep individual mathematics and science folders within larger portfolios. Mathematics and science materials also can be combined into a single portfolio or kept separately. Contents within the portfolio can be organized according to grading period or curriculum unit. They also can be organized by skill, concept, or standard/objective.

Stenmark suggests that keeping two portfolios for each student may be helpful (Stenmark, 1991). One, the *working portfolio*, contains all the student's work for a specific period of time (e.g., two weeks, a grading period, or during a unit of study). At the end of this time, students review their work and select items for their *assessment portfolio*. They write justifications for choosing these items. The teacher may require particular elements and/or select additional pieces. Students take the rest of their work home.

At the end of the year, Linda Koehler and her 5th-grade students in San Antonio select pieces from their portfolios that reflect progress. Students then evaluate their strengths and special challenges and write about their learning over the course of the year. Examples of included items are: photographs of student-constructed molecule models accompanied by written explanations, sketches of flower parts made during dissection, and recording sheets from the daily measurement lab. Students bring these archival portfolios to their next teacher. Sixth-grade teachers in Linda's district indicated a desire to have samples of incoming students' labeled lab drawings (e.g., drawings of organisms viewed

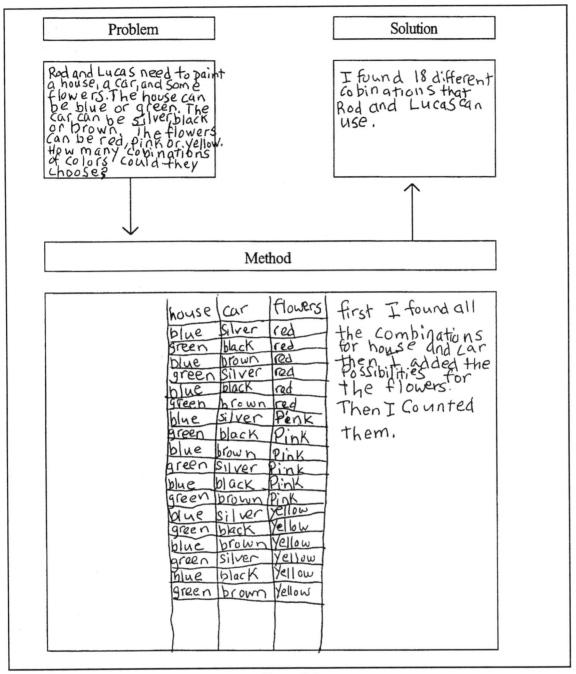

Figure 5.1

under a microscope) to determine how best to build upon students' skills.

Regardless of format, a portfolio should accommodate a sufficient number and type of items on which to base a valid judgment of achievement, but not so many that the portfolio becomes unwieldy and confusing (Tolman, Baird, & Hardy, 1994). Decisions about format are based on individual circumstances and often are modified with experience.

Suggestions for Types of Materials and Data. To figure out what material is most helpful to include in portfolios and to avoid collecting too much, teachers need to determine why each item should be included, who will see it, and what they will learn from seeing it (Clarkson, 1997). Portfolio contents should be representative of a student's work

PROBLEM SOLVING FLOW CHART

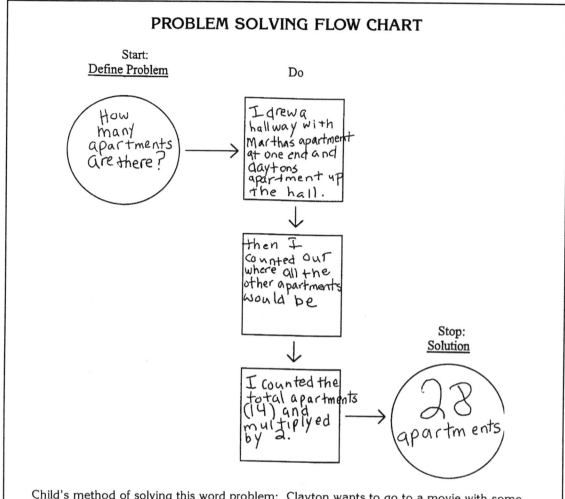

Child's method of solving this word problem: Clayton wants to go to a movie with some friends who live on the same floor of his apartment building. He walks down the hall 6 apartments to get Martha. Martha lives in the last apartment on the floor. From there, Clayton goes up the hall 10 apartments to get Juan. Next, he goes down the hall 3 apartments to find Rosa. From here he goes up the hall 6 apartments to pick up David, who lives in the last apartment on the other end of the floor. If there are the same number of apartments on both sides of the hall, how many apartments are there altogether on Clayton's floor?

Figure 5.2

in all areas of mathematics and science, and should highlight strengths, developing skills, personal reflections, and growth over time. As described in Chapter 2, portfolio contents should be diverse and may include work samples, journals, graphic organizers, checklists, rubrics, tests, photographs, summaries of contents, and self-evaluations. Work samples of various kinds should make up the bulk of any portfolio, as they constitute the primary evidence of what a student is able to do.

Types of materials that demonstrate students' mathematic literacy can be divided into broad categories, such as problem-solving activities, reflective writings, and teacher-selected work samples (Ferguson, 1992). Problem-solving samples should illustrate not only answers to problems, but also strategies used. To assess 3rd-grade children's understanding of using division for different purposes, for example, they might be asked to divide 21 by 4 under four different situations:

1. Divide 21 balloons among 4 people	3. Divide $21.00 among 4 people
2. Divide 21 cookies among 4 people	4. Divide 21 by 4 on a calculator

Children should be asked not only to record their answers, but also to explain why each answer made sense (Burns, 1995, p. 76). Graphic representations of solutions in various forms also can be included. Figures 5.1 and 5.2 illustrate two graphic organizers that display children's thinking strategies and steps taken to solve a problem.

Reflective writings can include journal entries, written justifications for selection of particular portfolio items, explanations of concepts or processes, narrative responses to completed units, descriptions of their performance or progress in a particular area, and an introductory letter to potential readers of the portfolio. Teachers may require certain portfolio elements to aid in assessing the entire group's understanding, as well as tracking the achievement of individual students.

Checklists of items to be included in each portfolio will help students select entries (Kennedy & Tipps, 1997). To ensure that a mathematics portfolio reveals a student's achievement in mathematical problem solving and communication, for example, a checklist might look like the one in Figure 5.3. These portfolio components have been used to assess 4th- and 8th-grade students in Vermont schools (Abruscato, 1993).

Yager and McCormack (1989) proposed five domains in planning science curriculum, instruction, and assessment. These domains also can be used to select portfolio items that indicate the breadth of students' scientific literacy. The five domains follow, with examples of portfolio components through which growth in each area can be assessed:

Concept Domain
Webs illustrating connections of concepts
Written work demonstrating understanding
Teacher descriptions of students' conceptual understanding (e.g., anecdotal remarks)
Process Domain
Charts, diagrams, graphs of data
Lab notebooks/logs
Project records
Drawings of observations
Teacher completed checklists
Application and Connection Domain
Productions
Performance tasks
Photographs or sketches of projects
Work from another subject area (e.g., analysis of data, a graph, map, or artwork using patterns or scale)
Student-formulated problems or questions
Creativity Domain
Written responses to "what if" questions
Cartoons, bumper stickers, posters
Explanations in various forms
Attitudinal Domain
Attitudinal surveys
Journal entries
Written responses to prompts (e.g., I like/dislike science because . . .)
A scientific (or mathematical) autobiography

MATHEMATICS PORTFOLIO CHECKLIST

Your portfolio should contain the following items:

5 to 7 "best pieces" showing the solution and the work involved. Include examples of problem solving, investigation, application, and group work.

_____ Title _____
_____ Title _____
_____ Title _____
_____ Title _____
_____ Title _____
_____ Title _____
_____ Title _____
_____ Other pieces of mathematics work
_____ A letter to the portfolio evaluator
_____ A table of contents

Figure 5.3

Each of these systems for selecting portfolio materials includes students' reflective writing: journal entries, justifications for selecting an item, autobiographies, letters to portfolio evaluators, and self-evaluations. Every mathematics and science portfolio should contain written elements that encourage students to self-assess and to reflect on their own thought/learning processes. The writing process helps students to gather, organize, and clarify their thinking and is critical in helping children to make sense of mathematics and science. Writing supports learning, helps to solve problems, explains thought processes, and reveals understanding (Burns, 1995).

REFLECTIONS ON PORTFOLIO SELECTIONS

Name: Isabel   Date: 4-8-98

Title of piece: palindrome project

I chose this piece because I did very well on it and I think it is neat how palindromes work.

The best things about it are that I found palindromes in numbers as well as words and sentences for egzample:(step on no pets)

If I were going to do it over again, I would Try to find other dates and make longer sentences.

Figure 5.4

Various prompts can be used to encourage students to communicate their mathematic and scientific thinking. Students can finish open statements like the following: "I learned (discovered, was surprised) that . . .," "I solved the problem by . . . ," and "I wonder . . ." They also can be asked to explain their reasoning, what is most important to know about a particular topic, the method they are most or least comfortable using, what a student who was absent should know about . . . , what they like most or least about . . . , or the next steps they will take to complete a project.

Suggested Timelines. How often items are collected will depend upon classroom activities, conference schedules, and reporting cycles. Some teachers, like Linda Koehler, base portfolio entries on units of study. Her district's curriculum guide includes the following seven strands in physical, earth, and life sciences to be taught during the year: matter, the periodic table, electricity, astronomy, the microscope, rocks, and plants. For each unit, Linda's students select several entries for their portfolios and complete a form explaining their reasons for choosing each item, as well as their evaluation of it (Figure 5.4).

Students may select a written project report or books they have made. Linda also requires a book report, a photograph of any finished project, lab drawings, and a form generated through tasks used to assess science process skills, such as the one appearing in Figure 5.5.

ALTERNATIVE ASSESSMENT/PROBLEM SOLVING:
Science Matter Unit

TAAS Areas Addressed: Summarization, drawing conclusions, using and applying formulas, inference, using four math operations to solve problems, creating charts and tables, attributes of matter, collection, organization, displaying and interpreting data, using logical reasoning to justify conclusions and solution processes, connecting mathematics to other disciplines.

Directions: Use density/volume boxes to do the following:
1. Define volume. _____
   _____
2. Write the formula for volume. _____
3. Measure the volume of your box in cm.
   Length: _____ Width: _____ Height: _____
4. Define mass. _____
5. Predict or infer the mass of your box before actual measurement. Mass your density/volume box on the triple beam balance.
   Prediction: _____ gms. Actual mass: _____ gms.
6. Define density. _____
7. Write the formula for density. _____
8. Using the formula, compute the density of your box. _____
9. Construct a chart to display the data you collected.
10. Summarize, in at least three paragraphs, the materials you needed to solve each step, what you needed to know prior to beginning the task, and how you proceeded to accomplish the assignment.

Adapted from assessment task developed by Linda Koehler & Ruby McDonald, Northside ISD, San Antonio, TX

Figure 5.5

Other teachers select or require a certain number and type of entries during each grading period or prior to portfolio conferences. Albert Losoya, a 3rd-grade teacher in San Antonio, and his students select between 8 and 12 pieces of data per six-week grading period. Some of the same types of items are selected every grading period (e.g., mathematics journals, rubrics assessing problem solving); others vary according to classroom activities or because he and/or the students decide particular pieces of work are important. To accommodate this timeline, components of long-term projects may be submitted before a final product is completed.

Selection of portfolio components does not need to depend upon units of study or reporting cycles. Instead, portfolio contents can be selected as the teacher and students judge items to be worthy of inclusion.

ASSESSMENT STRATEGIES TO BE USED

Evaluation of a portfolio in its entirety, or of its individual components, begins with clearly stated objectives that define the desired performance. The more specific and articulate these criteria are, the easier assessment will be for both teacher and student.

Some professionals recommend against assigning a single grade to a portfolio (Doris, 1991), arguing that comments by portfolio reviewers are more conducive to building student confidence and encouraging self-assessment. If portfolio grades are desired, however, teachers can develop a list of qualities against which to measure each one. Students can participate in generating criteria through class discussions and by evaluating their own portfolios accordingly.

Stenmark (1991, p. 43) suggests criteria for evaluating mathematics portfolios, advising teachers to choose only two or three criteria at a time to use in reviewing portfolios and to clearly communicate these standards to students in advance. These are some examples:

- Formulates and understands the problem or task (including assumptions and missing or extra data)
- Chooses a variety of strategies
- Carries out procedures using models, technology, and other resources
- Shows development of mathematical concepts
- Constructs mathematical ideas—inventing, discovering, extending, integrating, connecting, and critiquing ideas and procedures
- Shows thinking and reflection involved in mathematical reasoning, conjecturing, exploring, and processing
- Uses appropriate mathematical language and notation
- Interprets results—verifying, summarizing, applying to new cases
- Shows development of group problem-solving skills
- Relates mathematics to other subject areas and to the real world
- Shows development of positive attitudes—confidence, flexibility, willingness to persevere, appreciation of the value and beauty of mathematics
- Shows evidence of self-assessment and self-correction of work.

Similarly, criteria can be used in evaluating science portfolios. These have been adapted from Foster's and Heiting's (1994) definitions and indicators of basic and complex science processes:

- *Classifying*: Systematically classifies data based upon observed relationships (creates groups and subgroups using a single attribute or several attributes together)
- *Observing*: Shows active engagement with objects, by using senses, manipulation, and/or instruments
- *Communicating information*: Expresses opinions and explains observations and causal relationships, using a variety of media
- *Questioning*: Raises questions based on attributes of objects, relationships, patterns, and events related to experiments
- *Predicting*: Uses information gathered through observations to predict cause-and-effect relationships
- *Using numbers*: Expresses ideas, observations, and relationships in figures rather than words
- *Measuring*: Uses standard and nonstandard measurement instruments
- *Interpreting data*: Accurately identifies single pattern among objects
- *Controlling variables*: Identifies and selects variables that are held constant and those that are manipulated in order to carry out an investigation
- *Designing experiments*: Hypothesizes, plans data-gathering procedures, collects data, attempts to define and control variables, uses organized methods to test hypothesis and interpret results
- *Inferring*: Provides explanations based on limited facts
- *Hypothesizing*: Constructs generalizations about objects and events based on opinions, observations, and experiences
- *Formulating models*: Describes or constructs explanations of systems or phenomena that cannot be observed directly.

Portfolio evaluations also can be part of an overall grade for a marking period, particularly if some portfolio components have been graded already. In this case, portfolios can be evaluated according to diversity of selections, written reflections, and portfolio organization (Lambdin & Walker, 1994). Letter grades or numerical scores can be assigned to each of these categories and averaged for a final grade.

Checklists and Rubrics. Checklists and scoring rubrics are versatile assessment tools with various applications in mathematics and science. They are particularly useful in assessing performance tasks, productions, or investigations.

Checklists can be used to assess whether or not children have acquired a particular skill or conceptual understanding, or to analyze a task by breaking it up into component parts. Checklists also can be used by teachers and students in assembling portfolios and ensuring that contents are representative of children's progress (see "Organizing the Portfolio," p. 66).

Checklists are an easy and flexible method for recording observations of students' behaviors. They can be constructed to reflect attainment of targeted skills by individual students, as in the form "Evaluating Student Behaviors" in Figure 5.6, or by groups of students, as in the "Observation Checklist" in Figure 5.7.

To a limited extent, these checklists can incorporate ratings and comments. To assess students' abilities to demonstrate skills or complete tasks, teachers can develop a checklist composed of specific performance standards. Such a checklist might look like the one in Figure 5.8, which is based upon the Texas State Board of Education curriculum guidelines for 4th-grade mathematics (Texas Education Agency, 1993).

A useful tool for assessing performance tasks and portfolios in general is a scoring

EVALUATING STUDENT BEHAVIORS
Measuring Thought Processes in Behavior
Demonstrating Skill and Participation Levels

Name _____

Numerical Value
0 = Dependent
1 = Needs Support
2 - Independent

SPECIFIC SKILL	DATE			COMMENTS
Understands Problem • paraphrases • recalls problem				
Formulates a Plan • selects strategy				
Implements Plan • carries out strategies				
Explains Plan • orally and in writing				
Evaluates/Interprets Metarecognition Results • orally and in writing • demonstrates solution				
Extends • creates own problem • recalls related problem				

ATTITUDES (Interaction and Participation)

Cooperates				
Shares/Collaborates • tries, contributes ideas				
Questions Peers • encourages others to participate				
Takes Risks • confidence in own ability				
Stays on Task • perseveres				

Stenmark, J. K. (Ed.). (1991). *Mathematics assessment: Myths, models, good questions, and practical suggestions.* Reston, VA: National Council of Teachers of Mathematics. Used by permission.

Figure 5.6

OBSERVATION CHECKLIST

Curricular/Content Area _____ Date _____

Target Skills

Names of Students   Comments

1._____

2._____

3._____

4._____

5._____

6._____

7._____

8._____

9._____

10._____

11._____

12._____

13._____

14._____

15._____

Figure 5.7

rubric. Scoring rubrics contain a limited number of well-defined categories that describe students' performance (Barbra, 1997). They are designed to clarify expected outcomes for student performance for both teacher and students. Criteria, or specific descriptions of what children are expected to do, define the rubric's scoring system. These can include mastery of content, skills, processes, or attitudes. Criteria should be shared with students prior to beginning a task, in order to provide guidance and encourage self-assessments. The more specific the criteria, the greater the degree of guidance and the easier it will be to score students' work (Price & Hein, 1994). Students themselves can participate in defining and describing the criteria.

Rubrics can be based upon several types of scoring systems. One method is to assign a point to each component of a multi-part project. Students' scores are based upon the sum of the points earned. Such a rubric might look like the performance task assessment

---

MEASUREMENT

Concepts and Skills Using Metric and Customary Units

Name _____

Standard	Dates			Comments
Measures areas using grids				
Finds perimeters using standard and nonstandard units				
Uses the concept of perimeter to solve problems				
Measures the capacity of a container using nonstandard units				
Identifies concrete models that approximate capacity units				
Estimates and measures the capacity of a container				
Solves application and non-routine problems involving length _____ weight _____ time_____ capacity_____				
Determines the amount of time elapsed in a problem-solving situation				

Figure 5.8

---

for microscope usage in Figure 5.9. In this example, the student's final score is an average of points given by the student herself, a peer, and the teacher.

Another method is to establish pass/fail criteria. When this is done, a passing score often is required to complete an assignment. The score is not averaged into a student's grade, and students have multiple opportunities to complete the assignment if they are not successful on their first attempt (Jensen, 1995).

The most commonly used method is to assign a number along a 3- to 6-point scale to describe the quality of a finished product. Each number on the scale represents a clearly defined level of performance. For example, a 4-point scale used to assess observation and recording abilities in science might be:

---

4 = observes and records data with great expertise
3 = observes and records data accurately
2 = seems to observe correctly, but does not record data accurately
1 = fails to observe or record data (Barbra, 1997).

PERFORMANCE TASK ASSESSMENT
Microscope Usage

Name _____ Date _____

	Points	Points Earned		
		Self	Peer	Teacher
1. Carries microscope by arm and supports with hand.	1	_____	_____	_____
2. Holds slides by sides.	1	_____	_____	_____
3. Mounts slides under stage clips.	1	_____	_____	_____
4. Sets revolving nosepiece to lowest objective.	1	_____	_____	_____
5. Looks from the side and lowers the objective as low as it will go without touching the slide.	1	_____	_____	_____
6. Looks through the eyepiece and focuses upward until the slide is in focus.	1	_____	_____	_____
7. Turns the revolving nosepiece to the middle objective and focuses.	1	_____	_____	_____
8. Turns the revolving nosepiece to the highest objective and focuses.	1	_____	_____	_____
9. Lowers the stage and removes slides from stage.	1	_____	_____	_____
10. Unplugs microscope by pulling on plug, not wire.	1	_____	_____	_____
Total:	10	_____	_____	_____

_____ + _____ + _____ ÷ 3 = _____
Grade

Figure 5.9

As the above example indicates, scoring rubrics make it possible to translate observations of students' behavior into a numeric grade.

Some teachers use a generic point scale, but vary the criteria according to the task or behavior they are assessing. Judy Rose, a 3rd-grade teacher in San Antonio, uses a generic scoring rubric similar to the one in Fig. 5.10, adapted from Price and Hein (1994), to score performance tasks. Before students begin a task, Judy fully explains the assignment and, with her students' help, determines criteria and definitions (e.g., "unexpected") incorporated in the rubric. In a "Make Your Own Zoo" task, for example, students were required to include a map and an infogram of their zoo. These two elements were vehicles

GENERIC SCORING RUBRIC FOR PERFORMANCE TASKS

4 = Outstanding. All criteria met. In addition, the product/presentation exceeds the assigned task and contains additional, unexpected, or outstanding features.

3 = Good. Product/presentation completely or substantially meets the criteria.

2 = Adequate. Product/presentation meets some of the criteria and does not contain gross errors or crucial omissions.

1 = Inadequate. Product/presentation does not satisfy a significant number of the criteria, does not accomplish the task, contains errors, or is of poor quality.

0 = Poor. Student did not do or did not complete the task, or shows no comprehension of the requirements.

Figure 5.10

for students to demonstrate interdisciplinary concepts and skills related to animal classification systems, individual animal requirements, problem solving, and measurement. The rubric used to assess students' completion of this assignment incorporated the following criteria: the map must include a key, a logical method for grouping animals, and a systematic method for locating animals, and it must be neat and attractive; the infogram must demonstrate understanding of individual animals' habitats, food requirements, and behaviors, animal and human safety, and knowledge of zoo operation procedures; written language and presentation must be of high quality.

ANALYTIC SCALE FOR PROBLEM SOLVING

Understanding the problem
0 = No attempt
1 = Completely misinterprets the problem
2 = Misinterprets major part of the problem
3 = Misinterprets minor part of the problem
4 = Complete understanding of the problem

Solving the problem
0 = No attempt
1 = Totally inappropriate plan
2 = Partially correct procedure, but with major flaw
3 = Substantially correct procedure with minor omission or procedural error
4 = A plan that could lead to a correct solution with no arithmetic errors

Answering the problem
0 = No answer, or wrong answer based upon an inappropriate plan
1 = Copying error; computational error; partial answer for the problem with multiple answers; no answer statement; answer labeled incorrectly
2 = Correct solution

Source: Szetela, W., & Nicol, C. (1992). Evaluating problem solving in mathematics. *Educational Leadership, 49*(8), 42-45. Used by permission of the Association for Supervision and Curriculum Development. Copyright © 1992 by ASCD. All rights reserved.

Figure 5.11

PERFORMANCE TASK ASSESSMENT
Rock Identification

Scoring Scale:

    3 = uses correct procedures and attains complete and accurate results

    2 = uses correct procedures but results are incomplete or inaccurate

    1 = uses incorrect procedures and attains inaccurate and incomplete results

    0 = does not attempt task

Earned Points

1. Given 4 samples, uses physical characteristics to classify as mineral, sedimentary, igneous, or metamorphic. _____ _____ _____

2. Masses specimen to tenth of a gram. _____ _____ _____

3. Using graduated cylinder, determines volume of specimen to nearest cubic centimeter. _____ _____ _____

4. Calculates density using calculator and measurements of mass and volume. _____ _____ _____

5. Performs acid test on two specimens (able to identify positive/negative reaction). _____ _____ _____

6. Uses streak plate to identify color of a mineral streak. _____ _____ _____

7. Uses fingernail, copper penny, and nail to identify range of mineral's hardness. _____ _____ _____

8. Uses Mohs Hardness Scale to identify minerals that will scratch one another. _____ _____ _____

9. Compares/contrasts intrusive and extrusive rocks in the following ways: (One point for each correct answer)
   a. Describes where formed.
   b. Describes physical characteristics.
   c. Describes crystal size. _____ _____ _____

10. Using WEDSED, is able to describe how sedimentary rocks are formed. _____ _____ _____

11. Separates foliated from nonfoliated rocks. _____ _____ _____

12. Matches parent rock to metamorphic rock. _____ _____ _____

13. Diagrams and labels stages of the rock cycle. _____ _____ _____

Total: _____ _____ _____

_____ + _____ + _____ ÷ 3 = _____ (Grade)

Adapted from performance task developed by Linda Koehler & Ruby McDonald, Northside ISD, San Antonio, TX

Figure 5.12

ASSESSING FOR SUCCESS: PERFORMANCE TASK

Preparation

One way to assess a student's ability to construct inferences based on observations is to construct mystery boxes. Be sure to use identical boxes and objects when assessing children simultaneously. An example of a mystery box is one that uses two small objects that either roll or slide. Inexpensive and readily available rolling objects include BBs, ball bearings, plastic Easter eggs, and marbles. Metal washers and bottle caps and lids also are good sliding objects.

Directions to the Student

1. Write your name on this line _____
2. Check the box to be sure it is taped shut. Do not open the box.
3. The box contains one or more objects. Pick up the box and listen to the sounds as you gently shake it. Tilt the box and listen carefully.
4. Answer the following questions:

_____a. What shape is an object in the box?

_____b. What is one other property of an object in the box?

_____c. What is one kind of motion made by an object in the box?

_____d. Except for air, how many objects do you think are in the box?

_____e. Explain why you think your answer to question d is correct.

_____

_____

Scoring Procedure

1 point each for questions a, b, c, and e. Question d is not scored.

Acceptable responses for questions a, b, c, and e include:
a. flat, round, ball-shaped, like a coin, and so on
b. hard, heavy, sounds like metal
c. slides, rolls, glides, or drops
e. student response has to support response to question d

1. Adapted from an example presented by Douglas Reynolds at The United States Department of Education Secretary's Conference on Improving Assessment in Mathematics and Science Education, September 20-21, 1993, Arlington, Virginia.

From *Learning and Assessing Science Process Skills* by Rezba et al. Copyright © 1995 by Kendall/Hunt Publishing Company. Used with permission.

Figure 5.13

To assess problem-solving skills, Charles, Lester, and O'Daffer (1987) break down the process of problem solving into three stages: understanding the problem, solving the problem, and answering the question. Wilson's "Analytic Scale for Problem Solving" (Figure 5.11) is based on these stages, but reflects greater emphasis on understanding and solving the problem (Szetela & Nicol, 1992). Like other generic scoring rubrics, it can be applied in various situations.

Rubrics developed by Linda Koehler to assess science process skills in her 5th-grade class include items specific to each unit of study. The numerical value of the items totals 100. Linda's rubrics include spaces not only for her assessment of each item, but also for self and peer assessments. Students' total scores are averages of teacher, self, and peer ratings. Figure 5.12 illustrates an example of a performance task rubric used to assess students' skills in rock identification.

Another type of performance task scoring rubric is based on responses to particular questions that are designed to assess students' abilities to apply skills. One or more points are awarded for each acceptable response. Figure 5.13 outlines a performance task to assess students' abilities to make inferences and procedures to score their responses.

Any scoring system will need to be tried out in the classroom and refined or modified accordingly (Price & Hein, 1994). Teachers may find they need to revise expected levels of achievement, or have students complete an additional activity to document and score student learning more accurately.

Interpretation of Portfolio Contents. Whether portfolios are evaluated holistically or particular elements are scored individually, portfolios become vehicles to comprehensively assess mathematic and scientific literacy. Their contents enable reviewers to understand individual student performance in relation to program goals and performance standards. Teachers can use this information to align curriculum, instruction, and subsequent assessment. Administrators can use the data for program evaluation. Parents have access to easy-to-understand information about their children's progress. All parties have a relevant basis for dialogue.

Mathematics and science portfolios aid teachers and students in accomplishing goals recommended by the NCTM and the NSTA. Since implementing portfolio assessment in mathematics, Vicki Walker, a middle school teacher in Louisville (Lambdin & Walker, 1994), found her students were more cognizant of what problem solving and mathematical reasoning entail. They were less apt to resort to blind application of computational algorithms, learned to look for connections between mathematics and other aspects of life, and improved their abilities to communicate mathematical ideas.

Mathematics and science portfolios also enable students to take stock of their own progress and become involved in self-assessment. With teacher guidance and practice, students become adept at interpreting portfolio contents and setting high standards for themselves. To a large extent, "work in science requires some independence, the ability to interpret findings, and a willingness to make choices about what to pursue" (Doris, 1991). Self-assessment can become one more means for children to practice "doing what scientists do." Because portfolios highlight work, they help students pay attention to ways they are represented by their portfolios and to the quality of their work.

Portfolios themselves also can serve as a means for children to attain two of the NCTM goals: valuing mathematics and becoming confident in their ability to do mathematics. By maintaining and reviewing portfolio contents, children learn to understand relationships between mathematics and "real life," and learn how to track their growing understanding and proficiency.

> When students engage in self-assessment, they become aware of their knowledge of the content of mathematics, the processes they use, and the skills they possess. Internal, rather than external, knowledge of one's achievements is likely to create a student who values mathematics and gains a sense of power in doing mathematics. (Kennedy & Tipps, 1997, p. 119)

CONCLUSION

Mathematics and science portfolios have the potential to reveal more information about students' conceptual understandings, thought processes, skills, strengths, and weaknesses than traditional measures can. This information is essential in improving instructional approaches in mathematics and science. In addition to reflecting learning, portfolios also can enhance learning in ways suggested above.

Teachers who use mathematics and science portfolios for assessment learn by trial and error what is manageable and meaningful in their own situations. As in other areas of teaching, determining effective practices is an evolving process. It may take teachers three to five years to find the types of entries, a management system, and assessment strategies that work best (Clarkson, 1997). Thoughtful adaptations of approaches successfully used by others provide a beginning point for designing and using these flexible assessment tools.

REFERENCES

Abruscato, J. (1993). Early results and tentative implications from the Vermont Portfolio Project. *Phi Delta Kappan, 74*, 474-477.

Barbra, R. H. (1997). *Science in the multicultural classroom.* Needham Heights, MA: Allyn & Bacon.

Burns, M. (1995). *Writing in math class.* White Plains, NY: Math Solutions.

Charles, R., Lester, F. K., & O'Daffer, P. (1987). *How to evaluate progress in problem solving.* Reston, VA: National Council of Teachers of Mathematics.

Clarkson, J. (1997). Using math portfolios in first, second, and third grade classrooms. In J. Barton & A. Collins (Eds.), *Portfolio assessment: A handbook for educators* (pp. 25-32). Menlo Park, CA: Addison-Wesley.

Doris, E. (1991). *Doing what scientists do.* Portsmouth, NH: Heinemann.

Ferguson, S. (1992). Zeroing in on math abilities. *Learning, 21*(3), 38-40.

Foster, G. W., & Heiting, W. A. (1994). Embedded assessment. *Science and Children, 32*(2), 30-33.

Jensen, K. (1995). Effective rubric design. *The Science Teacher, 62*(5), 34-37.

Kennedy, L. M., & Tipps, S. (1997). *Guiding children's learning of mathematics.* Belmont, CA: Wadsworth.

Lambdin, D. V., & Walker, V. L. (1994). Planning for classroom portfolio assessment. *Arithmetic Teacher, 41*(6), 318-324.

National Council of Teachers of Mathematics. (1989). *Curriculum and evaluation standards for school mathematics.* Reston, VA: Author.

National Science Teachers Association. (1990-1991). Science/technology/society: A new effort for providing appropriate science for all (position statement). In *NSTA Handbook* (pp. 47-48). Washington, DC: Author.

Price, S., & Hein, G. E. (1994). Scoring active assessments. *Science and Children, 32*(2), 26-29.

Reichel, A. G. (1994). Performance assessment: Five practical approaches. *Science and Children, 32*(2), 21-25.

Rezba, R. J., Sprague, C., Fiel, R. L., & Funk, H. J., Okey, J. R., & Jaus, H. H. (1995). *Learning and assessing science process skills.* Dubuque, IA: Kendall/Hunt.

Rowan, T. E., & Bourne, B. (1994). *Thinking like mathematicians: Putting the K-4 NCTM standards into practice.* Portsmouth, NH: Heinemann.

Stenmark, J. K. (Ed.). (1991). *Mathematics assessment: Myths, models, good questions, and practical suggestions.* Reston, VA: National Council of Teachers of Mathematics.

Szetela, W., & Nicol, C. (1992). Evaluating problem solving in mathematics (using performance assessments). *Educational Leadership, 49*(8), 42-45.

Texas Education Agency. (1993). *State Board of Education rules for curriculum: Principles, standards, and procedures for accreditation of school districts.* Austin, TX: Author.

Tolman, M. N., Baird, J. H., & Hardy, G. R. (1994). Let the tool fit the task. *Science and Children, 32*(2), 44-47.

Yager, R. E., & McCormack, A. J. (1989). Assessing teaching/learning successes in multiple domains of science and science education. *Science Education, 73*(1), 45-58.

Project Portfolio Assessment in Multiage After-School Programs

INTRODUCTION

A national study of before- and after-school programs revealed that in 1991, approximately 1.7 million children, kindergarten through grade 8, were enrolled in 49,500 formal before- and/or after-school programs (RMC Research Corporation, 1993). This study also found that pre-kindergarten through 3rd-grade children constitute 90 percent of the before-school enrollments and 83 percent of the after-school enroll-ments. These statistics suggest that school-age care programs are playing an increasing role in providing educational experiences for children.

As with any educational program, many factors need to be ad-dressed in planning a quality experience for the children in after-school care. These factors include differences in various physical, mental, and perceptual capabilities; differences in ethnic origins and primary lan-guages; and differences in learning styles and experiential back-grounds. Although these factors appear, to varying degrees, in most heterogeneous public school classrooms, they become magnified in before- and after-school care programs, where different ages meet and mix. The challenge, therefore, is to implement a curriculum model and assessment that is responsive to the many individual differences that influence learning in these unique settings. The Project Approach provides one avenue for meeting this special challenge.

This chapter gives a brief description of the Project Approach, as described by Katz and Chard (1990), and provides examples of how this approach to learning is compatible with the goals of a quality before- and after-school care program. A model for a school-age care program for grades 3 through 6 using the three-phase project approach is presented, based on an actual case study, and emphasizing how to use portfolios to record and assess children's progress.

A BRIEF OVERVIEW OF THE PROJECT APPROACH

A project, as defined by Katz and Chard (1990), is an in-depth study of a topic or theme. The project approach to educa-tion "refers to a way of teaching and learning, as well as to the content of what is taught and

Blanche
Desjean-Perrotta
based on an idea by
Karen Storc

learned" (Katz & Chard, 1990, p. 3). This approach emphasizes children's active participation in the study of a particular topic that has meaning and relevance for them, usually drawn from the children's experience and interests. A large body of research on children's development suggests that children learn best when provided with opportunities to investigate, explore, experiment, and manipulate the environment within a social context (Bredekamp & Copple, 1997; Piaget, 1954; Vygotsky, 1962). In addition, education reformers also emphasize that children's learning must be demonstrated and evaluated in actual or applied situations, using authentic assessment (ACEI/Perrone, 1991; Meisels, 1993). These criteria apply to any type of program, for children of any age, where quality is valued. Five features of project work address these recommendations and provide a framework for responding to individual children's interests and learning needs.

Five Features of the Project Approach. Sylvia Chard (1994) describes five features of project work that help facilitate and support children's intellectual and social development. This flexible structure provides a framework for project work that is responsive to children's individual needs and interests (see Figure 6.1).

- **Group Discussion.** Conversations in large or small groups throughout the project enable the teacher to guide children's learning. As children share their ideas and the different kinds of work they are engaged in, new ideas and issues develop. Discussion serves as an informal assessment tool. Teachers can determine the level of children's knowledge acquisition or identify possible problems within the context of conversations about their investigations of real places, objects, and people. Notes taken during these conversations are included in a portfolio the teacher maintains for such purposes.
- **Field Work.** Field work may be thought of as research—that is, using primary sources to develop new knowledge and personal experience. Where possible, children investigate and study unfamiliar things through direct experience. A project about the cafeteria, for example, may mean visiting the school cafeteria, interviewing the food service personnel, touring the food preparation facility, and helping to prepare a meal. The difference between a field trip and field work is that field work does not necessarily involve expense for travel, and usually is focused on some type of investigation. This type of field work allows children to tap into expert knowledge that is close by and familiar. Notes, sketches, and other documentation of the field experience are included in children's project work portfolios.
- **Representation.** Children are challenged in project work to organize and share their knowledge of and experiences with the topic under study. At the beginning of the project, children use a variety of means to depict their current understanding of the topic. This can take the form of drama, writing, sculptures, drawings, and artifacts brought from home. Later, as children progress in their investigative work, they draw from the information in their portfolios and use a variety of representations such as graphs, charts, models, etc., to account for their work during the project. This feature of project work provides the children with a tool for measuring their own intellectual growth and for sharing information with others in an authentic way.
- **Investigation.** In project work, children can acquire new information about a topic and find answers to questions they have generated during class discussions through a variety of investigative activities, such as interviews, exploration of materials and objects using scientific tools, sketching their observations, photographing or videotaping subjects under investigation, or using library books.
- **Display.** Displays represent a record of the project's life. Contributions from members of the group participating in the project provide a growing source of information,

THE FUNCTIONS OF FIVE STRUCTURAL FEATURES IN THE DEVELOPMENT OF A PROJECT THROUGH THREE PHASES

	Group Discussion	Field Work	Representation	Investigation	Display
Phase I Beginning a Project	Sharing prior experience and current knowledge of the topic.	Children talking about their prior experience with their parents.	Drawing, writing, construction, dramatic play, etc. to share prior experience and knowledge.	Raising questions on the basis of current knowledge.	Sharing representations of personal experiences of the topic.
Phase II Developing the Project	Preparing for field work and interviews. Reviewing field work. Learning from secondary sources.	Going out of the classroom to investigate a field site. Interviewing experts in the field or in the classroom.	Brief field sketches and notes. Drawings, painting, writing, math diagrams, maps, etc. to represent new learning.	Investigating initial questions. Field work and library research. Raising further questions.	Sharing representations of new experience and knowledge. Ongoing record of the project work.
Phase III Concluding the Project	Preparing to share the story of the project. Review and evaluation of the project.	Evaluating the project through the eyes of an outside group.	Condensing and summarizing the story of the study to share the project with others.	Speculating about new questions.	Summary of the learning throughout the project.

Source: Chard, S. (1994). *The project approach: A second practical guide*. Alberta, Canada: Quality Color Press. Used by permission.

Figure 6.1

which can be displayed for all to see either on bulletin boards, walls, or cardboard stands that can be stored when necessary (as in the case of many school-age care programs). Displaying the results of children's investigative efforts lends credence and validity to the children's work. The display allows children to revisit the new information and reconcile the new ideas with any conflicting information they may have held previously. Displays also provide opportunities for children to explain to visitors what is happening in their project work. The results of these investigations become part of the child's project work portfolios.

These five features of project work are integrated into the learning that takes place in each of the three phases of the project approach, as defined by Katz and Chard (1990).

Phases in the Life of a Project.
- **Phase I.** Project work develops and grows correspondingly to children's interests and inquiries. In Phase I, the teacher uses a variety of methods to discover what children know about the topic for investigation and to stimulate interest in that topic. After the initial discussion of the topic (during which teachers may use webs and charts to graph information about children's knowledge), teachers then may provide opportunities for the children to represent their knowledge through various media, such as drawings, painting, dramatizations, etc. In this phase, the teacher wants to understand how much firsthand experience children have had with the topic. This first phase of project work usually culminates with the children listing questions about the topic that they would like to investigate further. These questions can be used for assessment later in the project.
- **Phase II.** Phase II in project work usually takes the most time to complete and consists of field work that provides firsthand experience with the topic for the children. Children visit and study real places, people, objects, and other resources. They collect data to bring back to the classroom by taking notes, doing rubbings, sketching, tape recording, or videotaping. This data is placed in the children's project work portfolios. Representative pieces from these investigations are displayed for all to study, discuss, and revisit. Documentation of the children's new understandings helps all of the children to construct ideas into a new system of knowledge. Documentation and representation also provide the teacher with an opportunity to "analyze the tracks left by the children" in their project work (Tarini, 1993).

   Children are encouraged to formulate new questions for study, adding to the initial web created in Phase I. During this phase, experts with firsthand experience of the topic under investigation come into the classroom to engage children in discussion and to answer children's questions.
- **Phase III.** Phase III brings together all that has been going on during project work and provides a sense of closure. In a culminating activity or event, children share and present the project work to their peers or interested adults. Children choose what they want to share from their portfolios and then devise a creative and imaginative way to represent their new learnings so that it is both personal and meaningful to another audience. This is also an opportunity for the children to evaluate their own efforts and achievements.

The Role of Assessment in Project Work. Perhaps the easiest way to explain the role of assessment and evaluation in project work is to compare it to the function of assessment in systematic instruction. Project work and systematic instruction provide different kinds of opportunities for evaluation. In systematic instruction, usually implemented in a school setting, the teacher is responsible for selecting tasks that the children must progress through in a specific sequence in order to obtain proficiency in certain subskills. The teacher is responsible for using formal assessment tools to determine the level at which the child is functioning.

The results of systematic instruction assessment provide the teacher with information about what the child is able to do when working at the limits of his or her capabilities. Such assessment usually is related to performance goals—how well the child is acquiring skills in response to instruction, as evidenced, for example, by how many right or wrong answers appear on a test. The teacher is held accountable for the failure or success of children to acquire skills. Children seldom have the opportunity to reflect on and determine the level of their own achievements, other than to label themselves as being abled or disabled. Assessment in this context concentrates on the product and does not include an evaluation of the processes children use to *achieve* the product.

Project work, on the other hand, focuses assessment not only on children's developing knowledge, but also on each child's ability to apply existing skills in learning situations, therby helping to ensure success. Rather than merely assessing what the children know, teachers involved in project work look at how well the children apply skills, how children approach their work, what kinds of tasks children choose for themselves, and how well children collaborate with each other to solve problems and answer questions. Through systematic instruction, children may have been taught how to create graphs and charts. During project work, children may apply this knowledge by conducting a survey and organizing the information into a bar graph or chart for presentation. It can be said that project work supports and extends formal, direct instruction, and that both forms of assessment are necessary when evaluating a child's level of achievement.

The different stages of project work provide the teacher with unique opportunities to assess children's knowledge and their depth of understanding, as well as their feelings, attitudes, and questions about the work. During the three phases of the project, the teacher can be compared to what Merritt and Dyson (1992) like to call a "teacher archeologist." The teacher works to uncover and support the children's developing knowledge by observing and assessing the artifacts contained in the children's portfolios. After-school care environments that focus on process and application of skills, rather than on how children acquire new skills, will find that project work provides the perfect model for meaningful activity and appropriate assessment. The following is a case study of an after-school care program for children in grades 3 through 6 that includes an explanation of how the teacher used portfolios for assessment in each of the three phases of their project work. At the end of the project work, the children's portfolios were shared with parents.

THE NEWSPAPER PROJECT

Children participating in this project were enrolled in a before- and after-school program provided by the Air Force for children living on base. This particular multiaged group consisted of children between the ages of 8 and 12. The daily routine for center staff involved meeting the children as they disembarked from the school bus, and accompanying them to the center housing the program. On their way to the center, the director noticed that the children picked up copies of the base newspaper (available in boxes all over the base).

As the children sat eating their snacks on this particular day, a discussion ensued about the newspaper's contents. The children indicated that they found the paper to be quite boring. One child in particular stated, "You know the paper is boring when the most interesting thing they can print is our elementary school lunch menus!" The teacher, picking up on this discussion, asked the children if they thought they could produce a better newspaper. The children immediately began to list topics that they felt would be more interesting than those in the original paper. Thus, the "Read All About It" newspaper project was born.

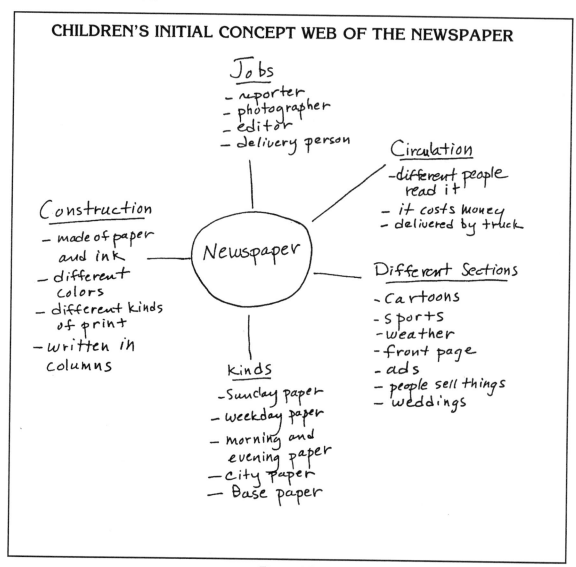

CHILDREN'S INITIAL CONCEPT WEB OF THE NEWSPAPER

Jobs
- reporter
- photographer
- editor
- delivery person

Circulation
- different people read it
- it costs money
- delivered by truck

Construction
- made of paper and ink
- different colors
- different kinds of print
- written in columns

Newspaper

Different Sections
- Cartoons
- Sports
- weather
- front page
- ads
- people sell things
- weddings

Kinds
- Sunday paper
- weekday paper
- morning and evening paper
- city paper
- Base paper

Figure 6.2

Phase I of the Newspaper Project. In Phase I, the teacher must find out what the children's background knowledge and personal experiences are related to the topic under study. A teacher can uncover this important information in a number of ways. The teacher and the children can engage in conversation and share personal stories related to the topic. They may also be encouraged to express or represent their knowledge and experiences through paintings, drawings, dramatizations, etc. Chard (1994) characterizes these representations as "reminiscent"; that is, children share experiences they have had in the past. Displays of children's experiences provide an opportunity for children to learn from each other, and help to form a common baseline of understanding.

In this case, the teacher began assessing the depth of children's prior knowledge about the newspaper by having the children map out a collective web of their knowledge and experience (Figure 6.2). Prior to this activity, the children asked their parents for news clips that they had found meaningful and, therefore, saved. These were posted on a display board, which was titled "In the News-In the Past."

To further stimulate the discussion, the teacher brought in copies of her old high school newspaper. The webbing activity revealed children's misconceptions, what they already did

CHILDREN'S LIST OF QUESTIONS FOR INVESTIGATION

What other jobs are there at a newspaper?
What do you do in each different job?
How do people get their jobs?
What kind of education do you have to have to work at a newspaper?
How much money do you make working at a newspaper?
Who puts the newspaper together?
What kinds of machines are used at a newspaper?
Where does the paper come from to make the newspaper?
How much does it cost to print a newspaper?
Are the different sections of the newspaper always in the same place?
How do you decide what goes in a newspaper?
How do you decide where things go in the newspaper?
Are there special names for the different parts of the newspaper?
How do you deliver newspapers to places like Alaska?
How do you decide how much a newspaper should cost?
How many people get the newspaper on the base?
How many people get the city newspaper?
How do you put an ad in the newspaper to sell things?
What kinds of computers do they have at the newspaper office?
What kinds of transportation are used to deliver newspapers?
Who owns the newspaper company?
Why is the newspaper written in columns?
How are newspapers recycled?
Do you keep old newspapers? Where do you keep them and for how long?
Why do people say "Stop the presses!"?
Why is the Sunday newspaper always bigger than the daily newspaper? Does more
    news happen on the weekends?
Can a city have more than one newspaper?
Who writes the newspaper stories?
What time of the day do you have to have the newspaper finished?

Figure 6.3

know about the newspaper, and their questions that could later be used for investigation. The teacher recorded the children's questions, labeled them with the children's names, and placed these in her portfolio for future reference. She also noted which children participated in the discussion, as well as who would need support to become more involved in the project.

Developing the Portfolios. Throughout this project, the teacher maintained a personal annotated portfolio that included information about each child and how the project was progressing in general; the children, meanwhile, collected project work in their own portfolios. The two portfolios provided evidence of different aspects of the project work.

- **The Teacher's Portfolio.** After the children explored the high school newspaper and the news clips, they began sharing their own experiences with newspapers. As the information web grew, the teacher began taking notes that she then transferred to her personal annotated portfolio. The notes included information about who participated in the discussion, who asked what questions, who expressed interest in the topic, and whether anyone appeared confused or overwhelmed by the topic. These notes, written on sticky labels, were easily stuck into her portfolio. The teacher also jotted down questions or concerns related to the project in general, such as 1) whether or not this topic was too big for investigation in this particular setting, 2) if they would have enough time to bring the project to completion (children had only 1 1/2 hours a day to work on the project), 3) why the children knew so little about the parts of a newspaper since they saw one every day, 4) how children can be helped to understand the written parts of the newspaper, 5) how to help the younger children take part in this project as fully as the older children, and 6) what resources were available to make this project work.

- **The Children's Portfolios.** Phase I concluded with the children developing a list of questions for investigation (Figure 6.3). As the project progressed, the children revisited and added information to the initial information web, which was displayed on a wall. The questions also were displayed on the wall in chart form, and the children were told to add to the list as often as they liked. These questions and the information web provided direction for the course of investigation in Phase II.

  Working from the questions generated by the group, children either chose one or two questions from the list to investigate, or developed two more questions of their own. These questions served as the children's statements of purpose for their project work portfolio. The children personalized their portfolio and developed their own individual curriculum based on the needs and interests expressed in these questions. As different work samples were included, the portfolio would reflect the child's growing understanding of the particular aspect chosen for investigation (Figure 6.4). Together, the child and the teacher could compare work done over a period of time and evaluate the child's growing competence and understanding of the topic, as well as determine where further help would be needed to complete the project.

  This type of individualized portfolio worked well in this multiage setting because it allowed the children to become actively involved in planning and implementing, at a comfortable level of involvement, activities that were personally meaningful. As a result, each child was able to contribute something to the total project, while at the same time developing personal interests. Developmental differences were addressed through an appropriate and challenging curriculum developed and monitored by the children themselves.

Phase II of the Newspaper Project. Field work is central to project work. In addition to using secondary sources to answer questions under investigation, children need to acquire new information through primary sources by interacting with real persons, objects, and other resources related to the topic under investigation. Teachers should prepare children for field work by discussing ahead of time what they are probably going to see, what ques-

---

POSSIBLE ARTIFACTS FOR INCLUSION IN A CHILD'S PROJECT PORTFOLIO

research notes	labeled photographs
field sketches	tapes or written copies of interviews
questions	rubbings
models to be copied	timelines for completion of work
graphs or charts	outlines
names of contact people for information	sketches of ideas for 3-D representations
checklists	self-evaluation
diagrams	measurements

Figure 6.4

REPRESENTATIONS OF INVESTIGATIONS

discussions	cycles
drawings	webs
paintings	dioramas
board games	role-playing
constructions	songs
models	raps
skits	dances
blocks	created books
dramatic play area	original poems
dictated stories	maps
collages	timelines
matrices	logs
flow charts	sequence charts
tree diagrams	mobiles

Figure 6.5

tions from their folders and list they might be able to investigate, and what artifacts or representations they may be able to bring back with them for further discussion and investigation. If it is not possible for the children to leave the site for field work, then an expert can be invited to the site to accomplish the same purpose.

- **Preparing for Field Work.** In preparation for a field trip to the offices of both the base newspaper and the city newspaper, the children studied and cut up copies of the local newspaper. This helped focus children's attention on the different parts of the newspaper and served to generate new questions for investigation. In the discussion preceding the field work, children reviewed this list of questions and familiarized themselves with the different recording techniques they could use to bring new information back to the center (e.g., writing notes, recording processes, making sketches or rubbings, taking measurements, drawing diagrams, taking photographs, making tape recordings, and collecting newspaper samples and other relevant artifacts). Children also reviewed the focus questions they had chosen for their project portfolio at the beginning of the project work, and were encouraged to try collecting data during the field experience that would address these questions. Children carried clipboards and paper to remind them of the purpose of the field experience.
- **Teacher Assessment During Field Work.** The teacher must ensure that the field work experience provides the children with some new understandings, and generates new questions for investigations. As children engage in the field experience, the teacher can keep notes on each child's level of interest, their misconceptions, and their questions, and then record comments related to individual learning needs. The teacher should also judge the quality of the field experience, and decide how to improve future experiences.
- **Field Work Follow-up.** It is especially important that children share, reflect upon, and re-create what they discovered during the field trip as soon after the excursion as possible. As children talk about a shared experience with the whole group, they come to appreciate how each person not only will recall different things, but also will have different ideas about what is important.

After the field trip to the newspaper offices, the teacher and children used the list of

CHILD'S PORTFOLIO SELF-ASSESSMENT SHEET

Name: _Gabriella_

1. What steps am I taking to get information about my project?

Going to the libary
Talking to people at the newspaper office
Using my compouter at home

2. Am I making responsible choices in my project work?

	Yes	No
• Who I work with?	☒	☐
• Where I work?	☒	☐
• How I use my time?	☒	☐
• What activities I do?	☒	☐
• What materials I use?	☒	☐

3. Strategies

	Yes	No
• Did I choose a good strategy for my project work?	☒	☐
• Is this strategy helping me to learn new information about my project topic?	☒	☐
• Have any problems come up?	☐	☒
• Is there something else that will work better for me next time?	☐	☐

Maybe asking more questions when we are on the field trip

4. What are some new things I have learned about my project topic?

That the people who write the cartoons for the newspaper don't live in San Antonio, they live everywhere in the country

5. What questions do I have about my project topic?

How do the cartoonists think up their ideas every day? How do they remember or keep track of all the cartoons they make?

6. What are some of the skills and processes I am using in my project work? (Circle)

(listening)	(speaking)	(reading)	(writing)
problem-solving	(researching)	(cooperating)	teamwork
graphing	analysizing	observing	(questioning)
risk-taking	(creativity)	responsibility	persistence

Figure 6.6

7. What do I need help with in order to complete my project?

I want to find a cartoonist on the web, and be able to ask him some questions?

8. What do I like best about my project so far? What do I like the least?

Cartoons are fun to read and learn about. I like drawing cartoons. I like everything about my project.

9. Are there any important pieces of information missing in my project work?

yes, what kind of school do cartoonists go to learn how to make cartoons

Figure 6.6 cont'd

questions on the wall as guidelines for discussion. While sharing new information, the teacher recorded it on the original web using a different colored marker than the original. This allowed the children to see what they had learned from the field trip. New questions were generated and added to the original question list, also using a different colored marker from the original. These questions were used later by the children for further investigation of the topic.

- **Long-term Multi-stage Work.** Phase II is the longest phase of project work, because it is here that children begin to study their portfolio questions in-depth. The children started with the information gleaned from the field experience, and began independent research, looking for further evidence or new information in secondary sources such as books and videos. Some of the children involved in the newspaper project, for example, decided they needed more information about how many people on base were served by the city newspaper. They decided to develop a survey to answer this question. Other members of the group wanted to know more about how people in the

PORTFOLIO CONFERENCING GUIDELINES

The following requests can be used to guide discussion during an individual conference about portfolio contents during project work.

1. Show me a piece from your portfolio that shows me something new you have learned.
2. Show me a piece from your portfolio that you worked on cooperatively with someone else, and describe how you did that.
3. Show me a piece from your portfolio that shows how you solved a problem that came up during your work.
4. Use one sample from your portfolio to show me how you are organizing your information about your project.
5. Show me a piece from your portfolio that took longer than one afternoon to finish, and explain the steps you took to complete it.

Figure 6.7

newspaper business got their jobs, and so conducted further interviews with newspaper personnel. Some of the younger children decided to investigate how newspapers are recycled, inviting a recycling plant manager to visit the center and explain this process.

As children developed in-depth knowledge about their personal topic for investigation, they were asked to represent this new knowledge in some fashion. The objective of this component of Phase II was to enable children to personalize their recently acquired knowledge. A wide range of representations are available for children to choose from, depending on their age and developmental level (Figure 6.5). As children's knowledge about the topic deepened, standards of accuracy and precision in the representation also increased. Different stages of the work involved in creating the representation became part of the child's portfolio. The purpose of the portfolio, especially during this phase, is to provide a record of the child's work as it develops.

The portfolio contents were particularly helpful in giving the child and the teacher a sense of how the project was developing and how the main concepts were being investigated and represented. During this stage of their project work, children received a self-assessment sheet to put in their portfolios (Figure 6.6). This self-assessment tool helped the children monitor their own processes related to their project work, and evaluate the quality of the resulting products. It also served as a springboard for discussion during individual conferences between the child and the teacher about the contents of the portfolio and the skills they practiced in the project work.

- **Portfolio Assessment.** Children's portfolio work was assessed frequently during their project work. This was done in one of three ways: 1) large-group discussion of individual children's portfolios offered the teacher an opportunity to feature different ways of representation that might be helpful to other children who were experiencing difficulties in this area, 2) small-group discussion of portfolio work with children of similar ages provided them with a set of standards for work relevant to their particular age group, 3) individual conferences about portfolio content gave both the child and the teacher a chance to ask questions, make clarifications, and assess the quality of work (Figure 6.7). These reviews helped the children to stay on track and accomplish their project goals.

    The teacher used these portfolio conferences to assess which children needed more help to complete their investigations, and which needed supplemental activities to help clarify some misconceptions.

- **Teacher Assessment of Portfolios During Phase II.** Katz and Chard (1990) suggest assessing children's project work using the mirror of four types of lifelong learning goals: knowledge, skills, dispositions, and feelings. They define each of these learning goals as follows:

> Knowledge can be defined as schemata, ideas, facts, concepts, information, stories, and myths. Skills are discrete units of action that can be fairly easily observed and that are executed in a relatively short amount of time. Dispositions are roughly defined as habits of the mind or tendencies to respond to situations in characteristic ways. Feelings are subjective emotional or affective states such as feeling accepted, confident, or anxious. (p. 20)

Using these four learning goals, the teacher developed a short assessment tool to use during the newspaper project to evaluate the children's development related to these four areas (Figure 6.8). These questions served as a guide for the teacher in facilitating the project work for the children, and also as a springboard for discussion with the

ASSESSING CHILDREN'S GROWTH RELATED TO KNOWLEDGE, SKILLS, DISPOSITIONS, AND FEELINGS

Child's name: _Gabriella_   Date: _3-11-97_

1. **Knowledge**: What new information, concepts, relationships, meaning is this child adding to his or her background as a result of the project work?.

She is learning how to trust her own instincts and ideas about how she wants to create her project. She is also learning how to think methodically and logically in order to get more information that is valuable so she is not wasting time.

2. **Skills**: What skills are being applied or developed as a result of this child's involvement in project work?

1. Periodically observed 2. Frequently observed 3. Always observed 4. Not observed

	1	2	3	4
Social				
• cooperation	☐	☐	☑	☐
• negotiation	☐	☐	☑	☐
• teamwork	☐	☐	☑	☐
• communication	☐	☐	☑	☐
• discussion	☐	☐	☑	☐
• assertiveness	☑	☐	☐	☐
• debating	☑	☐	☐	☐
• other: _willing to share ideas_	☐	☐	☑	☐
Academic				
• listening	☐	☐	☑	☐
• speaking	☐	☐	☑	☐
• reading	☐	☐	☑	☐
• writing	☐	☐	☑	☐
• other:	☐	☐	☐	☐
Mathematic				
• counting	☑	☐	☐	☐
• estimating	☑	☐	☐	☐
• measuring	☑	☐	☐	☐
• problem-solving	☐	☑	☐	☐
• graphing	☑	☐	☐	☐
• computing	☐	☑	☐	☐
• other	☐	☐	☐	☐

Figure 6.8

1. Periodically observed 2. Frequently observed 3. Always observed 4. Not observed

	1	2	3	4
Scientific				
• questioning	☐	☐	☑	☐
• researching	☐	☑	☐	☐
• observation	☐	☑	☐	☐
• analysis	☐	☑	☐	☐
• hypothesizing	☐	☑	☐	☐
• data management	☐	☑	☐	☐
• computer use	☐	☐	☑	☐
• other:				

3. **Dispositions**: What desirable patterns of behavior does this child exhibit in the project work?

	1	2	3	4
• cooperativeness	☐	☐	☑	☐
• initiative	☐	☑	☐	☐
• curiosity	☐	☑	☐	☐
• helpfulness — strength	☐	☐	☑	☐
• independence	☐	☑	☐	☐
• responsibility	☐	☐	☑	☐
• risk-taking	☐	☑	☐	☐
• humor	☐	☑	☐	☐
• resourcefulness	☐	☑	☐	☐
• appreciation	☐	☐	☑	☐
• persistence	☐	☐	☑	☐
• confidence	☐	☑	☐	☐
• generosity	☐	☐	☑	☐
• creativity	☐	☑	☐	☐
• respect	☐	☐	☑	☐
• Other:				

4. **Feelings**: How does this child feel about his or her project work?

___ recognizes personal strengths and limitations

X sets realistic goals for achievement

X learns from errors

X copes appropriately with frustrations or setbacks

X takes pride in his/her work

___ feels confident about his/her own potential for learning

X able to judge own successes

Gabriella needs to become more assertive and hold her own — she has good ideas and needs to build her confidence.

Figure 6.8 cont'd

parents about their children's project work. These documents became part of the teacher's project work portfolio.

- **Informal Evaluation—Sharing Portfolio Contents Through Display.** As children developed their portfolios and representations related to their questions and areas of interest, the teacher provided a display area so that children could share their portfolios and investigate the work of their peers more closely for themselves. This display

CHOOSING MY WORK FOR DISPLAY

1. What pieces of work really show what I have learned about my project topic?

The report I wrote and the cartoons I made.

2. Which pieces of work would I be proud to share with visitors?

My cartoons I made for the newspaper and the things I found on the web and made a poster about it

3. Are these pieces of work:

y complete?

y easy to understand?

y attractive?

y interesting?

y accurate?

4. Which pieces of my portfolio work contribute something of value to the project as a whole? *My cartoons and my story about the life of a real cartoon ists.*

5. What would be the best way for me to share my project with other people? *I can write my new infomation so that it looks like a cartoon.*

Figure 6.9

served many purposes. During the newspaper project, children used the display as a reference tool, as a model for attractive representations, as a springboard for discussion around a particular topic, and as a means of pulling information about the project together into some cohesive whole. This display also held artifacts from the field work that children could revisit. It served to keep interest high and encouraged children to take pride in their work.

Phase III of the Newspaper Project.

• **Concluding the Work.** The decision to draw the project to a close is made by the teacher in consultation with the children. Usually, the children themselves are a good indicator that it is time to put some closure to the project. It may become evident that the children's interest is waning, the children may have exhausted their personal topic of investigation and met most of their curriculum goals, or there may be a natural break in the school calendar.

When the time comes to draw the project to a close, the teacher can suggest some ideas for a culminating event that will allow the children to communicate what they have learned to another audience. The purpose of this third phase is to help children reflect upon their project work and evaluate what they have done (Katz & Chard, 1990). This event can be as simple as a Portfolio Evening, during which the children sit with members of their family and present their project portfolio (Hebert, 1992). Or the event can be as elaborate as a dramatic presentation, including music, food, song, and dance, to be shared with schoolmates. Usually, the topic for the project work inspires the choice of the culminating event. The purpose of the event is to help children elaborate upon and consolidate their newly acquired information (Katz & Chard, 1990).

- **Portfolios and the Culminating Event.** Having identified the audience for the culminating event, children review their portfolios and choose examples of their work that best represent their newly acquired knowledge, as well as the processes used during the project. The teacher can provide some guidance through personal conferences with the child or by providing guidelines to follow (Figure 6.9). It is appropriate that children showcase the life of their project work by choosing samples that represent their understanding as it developed through the three phases. The portfolio selections should focus not only on what the child has learned, but also on how the child learned the new information.
- **The Newspaper Project's Culminating Event.** The children involved in the newspaper project decided early on that their culminating event would be to publish their own newspaper. Having completed the work in Phase II, they were ready to begin production. They began by selecting an editor, in this case a child who was computer literate and had the resources to produce the newspaper at home. Since each of the children had chosen an area of interest to study related to a particular aspect of the newspaper, the rest of the group automatically took on the responsibilities for different sections of the newspaper. These jobs included reporter, advice columnist, health and safety editor, illustrator, copy editor, photographer, puzzles editor, advertisements editor, and comic strip writer. Each child developed a particular section of the newspaper, using their portfolio. The teacher assisted the editor with the layout, design, and reproduction of the newly created newspaper, called "Read All About It."

The children's parents were invited to a "Meet the Press" party. In addition to the display from Phase II, each child prepared their portfolio to share with their parents and friends, including samples of their project work that showcased their contribution to the newspaper project. A copy of ""Read All About It" was included in each portfolio. The base newspaper staff was invited to the celebration, and the children were thrilled when a reporter and photographer came out to cover the event. Their newspaper had made the newspaper!

CONCLUSION

Portfolios are a natural extension of project work, allowing children to keep a record of their learning in the form of resources, ideas for exploration, and possible representations of those ideas as they complete the project. Portfolios provide a means whereby the children can assess their own growth in learning by comparing where they were when the project began, and how much they accomplished by the end of the project. Teachers can use portfolios during project work to keep track of children's growth in skills and under-standing, as well as their feelings and approaches to the work. These records of achieve-ment are important for sharing with parents and are indicative of the program's quality. Project portfolios and the culminating events in project work assure parents that the after-school care program is not just a babysitting service or a warmed-over school program (Neugebaur, 1980).

In addition, the compilation of everyone's accomplishments, taken from portfolios and organized into a culminating event, can be used for reference in future projects. The initial web created at the beginning of the project work was expanded upon, using different colored markers. This provided a visual representation of the areas that most interested the children, and those that were the least investigated. This web also provided informa-tion about how activities and explorations grew and expanded from original ideas. An annotated web can serve as a resource for the teacher for future projects and can be added to the teacher's portfolio.

Children should have opportunities to assess their own growth in whatever project work they do. Portfolios serve to facilitate this process in project work in a developmentally appropriate manner, because they are learner-centered, interactive, and respectful of the child's individual abilities.

REFERENCES

Association for Childhood Education International/Perrone, V. (1991). On standardized testing. Position paper. *Childhood Education, 67,* 131-142.

Bredekamp, S., & Copple, C. (Eds.). (1997). *Developmentally appropriate practice in early childhood programs* (Rev. ed.). Washington, DC: National Association for the Education of Young Children.

Chard, S. (1994). *The project approach.* Alberta, Canada: University of Alberta.

Hebert, E. A. (1992). Portfolios invite reflection from students and staff. *Educational Leadership, 49*(8), 58-61.

Katz, L., & Chard, S. (1990). *Engaging children's minds: The project approach.* Norwood, NJ: Ablex.

Meisels, S. J. (1993). Remaking classroom assessment with the work sampling system. *Young Children, 48,* 34-40.

Merritt, S., & Dyson, A. H. (1992). A social perspective on informal assessment: Voices, texts, pictures, and play from a first grade. In C. Genishi (Ed.), *Ways of assessing children and curriculum* (pp. 94-125). New York: Teachers College Press.

Neugebaur, R. (1980). School age day care: Developing a responsive curriculum. *Child Care Information Exchange, 11.*

Piaget, J. (1954). *The construction of reality in the child.* New York: Basic Books.

RMC Research Corporation, in collaboration with the School-Age Care Project at Wellesley College and Mathematical Policy Research, Inc. (1993). A national look at before- and after-school programs. *Young Children, 48,* 19.

Tarini, E. (1993). What is documentation? *Innovations in Early Education: The International Reggio Exchange, 1,* 5.

Vygotsky, L. (1962). *Thought and language.* Cambridge, MA: MIT.

Conclusion

Many teachers have turned to portfolio assessment as a strategy for creating a classroom assessment system that includes multiple measures taken over time. Portfolios have the advantage of containing several samples of student work assembled in a purposeful manner. Well-conceived portfolios include pieces representing both work in progress and "showpiece" samples, student reflection about their work, and evaluation criteria. (Herman, Aschbacher, & Winters, 1992, p. 120)

In this handbook, we have described journeys taken by some teachers in planning and implementing portfolio assessment. We have described possibilities for portfolios in a variety of contexts. In all the examples, we have tried to demonstrate how teachers get started using portfolios and the steps that must be taken to use portfolios effectively. We also have discussed factors that teachers must consider when putting portfolio assessment into practice. Although the contexts and age groups represented by the examples provided in this book vary widely, we found commonalities in the steps or processes used. These common processes or themes were listed in Chapter 1. It might be appropriate to discuss some of these common elements to guide other teachers who are considering using portfolio assessment.

THE DECISION TO USE PORTFOLIO ASSESSMENT

The decision to begin portfolio assessment was the first step in all of the examples described. At some point in the teaching process, someone decided that portfolio assessment would be better than what was being used currently. The leaders in the child development center saw portfolio assessment as a method to link individualized instruction of infants, toddlers, and preschool children to their developmental advances. The processes used to conduct developmental assessments provided teachers of young children with the information they needed to provide appropriate activities.

The teachers in the multiage school saw portfolio assessment as a cohesive factor in their efforts to restructure their program. They used portfolio assessment to link their curriculum design, classroom arrangements, and learning activities with a more authentic type of learning and assessment. Teaching math and science in the intermediate grades was made more authentic by the use of portfolio assessment,

Sue Wortham

while portfolios provided a method for students of all ages in an after-school program to pull together the results of their newspaper project and share what they accomplished with their parents.

PHILOSOPHICAL BASES FOR USING PORTFOLIO ASSESSMENT

In Chapter 1, the common philosophical foundations of the authors and portfolios described were defined as constructivist in nature. The portfolios that were implemented in each case reflected a belief in the intrinsic nature of children's learning and the need for authenticity in learning experiences and assessment. Regardless of this common basis, each setting had an individual basis for using portfolios. The teachers in the child development center were concerned primarily with developmental progress. They wanted portfolio contents to reflect the developmental advances of individual children in their care, as well as the links that they made between developmental assessment and activity planning.

The teachers in the multiage school setting were concerned with multiple factors. They were using an integrated, thematic curriculum that focused on student performance and performance assessment. At the same time, they were concerned with moving from a skills-based curriculum to one that reflected their students' culture and development. They remained concerned with the acquisition of basic skills but, at the same time, they wanted to use learning centers to make their classroom more child-centered.

The after-school program was perhaps the most constructivist in philosophy. Its core philosophy was the Project Approach, as designed by Katz and Chard. Individual efforts initiated by the children in the program resulted from their own ideas and planning. The teacher's role was primarily one of facilitator.

The mathematics and science project reflects a more traditional public school curriculum that is transitioning into a constructivist approach to learning. Authentic learning and assessment strategies help students to have a different understanding of the value and purpose for their learning.

SELECTING THE PURPOSE FOR THE PORTFOLIO

Most of the portfolios were used for a combination of purposes, with a major goal being the evaluation of student progress and achievement. The after-school teacher, however, used portfolios mostly for "showcasing"; that is, they were used for the students to reflect on what they learned from the newspaper project and to share the project results with each other and their parents. The math and science portfolios were used mostly for evaluation, while the purposes behind using infant, toddler, and preschool portfolios were balanced between developmental assessment, individualized planning, and reporting to parents.

CRITERIA FOR SELECTING ASSESSMENT STRATEGIES

The portfolio assessments were partly a function of the developmental level of children or of their grade level in elementary school. Observation was the primary strategy used for the child development center. The multiage program used observation, concrete tasks, written work, and tests. Observation and concrete tasks were used for children in early stages of literacy, while written work was used more extensively by the end of 1st grade and in 2nd grade.

While the math and science model for intermediate grades depended upon written student work, performance assessments were important. The after-school project depended entirely upon performance activities related to the newspaper project. The type of activities represented in the portfolios depended upon the individual child's interests, abilities, and age level.

COLLECTING, INTERPRETING, AND REPORTING DATA

The decisions made about collecting, interpreting, and reporting data depended upon the purposes for the portfolio. The teachers in both the child development center and multiage program found that they had been too ambitious in their original planning. They had too many assessments, samples of children's work, and other materials. Both groups of teachers had to rethink how many samples they would include in each child's portfolio.

Validity and reliability became important issues when portfolios were interpreted and reported. Teachers who were required to give grades learned that they had to be consistent and reach consensus about their chosen instruments. Fortunately, all of the school-based portfolio projects were based on well-researched developmental milestones, or on state or national guidelines for curriculum goals. Checklists tied to these established indicators for development and learning were used. The portfolio projects that were used in the elementary grades relied on rubrics to establish validity and reliability.

The teachers at the child development center worked with the developmental assessments for a period of time before achieving consistent data interpretation. Likewise, the teachers in the multiage project met as a team to discuss their assessment strategies and consistency issues. They held many discussions during the first year of portfolio implementation, resulting in a refinement and a more complete consensus on the meaning of assessment results.

A FINAL WORD

It takes several years to establish a quality portfolio system. The steps outlined in this book rarely can be accomplished to the teacher's satisfaction in one year. In addition, the process is dynamic. As teachers and students grow in their understanding of portfolios and learn how to reflect on student development and achievement over time, portfolio assessment becomes more rewarding and useful. Teachers accustomed to giving tests and assigning grades may find it difficult to understand authentic learning and assessment quickly. Older students also need time and experience to be able to select work samples thoughtfully and to reflect upon their learning through self-assessment. It is a continuing challenge to use portfolio assessment for the students' best benefit (Stiggins, 1997). Moreover, the use of portfolios does not necessarily indicate better ways of teaching and learning (Wiggins, 1998). Teachers, students, and parents need to understand that this type of assessment process reflects a different approach to learning—one that offers the student opportunities to take responsibility for learning and assessment. Once the parties to portfolio assessment appreciate the broader implications for assessment in this process, learning and accomplishment will become more meaningful.

SUGGESTED RESOURCES

Portfolios: Assessing Learning in the Primary Grades (1995)
Author: Marianne Lucas Lescher
NEA Professional Library
National Education Association
P.O. Box 509
West Haven, CT 06516-9904
Phone: 1-800-229-4200

Student Portfolios (1993)
NEA Professional Library
National Education Association
P.O. Box 509
West Haven, CT 06516-9904
Phone: 1-800-229-4200

Literacy Portfolios (1997)
Authors: Roberta B. Wiener and Judith H. Cohen
Prentice-Hall, Inc.
Simon & Schuster
Upper Saddle River, NJ 07458

Eyes on the Child: Three Portfolio Stories (1996)
Author: Kathe Jervis
Teachers College Press
1234 Amsterdam Avenue
New York, NY 10027

The Portfolio and Its Use (1992)
Authors: Cathy Grace and Elizabeth F. Shores
Southern Early Childhood Association
P.O. Box 5403
Little Rock, AR 72215-5403

Portfolio Assessment and Evaluation (1992)
Author: Janine Batzle
Creative Teaching Press, Inc.
Cypress, CA 90630

A Practical Guide to Alternative Assessment (1992)
Authors: Joan L. Herman, Pamela R. Aschbacher, and Lynn Winters
Association for Supervision and Curriculum Development
1250 N. Pitt St.
Alexandria, VA 22314

Take a Look: Observation and Portfolio Assessment in Early Childhood (1994)
Author: Sue Martin
Addison-Wesley Publishers Limited
Don Mills, Ontario

Portfolio Practices: Thinking Through the Assessment of Children's Work (1997)
Authors: Steve Seidel, Joseph Walters, Edward Kirby, Nina Olff, Kimberly Powell, Larry
    Scripp, and Shirley Veenema
NEA Professional Library Publication
National Education Association
P.O. Box 509
West Haven, CT 06516-9904
Phone: 1-800-229-4200

REFERENCES

Herman, J. L., Aschbacher, P. R., & Winters, L. (1992). *A practical guide to alternative assessment.*
    Alexandria, VA: Association for Supervision and Curriculum Development.
Stiggins, R. J. (1997). *Student-centered classroom assessment* (2nd ed.). Upper Saddle River, NJ: Merrill.
Wiggins, G. (1998). *Educative assessment.* San Francisco: Jossey-Bass.

Appendix A

Form for
Chapter 2

GETTING STARTED
PORTFOLIO DESIGN WORKSHEET

1. What are your objectives for assessment?

_____

_____

_____

_____

_____

2. Which type(s) of portfolio best meets the above objectives?

_____

_____

3. Will the portfolio be organized by developmental areas or content areas?

_____

4. Who will make contributions to this portfolio?

_____

_____

_____

Teacher	Child	Parent
( ) Anecdotal records	( ) Attitudinal surveys	( ) Questionnaires
( ) Checklists	( ) Interest inventories	( ) Forms
( ) Rating scales	( ) Logs	( ) Work samples
( ) Rubrics	( ) Journals	( ) Comments
( ) Notes	( ) Literacy development	( ) Dialogue journals
( ) Conference notes	samples	( ) Notes
( ) Tests	( ) Project work	( ) Conference notes
( ) Required materials	( ) Written justifications	( ) Telephone logs
( ) Other	( ) Video/audio tapes	( ) Other
	( ) Self-reports	
	( ) Computer disks	
	( ) Other	

5. What type of container will be used for storage?

expandable file folders
x-ray folders
pizza boxes
grocery bags
large mailing envelopes

magazine holders
office supply boxes
paper briefcases
tag board folded in half
shoe boxes containing file folders
plastic crates

7. What methods will be used for:

Balancing?_____

Dating? _____

Annotating?_____

8. How often will data be collected? _____

9. Other notes

_____
_____
_____
_____
_____
_____
_____
_____
_____
_____
_____
_____

Appendix B

Portfolio Assessment

Forms for
Chapter 3

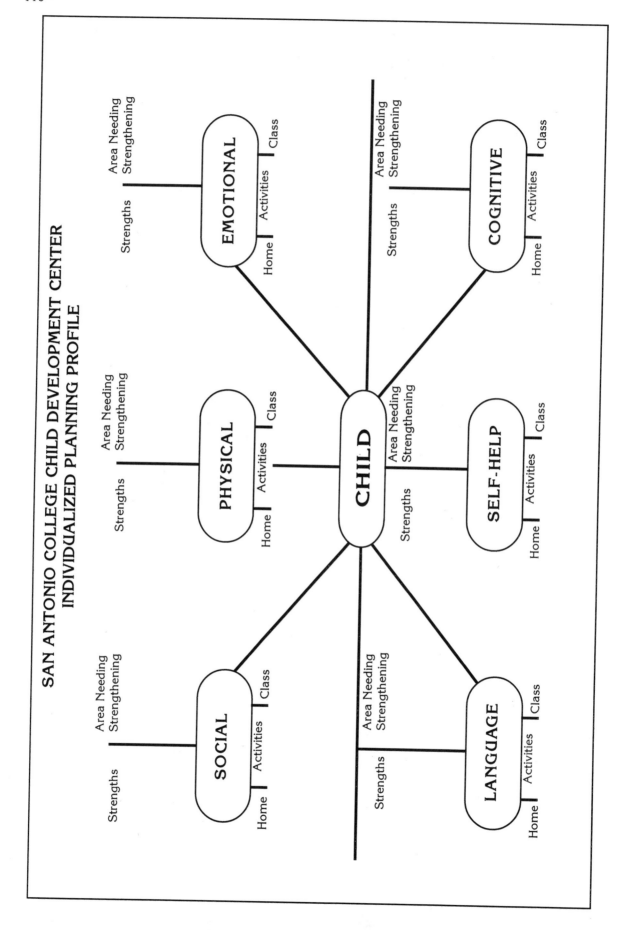

SAN ANTONIO COLLEGE CHILD DEVELOPMENT CENTER
INDIVIDUALIZED PLANNING PROFILE

INDIVIDUAL PLANNING PROFILE: INFANTS AND TODDLERS

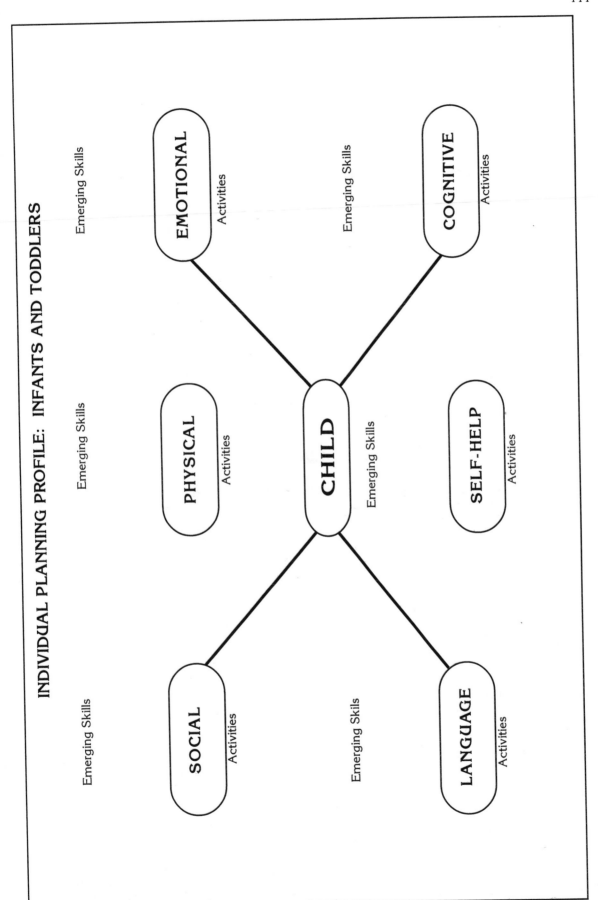

Emerging Skills

EMOTIONAL

Activities

Emerging Skills

COGNITIVE

Activities

Emerging Skills

PHYSICAL

Activities

CHILD

Emerging Skills

SELF-HELP

Activities

Emerging Skills

SOCIAL

Activities

Emerging Skils

LANGUAGE

Activities

Name_____ Date_____

BLOCK CONSTRUCTION

Directions: Circle the stage of development in block construction. Attach a photograph if possible.

1. Carries blocks from place to place; does not actually build

2. Begins building—child mostly makes rows

3. Creates bridging—two blocks with a space between them, connected by third block

4. Builds enclosures—blocks placed in such a way that they enclose a space

5. Names structures and uses them in dramatic play themes

6. Creates buildings that represent or symbolize actual structures

Reproduced by permission. *Math and Science for Young Children.* By Charlesworth/Lind. Delmar Publishers, Albany, New York, Copyright 1995.

Name_____ Date_____

SOCIAL PLAY

Directions: Circle the stage of play that the child is engaged in. Attach an anecdotal record observation as documentation.

1. **Unoccupied play**
   Children wander and watch.

2. **Onlooker**
   Children watch others play, ask questions, and make suggestions but do not participate.

3. **Solitary play**
   Children select toys with which to play, but are not interested in other children's activities.

4. **Parallel play**
   The child plays near another child and may play with the same objects, but does not interact.

5. **Associative play**
   Children play with others, are engaged in activities, and may exclude some children, but rarely negotiate about the direction their play takes.

6. **Cooperative play**
   Children organize their play, assigning roles and negotiating turns.

Source: Parton, M. (1932). In C. Grace, & E. F. Shores (Eds.). (1992). *The Portfolio and Its Use.* Little Rock, AR: Southern Association for Children Under Six. Used by permission.

Name_____ Date_____

CHILD DRAWING

Directions: Circle the developmental level of the child's drawing. Attach drawing.

1. **Random/Disordered Scribbling**
    -lacks direction of purpose for marks
    -does not mentally connect own movement to marks on page

2. **Controlled Scribbling**
    -explores and manipulates materials
    -tries to discover what can be done with color, texture, etc.
    -often repeats action
    -makes marks with intention and not by chance

3. **Basic Forms**
    -masters basic forms: circles, oval, lines, rectangle and square
    -discovers connection between own movements and marks on page

4. **Pictorial Stage (First Drawing Stage)**
    -combines basics forms to create first symbols
    -names drawings as a form of true communication

Reproduced by permission. *Creative Activities for Young Children.* By Mayesky.
Delmar Publishers, Albany, New York, Copyright 1998.

Name_____ Date_____

EASEL PAINTING

Directions: Circle the developmental level of the child's drawing. Attach child's drawing.

1. **Random/Disordered Scribbling**
    -lacks direction of purpose for marks
    -does not mentally connect own movement to marks on page

2. **Controlled Scribbling**
    -explores and manipulates materials
    -tries to discover what can be done with color, texture, etc.
    -often repeats action
    -makes marks with intention and not by chance

3. **Basic Forms**
    -masters basic forms: circle, oval, lines, rectangle, and square
    -discovers connection between own movements and marks on page

4. **Pictorial Stage (First Drawing Stage)**
    -combines basic forms to create first symbols
    -names drawings as a form of true communication

Reproduced by permission. *Creative Activities for Young Children.* By Mayesky.
Delmar Publishers, Albany, New York, Copyright 1998.

Name_____ Date_____

LANGUAGE DEVELOPMENT

Directions: Circle the stage of development that the child exhibits. Attach an Anecdotal Record or audiotape.

1. SOUNDS
Crying, gurgling, and cooing are important first steps in the language learning process.

2. BABBLING
Babbling encompasses all of the sounds found in all languages. Gradually, it becomes more specific with the syllables of the native language.

3. HOLOPHRASES
Single words that reflect much meaning (e.g., "car" may mean "I want my toy car" or "Look at the car outside").

4. TWO-WORD SENTENCES
Sentences of two words that often express ideas concerning relationships (e.g., "Mommy-sock" or "cat-sleeping").

5. TELEGRAPHIC SENTENCES
Short and simple sentences that omit function words and endings that contribute little to meaning (e.g., "Where Daddy go?" or "Me push truck").

6. JOINED SENTENCES
Child joins related sentences logically and expresses ideas.

7. OVERGENERALIZATIONS
As children become more sophisticated in their language, they overgeneralize rules in ways that are inconsistent with common usage (e.g., "I comed home").

Source: Feeney, S., Christensen, D., & Moravcik, E. (1991). *Who am I in the lives of children?* New York: Macmillan.

Name_____ Date_____

THREE-DIMENSIONAL ART (PLAY DOUGH)

Directions: Circle the developmental level of play with play dough. Attach photograph or describe the child's creation.

1. **Random Manipulation**
   Clay is squeezed through fingers in a very uncontrolled way; beats and pounds it.

2. **Patting and Rolling**
   Clay is patted and rolled by child, often making thin ropes or balls.

3. **Circles and Rectangles**
   Clay is rolled to make balls. Boxes are made out of clay.

4. **Synthetic and Analytic Manipulation**
   Synthetic way: Objects are made by child putting together separate pieces of clay
      to make a whole (e.g., separate pieces for bottom and sides).
   Analytic way: Child shapes the object from one whole piece of clay; child does not
      use separate pieces and then joins them together.

5. **Forming Clay Figures**
   Child combines basic form to build objects that are like figures in drawings.

Reproduced by permission. *Creative Activities for Young Children.* By Mayesky.
Delmar Publishers, Albany, New York, Copyright 1998.

Name_____ Date_____

WRITING DEVELOPMENT

Directions: Circle the developmental stage of early writing. Attach samples of work.

1. **Scribble Writes**
   Pretends to write by scribbling horizontally.

2. **Creates Letter-like Forms**
   Includes features of real letters in scribbling.

3. **Writes Strings of Letters**
   Writes real alphabet letters, but has problems with spacing, reversals, orientation of
   paper.

4. **Writes Words with Invented Spelling**
   Directionality or orientation is often a problem with first words.

5. **Writes Simple Message**

Source: Beaty, J. J. (1994). *Observing development of the young child.* New York:
Macmillan.

Name_____ Date_____
Time Period_____

ATTENTION SPAN DEVELOPMENT

Directions: Choose a time period (e.g., 1 hour) during learning center time and record, on class map, the places the child plays.

Attach a class map

Name_____ Date_____
Task/Activity

SCIENCE PROCESS SKILLS

Directions: Science process skills are the thinking skills necessary to learn science. Observe child interacting with the environment. Circle the skill that the child is practicing for this particular task. As you observe the child experiencing same task throughout the year, again circle the skill, looking for growth.

1. **Observing**
   Uses the senses to gather information about objects or events.

2. **Comparing**
   Looks at similarities and differences in real objects.

3. **Classifying**
   Groups and sorts according to properties, such as size, shape, color, use.

4. **Measuring**
   Quantifies observations. This can involve numbers, distances, time, etc. using nonstandard units (Example: 3 handfuls or salt, 4 boxes tall)

5. **Communicating**
   Communicates ideas, directions, and descriptions orally or in written form, such as through pictures, maps, graphs, etc., so others can understand what is meant.

Name_____ Date_____

STAGES OF SINGING DEVELOPMENT

Directions: Circle the stage of development in singing development.

1. **Musical Babbling**
   Listens to musical sounds—human voice, radio, TV, music boxes, tapes, etc., and invents musical sound.

2. **Tagging On**
   Begins to imitate what is heard, but lags a little behind or tags on to the end of a song.

3. **Talking/Singing**

4. **Increased Accuracy**

5. **Accurate Singing of Simple Songs, Alone**

6. **Accurate Singing with a Group**

Source: Wolf, J. (1992). Let's sing it again: Creating music with young children. *Young Children, 47*(2), 56-61. Used by permission.

Name_____ Date_____

IMITATION/IMAGINATIVE PLAY

Directions: Circle and date the developmental state that the infant exhibits. Add an anecdotal record or picture.

1. **Copies Facial Expressions of Adults**

2. **Copies Actions of Adults**

3. **Copies Actions of Other Children**

4. **Imitates Familiar Actions of Others While Alone**
   Example: purse on arm, keys in door

5. **Pretends To Brush Own Hair, Drink from a Cup, Talk on the Phone, etc.**

6. **Pretends To Use an Object Such As a Doll or Stuffed Animal**
   Examples: brushes doll's hair, gives doll a drink

7. **Pretends By Replaying Familiar Routines, Repeats Over and Over**

San Antonio College
Child Development Department
CHD 1307/2307

TEMPERAMENT: A KEY TO INDIVIDUALITY

Each child is born unique. There is no other person exactly like him/her. Part of each child's individuality is temperament. Temperament styles are often reflected in the way that children approach life. By becoming aware of each child's temperament, we help foster positive growth.

Some components of temperament style have been defined, based on the work of Thomas and Chess (*Temperament and Development*) and Brazelton (*Neonatal Behavioral Assessment Scale*). By becoming sensitive to these components as we interact with children, we can more accurately match our action to their style and thus ensure a more successful experience. Observe your infants and toddlers in terms of the following temperament components:

1. **Activity level:** Does he have a lot of energy or is he more "laid back"?
   Would you rate the activity level as high_____medium_____low_____?
   Examples:

2. **Rhythmicity:** Is it easy to predict when she needs to eat, sleep, and eliminate, or is her pattern erratic?
   Would you rate rhythmicity as regular_____irregular_____?
   Examples:

3. **Distractibility:** Is it easy to distract him? For instance, will he stop crying when being diapered if you sing a song, or will he continue to cry?
   Would you rate child as distractible_____not distractible_____?
   Examples:

4. **Approach/withdrawal:** Is her first response to new food, toy, or person eager (approach) or cautious (withdrawal)?
   Would you rate approach/withdrawal as eager_____cautious_____?
   Examples:

5. **Adaptability:** Does he easily adapt to changes? Does he eventually like something even if he did not like it at first, or does he resist change for long periods of time?
   Would you rate adaptability as adaptive_____not adaptive_____?
   Examples:

6. **Intensity of Reaction:** Does she show a "big reaction" (either positive or negative) to things, or are her responses mild?

    Would you rate intensity of reaction as intense_____mild_____?

    Examples:

7. **Threshold of Responsiveness:** Does it take much stimulation from the environment or from people to get him interested or upset? Or is he very sensitive to any stimulation?

    Would you rate the threshold of responsiveness as low_____high_____?

    Examples:

8. **Quality of Mood:** Is most of her behavior pleasant, joyful, or smiling, or is most of her behavior grumpy, unfriendly, fussy?

    Quality of mood is generally_____.

    Examples:

9. **Attention Span and Persistence:** Does he stay with an activity or behavior for a long time and cannot be distracted from it, or does he give up easily?

    Would you rate attention span and persistence as long_____short_____?

    Examples:

Based on these observations, you may decide that with some of your children, it will be best to approach new experiences cautiously, to provide stimulation carefully, and to make changes slowly. It is also important to remember that temperament is an integral part of the child. It is neither good nor bad—it just is. It is part of what makes each child special.

Implications for planning for this child based on his/her temperament style:

Form designed by Linda Ruhmann

Name_____ Date_____

PARENT PAGE

Let Me Tell You About My Child!

Topic_____

Appendix C

Portfolio Assessment

Forms for
Chapter 4

LEARNING CENTER DEVELOPMENT GUIDE SHEET

Objective(s): _____

_____

_____

Materials: _____

_____

_____

Duration: _____

_____

_____

Addressing different levels and assessment:

Level	Activity/Expectation	Assessment

123

Roosevelt Elementary School
MULTI-AGE THEMATIC WEB

Field Trips

Notes

Social Studies

Resources

Fine Arts

Resources

Language Arts/
Reading

Resources

SLA

Resources

Science

Resources

Assessments

Theme:

Math

Resources

ESL

Resources

ANECDOTAL RECORD

_____Student_____

_____

Date   Date

_____

Date   Date

_____

Date   Date

_____

Date   Date

_____

WRITTEN LANGUAGE INVENTORY
Emergent and Early Writer (Side 2)

Key
N-Not observed
B-Beginning
S-Secure

Name_____

	Grade/Date				Anecdotal Notes
PUNCTUATION/CAPITALIZATION					
Uses periods					
Is aware of question marks, exclamation points, commas, quotation marks					
Uses capitals at the beginning of sentences					
Uses capitals for most proper nouns					
SPELLING					
Random use of symbols, scribbles, letters					
Uses initial consonants					
L to R progression in words					
Spaces between words					
Takes risks in spelling					
Uses initial, final consonants					
Conventional spelling of some words					
Uses incorrect vowel, but in correct place					
Conventional spelling of word endings					
Vowel approximations are more accurate					
Recognizes misspellings					
Uses classroom resources to check spelling					

Roosevelt Elementary Multi-age
BEGINNING OF YEAR ASSESSMENT FOR PLACEMENT
1996-1997

Student: _____   Teacher: _____   Date of Assessment: _____

LANGUAGE ARTS:

Baseline Information: (These three items are to be completed every six weeks and added to portfolio to observe development. Check if completed.)

Level of Competency	Skill/Concept	Materials Needed	Level of Mastery Demonstrated	Date	Assessment/ Observation Results/Comments	Date	Assessment/ Observation Results/Comments	Date	Assessment/ Observation Results/Comments
all	Draws a self-portrait.	Paper	(add to portfolio)	1st 6 weeks	2nd 6 weeks	3rd 6 weeks	4th 6 weeks	5th 6 weeks	6th 6 weeks
all	Makes a picture	Paper	(add to portfolio)	1st 6 weeks	2nd 6 weeks	3rd 6 weeks	4th 6 weeks	5th 6 weeks	6th 6 weeks
all	Describes the picture (Dictates or writes a story)								

Communication:

PK/K	Speaks clearly	none							
PK/K	Follows oral directions	none							
PK/K	Engages in conversation with peers	none							

Emergent Reading/Writing

Level of Competency	Skill/Concept	Materials Needed	Level of Mastery Demonstrated	Date	Assessment/ Observation Results/Comments	Date	Assessment/ Observation Results/Comments	Date	Assessment/ Observation Results/Comments
PK/K	Is aware of environmental print	Texas Inventory	(Use Inventory checklist)						
PK/K	Follows reading conventions	Texas Inventory	left/right top/bottom front/back						
K/1 and 1/2	Knows reading conventions		(Use Inventory checklist)						
K/1	Word Sense	Texas Inventory	(Use Inventory checklist)						
1/2	Produces rhyming words	Texas Inventory							
PK/K	Retells a story	Texas Inventory							
K/1	Tells stories for picture books	picture books							
PK/K, K/1 and 1/2	Recognizes letters	letter cards	a b c d e f g h i j k l m n o p q r s t u v w x y z A B C D E F G H I J K L M N O P Q R S T U V W X Y Z						

Level of Competency	Skill/Concept	Materials Needed	Level of Mastery Demonstrated	Date	Assessment/ Observation Results/Comments	Date	Assessment/ Observation Results/Comments	Date	Assessment/ Observation Results/Comments
PK/K	Matches letters	letter cards							
1/2	Matches letters (Upper and lower case)	letter cards	A B C D E F G H I J K L M N O P Q R S T U V W X Y Z						
PK/K, K/1	Copies Letters		A B C D E F G H I J K L M N O P Q R S T U V W X Y Z						
K/1	Knows sounds of letters	Texas Inventory	A B C D E F G H I J K L M N O P Q R S T U V W X Y Z						
K/1, 1/2, 2/3	Identifies initial consonant sounds	Texas Inventory	List:						
K/1, 1/2, 2/3	Identifies final consonant sounds	Texas Inventory	List:						
2/3	Identifies initial blends	Texas Inventory	List:						

Level of Competency	Skill/Concept	Materials Needed	Level of Mastery Demonstrated	Date	Assessment/ Observation Results/Comments	Date	Assessment/ Observation Results/Comments	Date	Assessment/ Observation Results/Comments
PK/K	Recognizes name	name cards							
PK/K K/1	Writes name	paper							
K/1	Copies words	paper							
1/2	Recognizes level sight words	sight word lists	Read through Level:_____ (Attach list)						
1/2 and 2/3	Word Recognition Level	word recognition test (IRI)	Level:_____						
K/1	Reads simple books (10 words or less)	books							
1/2 and 2/3	Reading Level as determined by IRI	IRI	Instructional: Independent: Frustration:						
1/2 and 2/3	Comprehension Level as determined by IRI		Level:						
K/1	Sequences pictures	sequence cards							

Level of Competency	Skill/Concept	Materials Needed	Level of Mastery Demonstrated	Date	Assessment/ Observation Results/Comments	Date	Assessment/ Observation Results/Comments	Date	Assessment/ Observation Results/Comments
1/2	Retells story—story comprehension	IRI							
PK/K	Uses scribble writing	paper journals							
PK/K	Uses invented spellings	paper journals							
K/1	Writes stories using invented spelling	paper journals							
1/2	Spells phonetic words	paper word lists							
1/2	Spells level words	level word lists							
K/1	Writes stories using letter forms	paper journals							

Student's General Level of Performance

How many objectives did he/she master at each tested level:

PK/K: 1   2   3   4   5   6   7   8   9   10   11   12

K/1:   1   2   3   4   5   6   7   8   9   10   11   12   13

1/2:   1   2   3   4   5   6   7   8   9   10   11

2/3:   1   2   3   4

IRI Word Recognition Level: _____

IRI Oral Reading Instructional Level: _____

IRI Comprehension Level: _____

Based on this assessment, at which level is the child currently working? _____

_____   _____

Teacher's Signature   Date

Roosevelt Elementary Multi-age

BEGINNING OF YEAR ASSESSMENT FOR PLACEMENT
1996-1997

Student: _____   Teacher: _____   Date of Assessment: _____

MATHEMATICS:

Level of Competency	Skill/Concept	Materials Needed	Level of Mastery Demonstrated	Date	Assessment/ Observation Results/Comments	Date	Assessment/ Observation Results/Comments	Date	Assessment/ Observation Results/Comments
PK/K	Rote Counting (1-10, 1-20)	none	Counted to:						
K/1	Counts		Counted: 1-20, 1-50, 1-100						
1/2	Counts to 100		Counts to:						
PK/K	One-to-one Correspondence (1-10)	counters	Counted to:						
PK/K	Numeral Recognition (1-10)	number list or flashcards	1 2 3 4 5 6 7 8 9 10 Other:						
K/1	Numeral Recognition (1-20)		1 2 3 4 5 6 7 8 9 10 11 12 13 14 15 16 17 18 19 20						

Level of Competency	Skill/Concept	Materials Needed	Level of Mastery Demonstrated	Date	Assessment/ Observation Results/Comments	Date	Assessment/ Observation Results/Comments	Date	Assessment/ Observation Results/Comments
1/2	Numeral Recognition (1-100)	number list or flashcards	1-100:						
1/2	Reads number words (1-20)	word cards	1 2 3 4 5 6 7 8 9 10 11 12 13 14 15 16 17 18 19 20						
2/3	Reads number words to 100		1 2 3 4 5 6 7 8 9 10 11 12 13 14 15 16 17 18 19 20 30 40 50 60 70 80 90 100						
1/2	Place Value—1s and 10s	number cards	ones: tens:						
2/3	Place Value—1s, 10s, 100s, 1,000s	number cards	ones: tens: hundreds: thousands:						
PK/K	Constructs sets for numerals	counters	Sets through:						
K/1	Constructs sets for numerals		1-10 10-20						
PK/K	Sorts by size, shape and color	attribute shapes	size: shape: color:						

Level of Competency	Skill/Concept	Materials Needed	Level of Mastery Demonstrated	Date	Assessment/ Observation Results/Comments	Date	Assessment/ Observation Results/Comments	Date	Assessment/ Observation Results/Comments
PK/K	Recognizes 8 basic colors	color cards	red, blue, yellow, green, black, white, orange, purple						
PK/K	Recognizes 4 basic shapes	shape cards	square, circle, rectangle, triangle						
K/1	Writes numerals to 20	paper	Writes 1-20						
1/2	Writes numerals to 100		Writes to: ____(100)						
2/3	Writes numerals to 200		Writes to: ____(200)						
K/1	Orders numerals	number cards	1-20						
1/2	Orders numerals (1-100)		1-100						
K/1	Identifies coins	coins	1¢ 5¢ 10¢ 25¢ 50¢						
1/2 and 2/3	Knows value of coins	coins	1¢ 5¢ 10¢ 25¢ 50¢						
2/3	Counts change	test folder							
K/1	Tells time (hour and half hour)	clock	hour: 1/2 hour:						

Level of Competency	Skill/Concept	Materials Needed	Level of Mastery Demonstrated	Date	Assessment/ Observation Results/Comments	Date	Assessment/ Observation Results/Comments	Date	Assessment/ Observation Results/Comments
1/2	Tells time to quarter hour	clock	1/4 hour:						
2/3	Tells time to 5-minute and 1-minute intervals		5 min. Interval: 1-minute Interval:						
K/1	Combines sets to make larger sets to 10 (using manipulatives)	counters	1-10						
1/2	Adds to 10 using objects		1-10						
1/2	Subtracts from 10s using objects	counters	1-10						
1/2	Adds and subtracts using 2 digits, with no regrouping	paper	add: subtract:						
1/2	Addition and subtracting to 18	paper							
2/3	Adds and subtracts using 2 digits, with no regrouping	paper	adds: subtracts:						
2/3	Adds and subtracts using 2 digits, with regrouping	paper	adds: subtracts:						

Level of Competency	Skill/Concept	Materials Needed	Level of Mastery Demonstrated	Date	Assessment/ Observation Results/Comments	Date	Assessment/ Observation Results/Comments	Date	Assessment/ Observation Results/Comments
K/1	Counts by 2s to 20	none	counts to: ___ (20)						
1/2	Counts by 2s to 50	none	counts to: ___ (50)						
2/3	Counts by 2s to 100	none	counts to: ___ (100)						
1/2	Counts by 5s to 50	none	counts to: ___ (50)						
2/3	Counts by 5s to 100	none	counts to: ___ (100)						
1/2	Counts by 10s to 100	none	counts to: ___ (100)						
2/3	Counts by 10s to 200	none	counts to: ___ (200)						
1/2	Creates and extends simple patterns	pattern blocks							
2/3	Analyzes patterns	patterns							
2/3	Word problems	testing folder							
2/3	Multiplication facts to 9s	tests	1s 2s 3s 4s 5s 6s 7s 8s 9s						
2/3	Identifies fractional parts	fraction pieces	1/2, 1/4, 1/3, 3/4, 2/3, other						

Student's General Level of Performance

How many objectives did he/she master at each tested level:

PK/K: 1   2   3   4   5   6   7   8   9   10   11   12

K/1:   1   2   3   4   5   6   7   8   9   10   11   12   13

1/2:   1   2   3   4   5   6   7   8   9   10   11

2/3:   1   2   3   4

IRI Word Recognition Level: _____

IRI Oral Reading Instructional Level: _____

IRI Comprehension Level: _____

Based on this assessment, at which level is the child currently working? _____

_____   _____
Teacher's Signature   Date

Appendix D

Portfolio Assessment

Forms for
Chapter 5

Problem		Solution

Method

PROBLEM-SOLVING FLOW CHART

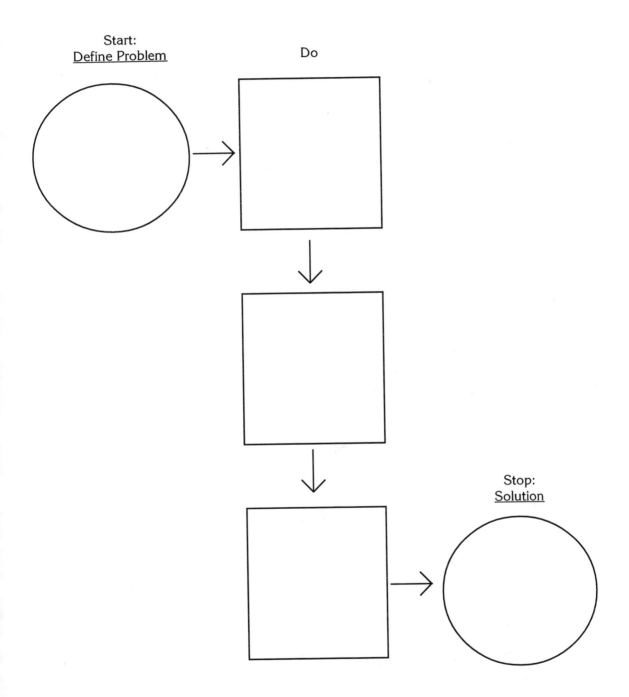

MATHEMATICS PORTFOLIO CHECKLIST

Your portfolio should contain the following items:

5 to 7 "best pieces" showing the solution and the work involved. Include examples of problem solving, investigation, application, and group work.

_____ Title _____

_____ Title _____

_____ Title _____

_____ Title _____

_____ Title _____

_____ Title _____

_____ Title _____

_____ Other pieces of mathematics work

_____ A letter to the portfolio evaluator

_____ A table of contents

REFLECTIONS ON PORTFOLIO SELECTIONS

Name: _____ Date: _____

Title of piece: _____

I chose this piece because _____

_____

_____

The best things about it are _____

_____

_____

If I were going to do it over again, I would _____

_____

_____

ALTERNATIVE ASSESSMENT/PROBLEM SOLVING
Science Matter Unit

TAAS Areas Addressed: Summarization, drawing conclusions, using and applying formulas, inference, using four math operations to solve problems, creating charts and tables, attributes of matter, collection, organization, displaying and interpreting data, using logical reasoning to justify conclusions and solution processes, connecting mathematics to other disciplines.

Directions: Use density/volume boxes to do the following:

1. Define volume. _____

_____

2. Write the formula for volume. _____

3. Measure the volume of your box in cm.

   Length: _____ Width: _____ Height: _____

4. Define mass. _____

5. Predict or infer the mass of your box before actual measurement. Mass your density/volume box on the triple beam balance.

   Prediction: _____ gms. Actual mass: _____ gms.

6. Define density. _____

7. Write the formula for density. _____

8. Using the formula, compute the density of your box. _____

9. Construct a chart to display the data you collected.

10. Summarize, in at least three paragraphs, the materials you needed to solve each step, what you needed to know prior to beginning the task, and how you proceeded to accomplish the assignment.

Adapted from assessment task developed by Linda Koehler & Ruby McDonald, Northside ISD, San Antonio, TX

EVALUATING STUDENT BEHAVIORS
Measuring Thought Processes in Behavior
Demonstrating Skill and Participation Levels

Name _____

Numerical Value
0 = Dependent
1 = Needs Support
2 - Independent

SPECIFIC SKILL	DATE			COMMENTS
Understands Problem • paraphrases • recalls problem				
Formulates a Plan • selects strategy				
Implements Plan • carries out strategies				
Explains Plan • orally and in writing				
Evaluates/Interprets Metarecognition Results • orally and in writing • demonstrates solution				
Extends • creates own problem • recalls related problem				

ATTITUDES (Interaction and Participation)

Cooperates				
Shares/Collaborates • tries, contributes ideas				
Questions Peers • encourages others to participate				
Takes Risks • confidence in own ability				
Stays on Task • perseveres				

Stenmark, J. K. (Ed.). (1991). *Mathematics assessment: Myths, models, good questions, and practical suggestions.* Reston, VA: National Council of Teachers of Mathematics. Used by permission.

OBSERVATION CHECKLIST

Curricular/Content Area _____ Date _____

Target Skills

Names of Students   Comments

1._____

2._____

3._____

4._____

5._____

6._____

7._____

8._____

9._____

10._____

11._____

12._____

13._____

14._____

15._____

MEASUREMENT
Concepts and Skills Using Metric and Customary Units

Name _____

Standard	Dates			Comments
Measures areas using grids				
Finds perimeters using standard and nonstandard units				
Uses the concept of perimeter to solve problems				
Measures the capacity of a container using nonstandard units				
Identifies concrete models that approximate capacity units				
Estimates and measures the capacity of a container				
Solves application and non-routine problems involving				
length _____				
weight _____				
time _____				
capacity _____				
Determines the amount of time elapsed in a problem-solving situation				

PERFORMANCE TASK ASSESSMENT
Microscope Usage

Name _____ Date: _____

	Points	Self	Peer	Teacher
		Points Earned		
1. Carries microscope by arm and supports with hand.	1	___	___	___
2. Holds slides by sides.	1	___	___	___
3. Mounts slides under stage clips.	1	___	___	___
4. Sets revolving nosepiece to lowest objective.	1	___	___	___
5. Looks from the side and lowers the objective as low as it will go without touching the slide.	1	___	___	___
6. Looks through the eyepiece and focuses upward until the slide is in focus.	1	___	___	___
7. Turns the revolving nosepiece to the middle objective and focuses.	1	___	___	___
8. Turns the revolving nosepiece to the highest objective and focuses.	1	___	___	___
9. Lowers the stage and removes slides from stage.	1	___	___	___
10. Unplugs microscope by pulling on plug, not wire.	1	___	___	___
Total:	10	___	___	___

_____ + _____ + _____ ÷ 3 = _____
Grade

Adapted from performance task developed by Linda Koehler & Ruby McDonald, Northside ISD, San Antonio, TX.

GENERIC SCORING RUBRIC FOR PERFORMANCE TASKS

4 = Outstanding. All criteria met. In addition, the product/presentation exceeds the assigned task and contains additional, unexpected, or outstanding features.

3 = Good. Product/presentation completely or substantially meets the criteria.

2 = Adequate. Product/presentation meets some of the criteria and does not contain gross errors or crucial omissions.

1 = Inadequate. Product/presentation does not satisfy a significant number of the criteria, does not accomplish the task, contains errors, or is of poor quality.

0 = Poor. Student did not do or did not complete the task, or shows no comprehension of the requirements.

ANALYTIC SCALE FOR PROBLEM SOLVING

Understanding the problem
0 = No attempt
1 = Completely misinterprets the problem
2 = Misinterprets major part of the problem
3 = Misinterprets minor part of the problem
4 = Complete understanding of the problem

Solving the problem
0 = No attempt
1 = Totally inappropriate plan
2 = Partially correct procedure but with major flaw
3 = Substantially correct procedure with minor omission or procedural error
4 = A plan that could lead to a correct solution with no arithmetic errors

Answering the problem
0 = No answer, or wrong answer based upon an inappropriate plan
1 = Copying error; computational error; partial answer for the problem with multiple answers; no answer statement; answer labeled incorrectly
2 = Correct solution

Source: Szetela, W., & Nicol, C. (1992). Evaluating problem solving in mathematics. *Educational Leadership, 49*(8), 42-45. Used by permission of the Association for Supervision and Curriculum Development. Copyright © 1992 by ASCD. All rights reserved.

PERFORMANCE TASK ASSESSMENT
Rock Identification

Scoring Scale:
  3 = uses correct procedures and attains complete and accurate results
  2 = uses correct procedures but results are incomplete or inaccurate
  1 = uses incorrect procedures and attains inaccurate and incomplete results
  0 = does not attempt task

Earned Points

1. Given 4 samples, uses physical characteristics   _____ _____ _____
    to classify as mineral, sedimentary, igneous,
    or metamorphic.

2. Masses specimen to tenth of a gram.   _____ _____ _____

3. Using graduated cylinder, determines volume   _____ _____ _____
    of specimen to nearest cubic centimeter.

4. Calculates density using calculator and   _____ _____ _____
    measurements of mass and volume.

5. Performs acid test on two specimens (able   _____ _____ _____
    to identify positive/negative reaction).

6. Uses streak plate to identify color of   _____ _____ _____
    a mineral streak.

7. Uses fingernail, copper penny, and   _____ _____ _____
    nail to identify range of mineral's hardness.

8. Uses Mohs Hardness Scale to identify   _____ _____ _____
    minerals that will scratch one another.

9. Compares/contrasts intrusive and   _____ _____ _____
    extrusive rocks in the following ways:
    (One point for each correct answer)
    a. Describes where formed.
    b. Describes physical characteristics.
    c. Describes crystal size.

10. Using WEDSED, is able to describe   _____ _____ _____
    how sedimentary rocks are formed.

11. Separates foliated from nonfoliated rocks.   _____ _____ _____

12. Matches parent rock to metamorphic rock.   _____ _____ _____

13. Diagrams and labels stages of the rock cycle.   _____ _____ _____

                          Total: _____ _____ _____

_____ + _____ + _____ ÷ 3 = _____ (Grade)

Adapted from performance task developed by Linda Koehler & Ruby McDonald, Northside ISD, San Antonio, TX

ASSESSING FOR SUCCESS: PERFORMANCE TASK

Preparation

One way to assess a student's ability to construct inferences based on observations is to construct mystery boxes. Be sure to use identical boxes and objects when assessing children simultaneously. An example of a mystery box is one that uses two small objects that either roll or slide. Inexpensive and readily available rolling objects include BBs, ball bearings, plastic Easter eggs, and marbles. Metal washers and bottle caps and lids also are good sliding objects.

Directions to the Student

1. Write your name on this line _____

2. Check the box to be sure it is taped shut. Do not open the box.

3. The box contains one or more objects. Pick up the box and listen to the sounds as you gently shake it. Tilt the box and listen carefully.

4. Answer the following questions:

_____a. What shape is an object in the box?

_____b. What is one other property of an object in the box?

_____c. What is one kind of motion made by an object in the box?

_____d. Except for air, how many objects do you think are in the box?

_____e. Explain why you think your answer to question d is correct.

_____

_____

Scoring Procedure

1 point each for questions a, b, c, and e. Question d is not scored.

Acceptable responses for questions a, b, c, and e include:
   a. flat, round, ball-shaped, like a coin, and so on
   b. hard, heavy, sounds like metal
   c. slides, rolls, glides, or drops
   e. student response has to support response to question d

1. Adapted from an example presented by Douglas Reynolds at The United States Department of Education Secretary's Conference on Improving Assessment in Mathematics and Science Education, September 20-21, 1993, Arlington, Virginia.

Appendix E

Portfolio Assessment

Forms for
Chapter 6

ASSESSING CHILDREN'S GROWTH RELATED TO KNOWLEDGE, SKILLS, DISPOSITIONS, AND FEELINGS

Child's name: _____ Date: _____

1. Knowledge: What new information, concepts, relationships, meaning is this child adding to his or her background as a result of the project work?

2. Skills: What skills are being applied or developed as a result of this child's involvement in project work?

1. Periodically observed   2. Frequently observed   3. Always observed
4. Not observed

	1	2	3	4
Social				
• cooperation	❏	❏	❏	❏
• negotiation	❏	❏	❏	❏
• teamwork	❏	❏	❏	❏
• communication	❏	❏	❏	❏
• discussion	❏	❏	❏	❏
• assertiveness	❏	❏	❏	❏
• debating	❏	❏	❏	❏
• other:	❏	❏	❏	❏
Academic				
• listening	❏	❏	❏	❏
• speaking	❏	❏	❏	❏
• reading	❏	❏	❏	❏
• writing	❏	❏	❏	❏
• other:	❏	❏	❏	❏
Mathematic				
• counting	❏	❏	❏	❏
• estimating	❏	❏	❏	❏
• measuring	❏	❏	❏	❏
• problem solving	❏	❏	❏	❏
• graphing	❏	❏	❏	❏
• computing	❏	❏	❏	❏
• other:	❏	❏	❏	❏

1. Periodically observed   2. Frequently observed   3. Always observed
4. Not observed

	1	2	3	4

Scientific
- questioning   ❑ ❑ ❑ ❑
- researching   ❑ ❑ ❑ ❑
- observation   ❑ ❑ ❑ ❑
- analysis   ❑ ❑ ❑ ❑
- hypothesizing   ❑ ❑ ❑ ❑
- data management   ❑ ❑ ❑ ❑
- computer use   ❑ ❑ ❑ ❑
- other: ❑ ❑ ❑ ❑

3. Dispositions: What desirable patterns of behavior does this child exhibit in the project work?

- cooperativeness   ❑ ❑ ❑ ❑
- initiative   ❑ ❑ ❑ ❑
- curiosity   ❑ ❑ ❑ ❑
- helpfulness   ❑ ❑ ❑ ❑
- independence   ❑ ❑ ❑ ❑
- responsibility   ❑ ❑ ❑ ❑
- risk-taking   ❑ ❑ ❑ ❑
- humor   ❑ ❑ ❑ ❑
- resourcefulness   ❑ ❑ ❑ ❑
- appreciation   ❑ ❑ ❑ ❑
- persistence   ❑ ❑ ❑ ❑
- confidence   ❑ ❑ ❑ ❑
- generosity   ❑ ❑ ❑ ❑
- creativity   ❑ ❑ ❑ ❑
- respect   ❑ ❑ ❑ ❑
- other: ❑ ❑ ❑ ❑

4. Feelings: How does this child feel about his or her project work?
___ recognizes personal strengths and limitations
___ sets realistic goals for achievement
___ learns from errors
___ copes appropriately with frustrations or setbacks
___ takes pride in his/her work
___ feels confident about his/her own potential for learning
___ able to judge own successes

154

CHILD'S PORTFOLIO SELF-ASSESSMENT SHEET

Name: _____

1. What steps am I taking to get information about my project?

2. Am I making responsible choices in my project work?

	Yes	No
Who I work with?	❏	❏
Where I work?	❏	❏
How I use my time?	❏	❏
What activities I do?	❏	❏
What materials I use?	❏	❏

3. Strategies

	Yes	No
Did I choose a good strategy for my project work?	❏	❏
Is this strategy helping me to learn new information about my project topic?	❏	❏
Have any problems come up?	❏	❏
Is there something else that will work better for me next time?	❏	❏

4. What are some new things I have learned about my project topic?

5. What questions do I have about my project topic?

6. What are some of the skills and processes I am using in my project work? (Circle)

listening	speaking	reading	writing
problem solving	researching	cooperating	teamwork
graphing	analyzing	observing	questioning
risk-taking	creativity	responsibility	persistence

7. What do I need help with in order to complete my project?

8. What do I like best about my project so far?   What do I like the least?

9. Are there any important pieces of information missing in my project work?

CHOOSING MY WORK FOR DISPLAY

1. Which pieces of work really show what I have learned about my project topic?

2. Which pieces of work would I be proud to share with visitors?

3. Are these pieces of work:

   ___ complete?

   ___ easy to understand?

   ___ attractive?

   ___ interesting?

   ___ accurate?

4. Which pieces of my portfolio work contribute something of value to the project as a whole?

5. What would be the best way for me to share my project with other people?

FIRST GRADE SKILLS

Thinking Kids®
Carson-Dellosa Publishing LLC
Greensboro, North Carolina

Thinking Kids®
Carson-Dellosa Publishing LLC
PO Box 35665
Greensboro, NC 27425 USA

Printed in the USA • All rights reserved.   ISBN 978-1-4838-4116-8
02-253187811

Contents

Letter to Parents & Caregivers 4

Checklist of Essential First Grade Skills 5

Sounds & Letters 6–71
Writing Letters • Matching Uppercase & Lowercase Letters • Beginning & Ending
Consonant Sounds • Consonant Blends & Digraphs • Short & Long Vowel Sounds

Vocabulary 72–101
Sight Words • Context Clues • Classifying Words • Prefixes & Suffixes • Shades of Meaning

Language Arts 102–137
Common & Proper Nouns • Plurals & Possessives • Pronouns • Verb Tenses
• Noun-Verb Agreement • Adjectives • Articles • Prepositions & Conjunctions
• Types of Sentences • Capitalization & Punctuation • Comma Use

Reading Comprehension 138–151
Sequencing • Using Picture Clues • Classifying • Following Directions • Predicting
• Drawing Conclusions • Answering Questions

Writing 152–163
Writing a Story • Writing to Inform • Writing an Opinion

Addition & Subtraction to 20 164–199
Counting Ahead & Back • Commutative & Associative Properties of Addition • Making 10
• Using Addition for Subtraction • Word Problems • Fact Families

Place Value 200–225
Counting by Tens • Counting to 120 • Two-Digit Numbers • Comparing Numbers • Adding
& Subtracting 10

Addition & Subtraction to 100 226–235
Adding One-Digit Numbers to Two-Digit Numbers • Regrouping • Adding & Subtracting
Multiples of 10

Measurement & Data 236–261
Measuring Length • Telling Time • Bar Graphs • Picture Graphs • Tally Charts

Shapes 262–275
Flat & Solid Shapes • Describing & Making Shapes • Equal Shares

Answer Key 276–320

Dear Parents & Caregivers

Dear Parents and Caregivers,

Welcome to *First Grade Skills!* Inside this comprehensive resource, you'll find an abundance of joyful, child-centered learning activities that will guide your child step-by-step as he or she explores these essential skills for school success:

Reading & Writing Skills: Your child will practice handwriting and phonics and identify nouns, verbs, and other parts of speech. He or she will write sentences using correct capitalization and punctuation. Your child will improve reading comprehension and write stories, informational reports, and opinions.

Vocabulary Development: Your child will recognize high-frequency words, use context clues, and use prefixes and suffixes as clues to word meanings.

Math Skills: Your child will understand the place value of two-digit numbers and use strategies to add and subtract to 100.

Applying Math Skills: Your child will measure length, tell time, make graphs, and identify two-dimensional and three-dimensional shapes.

While academics are important, social and emotional skills also play a huge role in school success. Throughout this book, you and your child will find fun activities and practical tips that promote development in these vital areas:

everything that makes your child special and unique

healthy eating, exercise, safety, and more

making friends and getting along with others

honesty, responsibility, tolerance, and more

effort and attitude as the keys to learning and growth

So, invite your child to grab a pencil and get going! Over 250 fun and educational activities are at your fingertips!

Sincerely,
Thinking Kids®

Essential First Grade Skills

Reading & Writing Skills:
I can...

- ❑ print all uppercase and lowercase letters.
- ❑ associate sounds and letters in order to read and spell one-syllable words.
- ❑ break longer words into syllables.
- ❑ write sentences that begin with a capital letter and end with a punctuation mark.
- ❑ compare characters and events in stories.
- ❑ answer questions about what I read.
- ❑ write stories, facts, and opinions.

Motor Skills: I can...

- ❑ use all eating utensils well.
- ❑ hold a pencil correctly and write with greater control.
- ❑ draw detailed shapes and pictures.
- ❑ catch a small ball using only my hands.
- ❑ run around obstacles while maintaining balance.
- ❑ kick a ball with reasonable accuracy.

Math Skills: I can...

- ❑ count and write numbers to 120.
- ❑ add and subtract to 20.
- ❑ add to 100 using an understanding of place value.
- ❑ compare two-digit numbers.
- ❑ order objects by length.
- ❑ tell time in hours and half-hours.
- ❑ understand data in simple charts and graphs.
- ❑ identify and compare shapes.
- ❑ divide shapes into halves and fourths.

Social/Emotional Skills: I can...

- ❑ distinguish between fact and fiction.
- ❑ adjust behavior based on positive feedback and encouragement.
- ❑ begin to see things from another person's point of view.
- ❑ go along with routines, rules, and organized activities.
- ❑ choose activities that involve social interaction and cooperation.
- ❑ try first to solve problems by myself.

Write Aa, Bb, Cc

Trace and write.

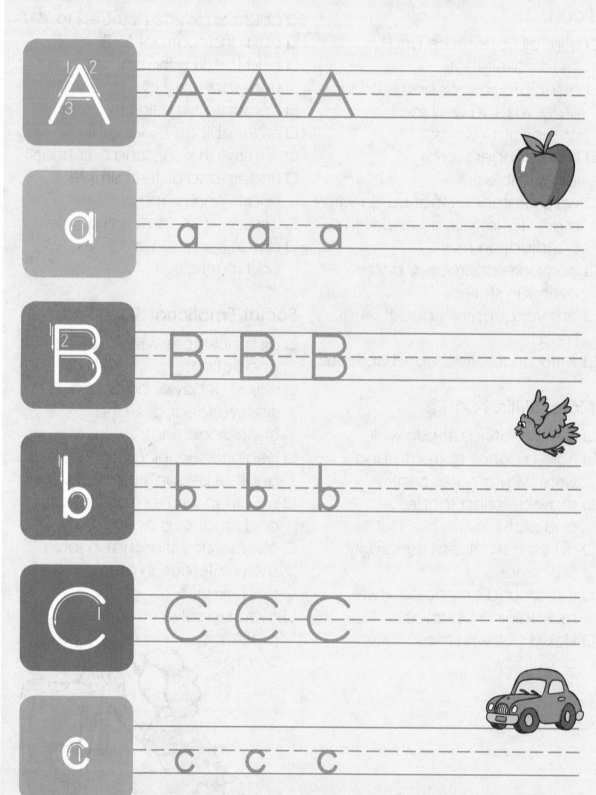

A A A A

a a a a

B B B B

b b b b

C C C C

c c c c

6

Write Dd, Ee

Trace and write.

D D D D

d d d

E E E

e e e

When you have a growth mindset, you know that if you try and work hard, you learn and improve. Check sentences that show a growth mindset. In each one, find a word that begins with **d**.

- ☐ I will never learn this.
- ☐ This is difficult, but I will get better at it.
- ☐ She is talented at this, but I am not.
- ☐ I made a mistake, so I will do it again.

Write Ff, Gg, Hh

Trace and write.

Write Ii, Jj

Trace and write.

Write **I** to begin each sentence. Then, finish the sentence to tell about you!

_____ _____

___ _____

_____ am _____ years old.

_____ _____

___ _____

_____ like to _____.

9

All About Me

Write kk, Ll, Mm

Trace and write.

Write Nn, Oo

Trace and write.

N-O spells **NO**! If you see someone being bullied, look the bully in the eye and say, "No!" Try to get the person to a safe place. Kids who bully use their power to control or harm others. You can use your powers to help others! Take all bullying seriously. If you see it happen, tell a trusted adult.

Social Skills

Write Pp, Qq, Rr

Trace and write.

Write Ss, Tt

Trace and write.

S   S   S   S

s   s   s   s

T   T   T   T

t   t   t   t

Write **s** or **t** in each car safety rule.

Wear a seatbelt during every ___rip.

Buckle up righ___ away.

Never ___hare a seatbelt.

Health & Fitness

Write Uu, Vv, Ww

Trace and write.

14

Write Xx, Yy, Zz

Trace and write.

Uppercase & Lowercase Letters

Write the missing letter in each pair.

a B   C   d E

f   g H   i   j

K   l M   n   o

P Q   r S   T

U   v W

x Y   z

Write Your Name

Circle the letters in your first and last names.

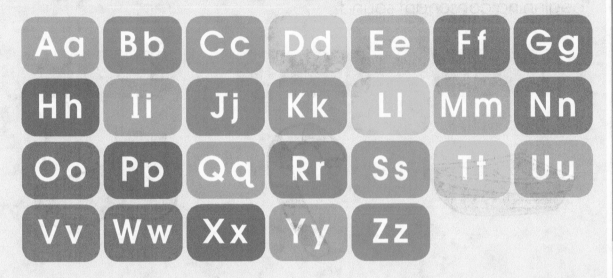

Aa Bb Cc Dd Ee Ff Gg
Hh Ii Jj Kk Ll Mm Nn
Oo Pp Qq Rr Ss Tt Uu
Vv Ww Xx Yy Zz

Write your first and last names.

_____

_____

_____

_____

When you introduce yourself, tell your full **name**. Stand up straight, look the person in the eye, and give a firm handshake. Imagine you are meeting one of your heroes. Complete the introduction.

_____

Hi, I am _____.

your name

_____

It is nice to meet you, _____.

your hero's name

Beginning Sounds b, c, d, f

Say the name of each picture. Circle the letter that makes its beginning consonant sound.

18

Beginning Sounds b, c, d, f

Say the name of each picture. Draw a line to the letter that makes its beginning consonant sound.

b

c

d

f

19

Beginning Sounds g, h, j

Say the name of each picture. Trace the letter that makes its beginning consonant sound.

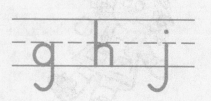

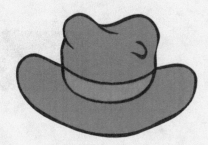

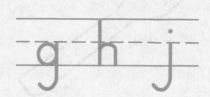

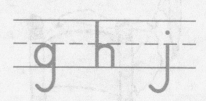

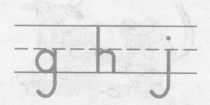

Beginning Sounds g, h, j

Say the name of each picture. Draw a line to the letter that makes its beginning consonant sound.

g

h

j

Goal begins with the **g** sound. Choose a goal, like reading a chapter book, catching a ball, or learning a new game. With an adult, find and print out 10 pictures that show your goal. Then, practice 10 times. Each time, tape one picture on the bathroom mirror. On day 10, celebrate how far you have come. Look in the mirror and smile!

Growth Mindset

Beginning Sounds k, l, m, n

Say the name of each picture. Circle the letter that makes its beginning consonant sound.

Beginning Sounds k, l, m, n

Say the name of each picture. Draw a line to the letter that makes its beginning consonant sound.

k

l

m

n

23

Beginning Sounds p, q, r, s

Say the name of each picture. Color the picture whose name begins with the consonant shown.

p

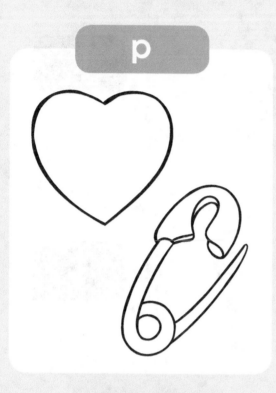

q

r

s

Beginning Sounds p, q, r, s

Say the name of each picture. Draw a line to the letter that makes its beginning consonant sound.

p

q

r

s

25

Beginning Sounds t, v, w

Say the name of each picture. Trace the letter that makes its beginning consonant sound.

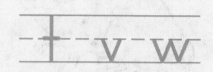

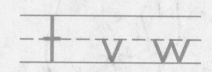

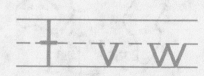

Beginning Sounds t, v, w

Say the name of each picture. Draw a line to the letter that makes its beginning consonant sound.

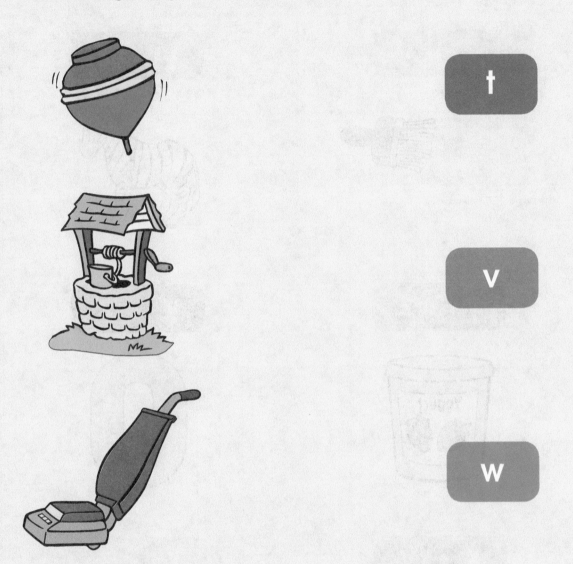

t

v

w

Wash begins with the **w** sound. Wash your hands often to stay healthy. Read the names of things at school that are likely to have germs on them. Circle the ones you have touched recently.

doorknob   computer keyboard

handrail   playground equipment

water fountain

Health & Fitness

Beginning Sounds y, z

Say the name of each picture. Circle the letter that makes its beginning consonant sound.

x   y

y   z

y   z

y   z

x   y

x   z

28

Beginning Sounds y, z

Say the name of each picture. Draw a line to the letter that makes its beginning consonant sound.

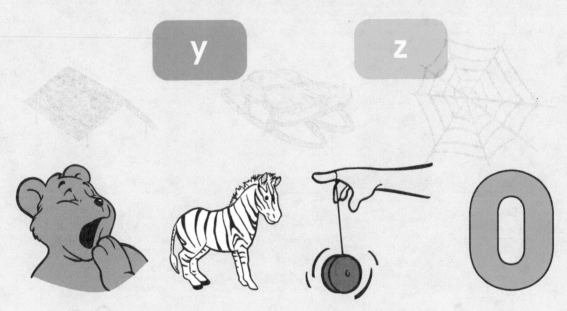

| y | z |

Yawn begins with the **y** sound. If you yawn a lot, you might not be getting enough sleep! First graders need about 10 hours of sleep each night. Color one section of the clock for each hour you slept last night. Begin at the hour you went to bed and end at the hour when you woke up. Count the sections you colored. Did you get enough sleep?

29

Health & Fitness

Ending Sounds b, d, f

Say the name of each picture. Write the letter that makes its ending consonant sound.

_____

_ _ _ _ _

_____

_ _ _ _ _

_____

_ _ _ _ _

_____

_ _ _ _ _

_____

_ _ _ _ _

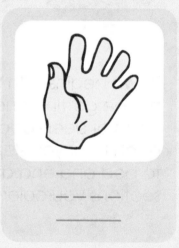

_____

_ _ _ _ _

_____

_ _ _ _ _

_____

_ _ _ _ _

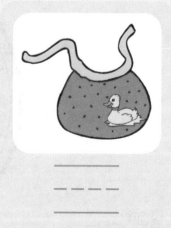

_____

_ _ _ _ _

Ending Sounds g, m, n

Say the name of each picture. Draw a line to the letter that makes its ending consonant sound.

g

m

n

Ending Sounds k, l, p

In each row, color the pictures that end with the sound of the consonant letter shown.

k

l

p

Help ends with the **p** sound. It is OK to ask for help. Help from others lets us learn and grow. Draw pictures that show a time you asked for help and what happened after you asked.

I asked for help.	This is what happened.

Ending Sounds r, s, t, x

Say the name of each picture. Circle the letter that makes its ending consonant sound.

r s **t** x	r s t x	r s t x
r s **t** x	r s t x	r s t x
r s t x	r s t x	r s t x

Beginning & Ending Sounds

Say the name of each picture. Draw a triangle around the letter that makes the beginning consonant sound. Draw a square around the letter that makes the ending consonant sound.

l g b

m n s

v n l

b p t

d l s

p r z

34

Beginning & Ending Sounds

Say the name of each picture. Write the letters that make its beginning and ending consonant sounds.

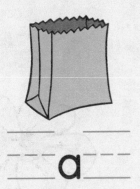

__ a __

__ o __

__ i __

__ a __

__ oa __

__ ir __

Consonant Blends

A consonant blend is two or more consonant letters whose sounds blend together in a word. Say the name of each picture. Circle the consonant blend you hear.

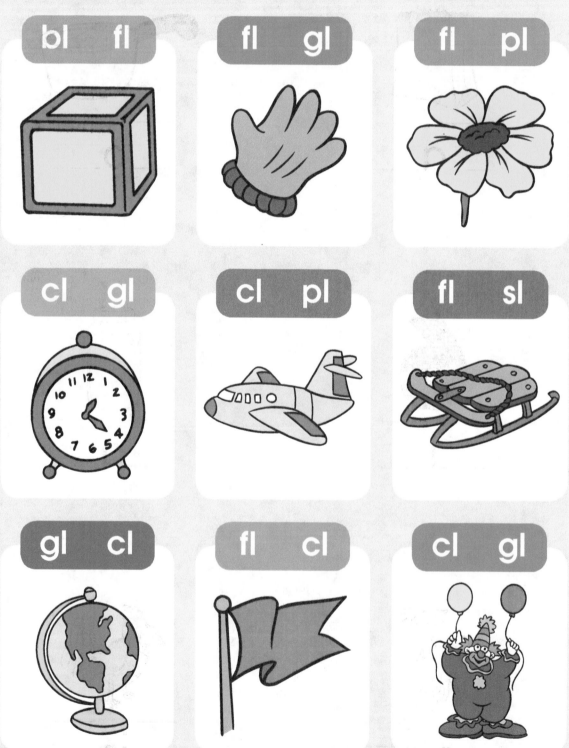

bl   fl

fl   gl

fl   pl

cl   gl

cl   pl

fl   sl

gl   cl

fl   cl

cl   gl

Consonant Blends

Answer each riddle by writing a word with a consonant blend.

sleep	clap	clock	blow	glass

I have two hands on my face. What am I?

_____

_____

I can be empty or full. What am I?

_____

_____

I am the opposite of **wake**. What am I?

_____

_____

I am what you do with a whistle or bubble gum.
What am I?

_____

_____

I am what people do after a good show. What am I?

_____

_____

37

Consonant Blends

Write a consonant blend to complete each word.

_____ ain

_____ og

_____ um

_____ esent

_____ ab

_____ ush

Consonant Blends

Say the name of each picture. Circle the consonant blend you hear.

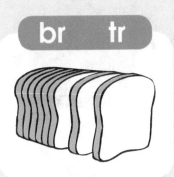

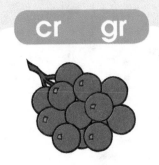

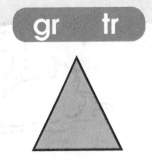

Tradition begins with a **consonant blend**. A family tradition is something your family does each year, especially around holidays. Complete the sentence and draw a picture to tell about one of your family's traditions.

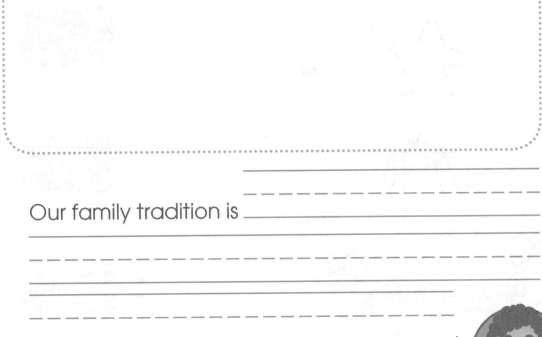

Our family tradition is _____

_____

_____

_____.

All About Me

Consonant Blends

Say the name of each picture. Draw a line to the consonant blend you hear.

sk

sw

sm

sn

sp

st

Consonant Blends

Write a consonant blend to complete each word.

_____unk

_____ow

_____ed

_____ide

_____ate

_____ake

Consonant Blends

Write a consonant blend to complete each word.

she _____

be _____

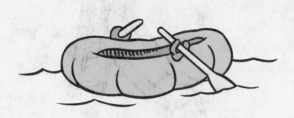

ra _____

mi _____

ma _____

qui _____

Consonant Blends

Say the name of each picture. Draw a line to the consonant blend you hear at the end of the word.

ft

st

lt

nt

Consonant Digraphs

A consonant digraph is two or more consonant letters that come together to make one sound in a word. The word at the top of each column has a consonant digraph. Circle pictures in the column whose names have the same consonant digraph.

sh

shoe

ch

chin

th

thumb

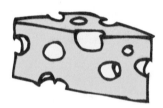

Consonant Digraphs

Write a consonant digraph to complete each word.

_____eep

_____ale

_____air

_____orn

_____ip

_____icken

45

Consonant Digraphs

Underline a consonant digraph in each word in the box. Then, write a word to name each picture.

bench whale shoe wheel brush chair

46

Consonant Digraphs

Underline a consonant digraph in each word in the box. Then, write a word to name each picture.

watch shell peach thimble teeth match

_____

_____

_____

_____

_____

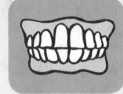

_____

Short a

Short **a** is the vowel sound you hear in the middle of **bat**. In each column, circle the picture whose name has the short **a** sound.

Short a

Write a short **a** word to name each picture.

| rat | grass | can | bag | man | bat |

_____
- -
_____

_____
- -
_____

_____
- -
_____

_____
- -
_____

_____
- -
_____

_____
- -
_____

49

Short e

Short **e** is the vowel sound you hear in the middle of **pet**. Color the pictures whose names have the short **e** sound.

Short e

Write a short **e** word to name each picture.

| ten | net | bell | beg |

You hear the short **e** sound in **help**. Circle ways that you help at home.

feed my pet   weed the garden   set the table

sweep the floor   wash dishes   make my bed

carry groceries   put toys away

turn out lights

Character Development

Short i

Short **i** is the vowel sound you hear in the middle of **six**. In each sentence, find and circle two words that have the short **i** sound.

Is that a shark's fin?

Dante put cans in the bin.

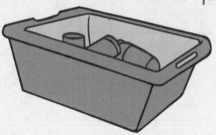

The chick ran to its mother.

Lift the jar's lid.

Short i

Write a short **i** word to name each picture.

pig   bib   wig   pin   gift   hit

Short o

Short **o** is the vowel sound you hear in the middle of **hot**. Write a short **o** word that rhymes with each word shown. Draw a picture to match the word you wrote.

frog

sock

You hear the short **o** sound in **not**. Cross out **not** in each sentence. Then, read the sentences about learning and trying hard.

I am not getting better at this.

It is not OK to make mistakes.

I do not want to try again.

Growth Mindset

Short o

Write a short **o** word to name each picture.

box   pot   ox   rod   rock   lock

_____
- -
_____

_____
- -
_____

_____
- -
_____

_____
- -
_____

_____
- -
_____

_____
- -
_____

Short u

Short **u** is the vowel sound you hear in the middle of **pup**. Draw a line from **u** to pictures whose names have the short **u** sound.

Short u

Write a short **u** word to name each picture.

cup	hug	cut	rug	duck	sun

57

Long a

Long **a** is the vowel sound you hear in **hay**. It says its own name. Circle the pictures whose names have the long **a** sound.

cake

gate

kite

bat

skate

plate
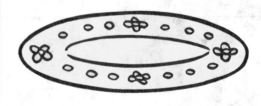

Long a

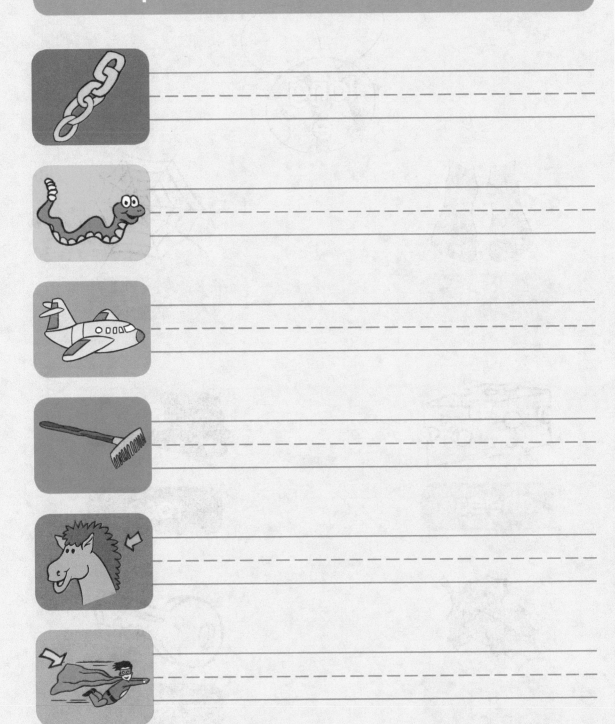

Write a long **a** word to name each picture.

rake plane chain snake mane cape

Long e

Long **e** is the vowel sound you hear in **bee**. It says its own name. Draw lines from the bee to the pictures whose names have the long **e** sound.

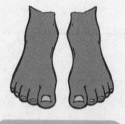

feet

web

cheese

rose

leaf

key

60

Long e

Write a long **e** word to name each picture.

beans   sheep   green

You hear the long **e** sound in **feeling**. Draw a face to match each feeling. Then, play a game with a friend. Act out a feeling. Can your partner guess what it is?

happy   surprised   angry

confused   sad   proud

Social Skills

Long i

Long **i** is the vowel sound you hear in **kite**. It says its own name.
In each sentence, circle two words that have the long **i** sound.

Five friends shared the pie.

Are you ready to ride down the slide?

I rode a bike to the park.

The mice ran from the light.

62

Long i

Write a long **i** word to name each picture.

kite	ice	tie	nine

You hear the long **i** sound in **bike**. Color only the boxes with letters. You will find a hidden message about bike safety!

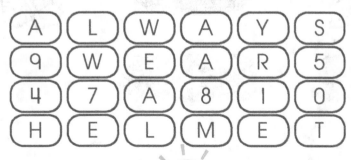

A	L	W	A	Y	S
9	W	E	A	R	5
4	7	A	8	I	0
H	E	L	M	E	T

Health & Fitness

Long o

Long **o** is the vowel sound you hear in **rope**. It says its own name. Circle the long **o** word in each column.

rose

clock

frog

fox

bike

slide

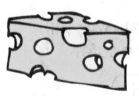

cheese

boat

coat

Long o

Write a long **o** word to name each picture.

smoke   throne   bone   soap   goat   globe

Long u & Long oo

Long **u** and long **oo** are the vowel sounds you hear in **cute** and **rule**. Color pictures whose names have the long **u** and long **oo** sounds.

mule

hive

moose

drum

cube

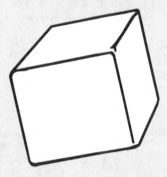

moon

Long u & Long oo

Write a long **u** or long **oo** word to name each picture.

| fruit | tube | juice | glue | music | suit |

Super Silent e

When you add **e** to the end of some words, the vowel sound changes from short to long. The **e** is silent. That is why it is called super silent **e**! Rewrite each short vowel word, but add **e** to the end. Listen for a long vowel sound in each word you write. The first one is done for you.

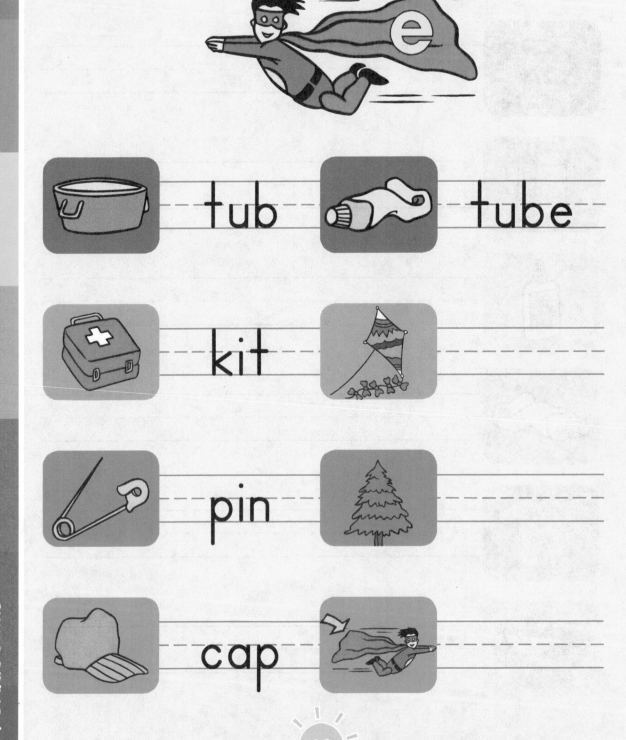

tub   tube

kit

pin

cap

Vowel Teams

Long vowel sounds can be spelled with two vowels together, or vowel teams. Usually, the first vowel letter makes the sound. The second letter is silent. Circle a vowel team in each long vowel word.

soap

meat

rain

tear

pail

leaf

Syllables

Parts of words are called syllables. Each syllable has one vowel sound. Say each word. Clap for each syllable you hear. The letters that spell the vowel sounds are in **bold**. Use them as clues. Write the number of syllables in each word.

Examples: c**a**t   1 clap   1 syllable

s**a**ndb**o**x   2 claps   2 syllables

und**e**rst**a**nd   3 claps   3 syllables

dog

_____

rainbow

_____

tree

_____

football

_____

sail

_____

basketball

_____

Syllables

Look at the number of syllables in each word. Draw lines between the syllables. Then, circle the letter or letters that spell one vowel sound in each syllable. The first one is done for you.

| **2** | **1** | **2** |

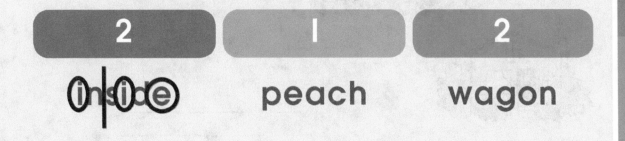

in|side   peach   wagon

| **1** | **3** | **2** |

sad   violin   sunshine

| **1** | **3** | **2** |

stain   elephant   bedroom

Sight Words: after & again

Write **after** or **again** to complete each sentence.

after   again

Pedro came to my house _____ today.

What will we do _____ lunch?

I was ready for bed _____ a long day.

We left the door open, and Bruno

ran away _____!

Sight Words: any & ask

Look at the word at the top of each box. Circle the same word in the list below.

ask

as
ask
task
sack

any

many
ant
an
any

ask

ask
mask
act
ash

any

money
any
anyway
yam

73

Sight Words: by & fly

Color the leaves with **by** orange. Color the leaves with **fly** green.

Sight Words: could & every

Write **could** or **every** to complete each sentence.

could   every

We jump in the pool ＿＿＿＿＿＿ time!

＿＿＿＿＿＿ you help me look for my book?

Kat feeds her fish ＿＿＿＿＿＿ day.

We ＿＿＿＿＿＿ choose an apple or a pear.

What is important to do two times **every** day? Write the missing letters to find out.

＿＿＿＿＿r＿＿s h   y＿＿＿u＿＿＿   ＿＿＿e e＿＿＿h!

Health & Fitness

Sight Words: from & give

Color the boxes with **from purple**. Color the boxes with **give** pink.

from	fort	give	from
five	give	grime	hive
frame	gave	from	frog
give	from	gave	fright
from	give	have	give

When you respect others, you let them know that they are important to you. Check the ways you **give** respect to people you know.

☐ Be on time.

☐ Listen carefully.

☐ Follow the rules.

☐ Say "please" and "thank you."

☐ Offer to help.

☐ Try hard.

Character Development

Sight Words: had & has

Decide whether each sentence is missing **had** or **has**. Then, write **d** or **s** to complete the word.

Last year, Trey ha____ two cats.

Now, Trey ha____ a third cat, Ginger.

Ginger ha____ brown fur.

Trey's friend Antonio ha____ one cat, but it ran away.

Antonio ha____ a new cat now.

Sight Words: her & his

Write **her** or **his** in each sentence. Then, draw a line to the correct object.

Jared brought lunch.

_____

This is _____ lunch.

It is Kara's birthday.

_____

This is _____ cake.

Travon's jacket is green.

_____

This is _____ jacket.

Sheila's shoes are old.

_____

These are _____ shoes.

Sight Words: know & let

Circle **know** or **let** in each sentence.

Let me tell you a story about yesterday.

Maria wanted to know if I would skate with her.

I love to skate, but I know my mom had already made plans.

I asked Mom if I could go, and she let me!

When you talk, you want others to listen to you. Then, it is your turn to **let** others talk while you listen. Practice with a partner. Tell a story while your partner interrupts. How do you feel? Then, tell a story while your partner listens carefully. How do you feel now?

Social Skills

Sight Words: live & may

In each row, color the letters that spell **live**.

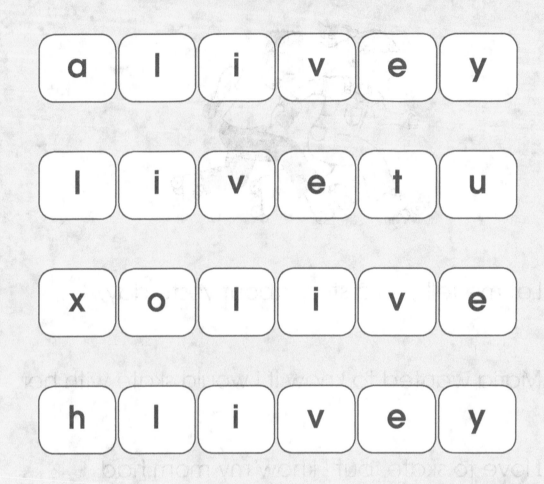

| a | l | i | v | e | y |

| l | i | v | e | t | u |

| x | o | l | i | v | e |

| h | l | i | v | e | y |

Circle **may** in each sentence.

The baby may have some juice.

Brendan may know the answer.

May I play with you?

80

Sight Words: of & put

Color the books with **of** blue. Color the books with **put** green.
Color the other books **red**.

put

pat

of

put

off

put

of

of

81

Sight Words: old & once

Circle the picture that matches each sentence. Pay attention to the **bold** word.

Is it time to replace my **old** shoes?

We will go outside **once** it stops raining.

Complete the sentences. Draw a picture of yourself at each age.

In 10 years, I will be _____ years **old**.

In 20 years, I will be _____ years **old**.

Sight Words: round & stop

Draw a picture to match each sentence. Pay attention to the **bold** word.

The ducks swim in the round pond.

Cars stop at the red light.

Sight Words: some & them

Circle the chicks with **some**.

Circle **them** in each sentence.

We will meet them at the barn.

There are seven chicks, and five of them are awake.

It is best for them to be near their mother.

Sight Words: take & thank

Find words in the puzzle. Circle **take** six times in green. Circle **thank** six times in blue. Look across and down.

```
e  a  d  a  t  a  k  e  j  t  q
t  h  a  n  k  t  i  p  o  a  l
a  v  r  j  p  h  t  a  k  e  u
k  d  a  t  k  a  m  a  t  x  m
e  y  s  a  a  n  p  w  h  h  p
s  s  t  k  i  k  k  a  a  t  v
e  x  h  e  b  n  s  h  n  a  f
w  a  a  k  t  h  a  n  k  s  h
r  l  n  h  z  q  z  e  i  n  t
t  a  k  e  p  a  h  h  k  x  a
p  g  e  g  d  s  t  h  a  n  k
a  i  j  p  i  z  k  e  x  w  e
```

It is polite to **thank** someone who does something for you. When someone is nice to you, be nice in return! Emilie's mom brought her grapes for a snack. Write what Emilie should say.

Sight Words: then & were

Write **then** or **were** to complete each sentence.

| then | were |

It rained, and _____ the grass got wet.

_____ you ready for the test today?

If I eat my dinner, _____ I can have dessert.

The socks _____ full of holes.

86

Sight Words: think & walk

Look at the word at the top of each box. Circle the same word in the list below.

think

thank

think

thin

talk

walk

wall

want

wink

walk

think

think

they

them

sink

walk

whale

wake

walk

talk

Sight Words

Write the missing letters to complete the words.

| ask | from | think | put | then |
| round | give | old | some | thank |

ol__ __

so__e

t__an__ __

fro__ __

__ __sk

__ __h__nk

p__ __t

__ __i__e

__ __oun__ __

__ __ __en

88

Sight Words

Write the missing letters to complete the words.

after   know   once   could   take   walk

w__l__   __nc__

t__k__   kn_____

a__te__   c____ld

Write **sight words** from the box to complete the safety rules.

Always _____ outside with a buddy.

Do not go anywhere with a person you
do not _____.

Never _____ something from a
person you do not know.

Health & Fitness

Context Clues

Write words from the box to complete the story. Use clues in the story to help you.

cloudy   grow   rain   water   wet

"May I please go outside?" I asked.

"It is too _____," Dad told me.

Later, the sun came out, but then it began to

_____. "May I go out now?" I

asked again.

Dad looked out the window. "You will get

_____," he said.

"But I want to see if the rain helped our

flowers _____," I said.

"You mean you want to play in the

_____," Dad said with a

smile. How did he know that?

Context Clues

Write words from the box to complete the story. Use clues in the story to help you.

> practice   teach   finish   write   read

James was trying to _____ his little sister how to write her name.

"Watch what I do," James said. He took the pencil and got ready to _____. He showed her how to make **W**, then **e, n, d**, and **y**.

At first, Wendy's letters were large and shaky. But with _____ and hard work, Wendy's letters became more and more clear.

"I can do it!" Wendy said with a smile. "I can write my name from start to _____.

Would you teach me how to _____ now, James?"

James laughed. "Of course! But let's do it tomorrow."

91

Classify

Write words from the box under the pictures they describe.

day	night	rays	moon
sun	dark	light	stars

Classify the children's actions. Circle the pictures that show kindness. Draw a box around the pictures that show curiosity.

reading   sharing   giving a gift   asking a question

Classify

Draw an **X** on the word in each row that does not belong.

flashlight	candle	radio	fire

dogs	bees	flies	ants

shirt	pants	coat	bat

beans	grapes	ball	bread

gloves	hat	book	boots

93

Prefixes

Write a prefix in front of each base word. Then, match the new word to its meaning.

un	dis	re	over

_____ real

- do not like

_____ heat

- coat worn over clothes

_____ like

- not real

_____ coat

- heat again

_____ turn

- turn back

Prefixes

Write a prefix in front of the base word in each sentence.

un	dis	re	over

The magician made the rabbit _____appear.

That bucket is about to _____flow with water.

He will _____take the blurry photo.

Jasmine was _____happy
when the snowman melted.

Show what you should do. Draw a line to a word with
a **prefix**.

You do not understand the directions.   redo

You made a mistake.   recheck

You are not sure your answer is right.   reread

Suffixes

Write a suffix after the base word in each sentence.

| s | es | ing | ed |

Mom needs eight peach_____ to make a pie.

I like eat_____ lunch outside at the park.

Yesterday, I climb_____ to the top of that pole.

Please help me find my mitten_____.

Suffixes

Write a suffix after the base word in each sentence.

s	es	ing	ed

Where are you go_____ after lunch?

I jump_____ even higher than Brady!

Ms. Moore mix_____ paints for art class.

Cupcake_____ are my favorite treat.

Shades of Meaning

Write each word in the list where it belongs.

scream sprint whisper run flutter glide

say

shout

_____
- - - - - - - - - - -
_____

_____
- - - - - - - - - - -
_____

fly

soar

_____
- - - - - - - - - - -
_____

_____
- - - - - - - - - - -
_____

jog

gallop

_____
- - - - - - - - - - -
_____

_____
- - - - - - - - - - -
_____

Shades of Meaning

Write each word in the list where it belongs.

speedy afraid spooked quick

fast

rapid

_____

_____

_____

scared

frightened

_____

_____

_____

Read the words with similar **meanings**. Choose one to describe yourself. Then, finish the sentence.

| honest | truthful | reliable |
| fair | trustworthy | dependable |

_____

I am _____ because

_____

_____

_____.

99

Shades of Meaning

In each row, color a flower to show which verb has the strongest meaning.

make

build

create

walk

stride

tiptoe

hop

leap

skip

Shades of Meaning

In each row, color a balloon to show which adjective has the strongest meaning.

terrible

bad

lousy

cold

cool

freezing

joyful

thrilled

happy

Common Nouns

A noun names a person, place, or thing. Read the story and circle all the nouns. Then, write the nouns you circled under the pictures.

Our family likes to go to the park. We play on the swings. We eat sandwiches. We throw the ball to our dog. Then, we go home.

Common Nouns

Draw the missing pictures to match the nouns. Write the missing nouns to match the pictures.

astronaut

beach

Plural Nouns

Plural nouns name more than one person, place, or thing. To form most plurals, add **s** or **es** to the end of the word. If a word ends in **y**, change **y** to **i** before adding **es**. Examples: **baby/ babies**, **story/stories**. Read each noun. Write the plural.

desk _____

wish _____

lady _____

dress _____

bunny _____

pencil _____

Community helpers keep people safe and healthy. Write a **plural** to complete each sentence.

police officers   doctors   firefighters

_____ care for the sick and injured.

_____ make sure people follow the law.

_____ put out fires and rescue people from danger.

Health & Fitness

Proper Nouns

Proper nouns name specific people, places, and things. Proper nouns always begin with a capital letter. Write the proper nouns.

denver, colorado

_____

_____

miss davis

_____

_____

aiden james

_____

_____

patches

_____

_____

For each common noun, write a **proper noun** that names a person or place you know.

_____

school _____

_____

friend _____

_____

pet _____

_____

park _____

105

All About Me

Possessive Nouns

Possessive nouns show who or what owns something. To form a possessive noun, add an apostrophe (') and then s: 's. Write each underlined noun as a possessive noun. The first one is done for you.

<u>Ann</u> gerbil is named Happy.

Ann's

The <u>baby</u> cry was loud.

<u>Andy</u> shoe is untied.

The <u>school</u> flag flies high.

Personal Pronouns

Pronouns are words that can take the place of nouns. Read the first sentence in each pair. Complete the second sentence by writing a pronoun to replace the underlined noun.

| he | she | it | they |

Oliver likes funny jokes.

_____

_____ likes funny jokes.

Mei and Sam are on the trampoline.

_____

_____ are on the trampoline.

Sarah is a very good dancer.

_____

_____ is a very good dancer.

The dolphin dove into the water.

_____

_____ dove into the water.

107

Possessive Pronouns

Possessive pronouns take the place of nouns and tell who or what owns something. Circle and write a possessive pronoun to complete each sentence.

Are these books _____?

you   yours

That is _____ box of crayons.

her   she

There is a globe in _____ classroom.

me   my

Ask Miles if we can use _____ glue.

his   he

108

Indefinite Pronouns

An indefinite pronoun does not take the place of a specific (or definite) person, place, or thing. Write the indefinite pronoun that best completes each sentence.

everything anyone someone something

Can _____ please turn on the lights?

Does _____ know where I left my umbrella?

I can carry _____ in one bag.

Do you see _____ you can buy with your money?

Present-Tense Verbs

Some verbs tell what actions are happening now. Write verbs to complete the sentences.

make   race   jump   watch   ride   rest

The girls _____ the frogs _____ _____.

The boys _____ to the park, then they _____.

They _____ cars to _____ in.

110

Present-Tense Verbs

The underlined verb in each sentence is wrong. Add **s** to write the correct verb that tells what is happening now.

The baby <u>sleep</u> with a teddy bear.

_____

_ _ _ _ _ _ _ _ _ _

_____

Sari <u>cook</u> breakfast for us.

_____

_ _ _ _ _ _ _ _ _ _

_____

Chad <u>stop</u> and looks both ways.

_____

_ _ _ _ _ _ _ _ _ _

_____

Match each **verb** with the character trait it shows.

share	patience
wait	courage
try	kindness

Use Verbs with Nouns

Nouns (or pronouns) and verbs go together. Rewrite each verb that tells what is happening now. Make it go with each pronoun shown. The first one is done for you.

ride

I ___ride___ .

She ___rides___ .

They ___ride___ .

sleep

We _____ .

He _____ .

You _____ .

make

He _____ .

They _____ .

I _____ .

play

We _____ .

He _____ .

She _____ .

Use Verbs with Nouns

These sentences need a verb to tell what is happening now. Circle and write the verb that goes with the noun to complete each sentence.

I _____ a newspaper about our street.

writes   write

My sister _____ me.

helps   help

She _____ the pictures.

draws   draw

I _____ the news about people on our street.

tells   tell

We _____ the newspapers together.

delivers   deliver

Past-Tense Verbs

Some verbs tell what already happened. Look at each pair of verbs. Circle the verb that tells what already happened. Then, write letters to answer the question.

wash   washed

dried   dry

floated   float

rain   rained

_____

_ _ _ _

All the verbs I circled end with these two letters: _____.

Kids need exercise every day to stay fit and healthy. Circle the **past-tense verbs** that tell how you exercised yesterday.

walked	played outside	climbed
jumped	skipped	danced
biked	hiked	raced

Past-Tense Verbs

The underlined verb in each sentence is wrong. Write the correct verb that tells what already happened. **Hint:** The verbs you write will end with **ed**.

It <u>snow</u>, so I made a snowman.

_____

- - - - - - - - - - - - - -

_____

Ben <u>rake</u> the leaves when they fell off the tree.

_____

- - - - - - - - - - - - - -

_____

My brother <u>bake</u> a cake on my birthday.

_____

- - - - - - - - - - - - - -

_____

My family <u>visit</u> the beach last summer.

_____

- - - - - - - - - - - - - -

_____

115

Future-Tense Verbs

Some verbs tell what has not happened yet. These verbs are made up of two words. The first word is **will**. In each sentence, write **will** in front of the underlined verb.

We _____ <u>wash</u> our dog Fritz later today.

First, we _____ <u>fill</u> the tub with soapy water.

Then, I _____ <u>call</u> Fritz.

He _____ <u>cry</u> at first.

Then, he _____ <u>like</u> his bath.

Fritz _____ <u>look</u> a lot better after his bath!

Future-Tense Verbs

The underlined verb in each sentence is wrong. Write the correct verb that tells what has not yet happened. **Hint:** Write two words for each verb.

The dog <u>bring</u> mud into the house.

_____   _____

A box <u>fall</u>.

_____   _____

The chair <u>break</u>.

_____   _____

Check things you will do in the **future** to make new friends.

☐ I will ask a new friend to play.

☐ I will share my snack with a new friend.

☐ I will play a game with a new friend.

☐ I will say something nice to a new friend.

☐ I will ask a new friend to sit by me.

Social Skills

Verb Tenses

Look at the verb in each sentence. Use the key to color the box around the sentence.

present (happening now)

past (already happened)

future (has not yet happened)

Mia likes her new friend.

Cameron will talk to Mom.

We play baseball every day.

Holly and Luisa walked this way.

Ada painted a picture.

Our class will have a party next week.

Verb Tenses

Look at the verb in each sentence. Draw a line to match it to the correct verb tense.

It will rain tomorrow.

past
(already happened)

He played soccer yesterday.

Molly sleeps under the quilt.

present
(happening now)

Tomas sings a song.

I will buy a kite.

future
(has not yet happened)

Dad worked hard today.

Adjectives

Adjectives are describing words. They tell more about a noun. Write two adjectives that could describe each noun.

shiny   horned   bright   scaly   giant   slow   sweet   juicy

turtle

_____

- - - - - - - - - - - -

_____

- - - - - - - - - - - -

orange

_____

- - - - - - - - - - - -

_____

- - - - - - - - - - - -

sun

_____

- - - - - - - - - - - -

_____

- - - - - - - - - - - -

dinosaur

_____

- - - - - - - - - - - -

_____

- - - - - - - - - - - -

Adjectives

Circle the adjective in each sentence. Draw a line from the sentence to a picture.

The hungry dog is eating.

The blue bird flies.

Horses have long legs.

She is a fast runner.

Circle **adjectives** that describe you. Write two more adjectives that describe you.

tall	silly	happy	kind
quiet	brave	smart	strong

_____

- -

_____

- -

_____

All About Me

Articles

The small word **the** is often used before nouns. Write **the** to complete each sentence.

Spread _____ peanut butter on each slice of bread.

Put _____ two slices of bread together.

Eat _____ sandwich for a yummy lunch.

Remember to clean up _____ kitchen!

Articles

The small words **a** and **an** are often used before nouns. Use **an** before a word that begins with a vowel. Use **a** before a word that begins with a consonant. Write **a** or **an** to complete each sentence.

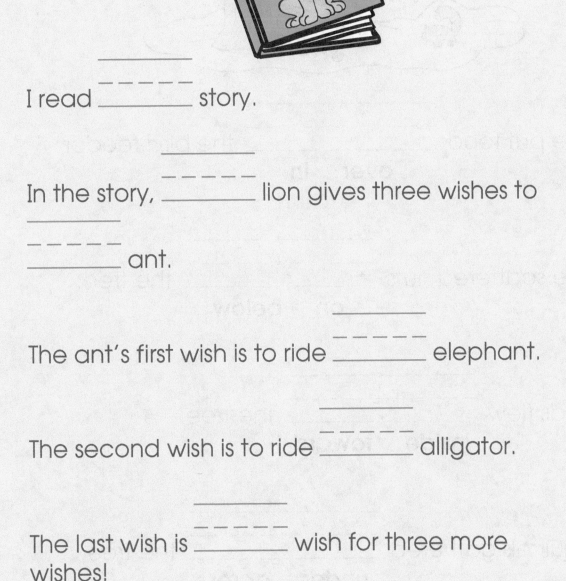

I read _____ story.

In the story, _____ lion gives three wishes to _____ ant.

The ant's first wish is to ride _____ elephant.

The second wish is to ride _____ alligator.

The last wish is _____ wish for three more wishes!

Prepositions

Prepositions are words that can describe position or direction.
Circle and write a preposition to complete each sentence.

We put food _____ the bird feeder.

over   in

We scattered nuts _____ the tree.

on   below

Birds flew _____ the tree.

inside   toward

Squirrels gathered _____ the tree.

under   across

Prepositions

Circle and write a preposition to complete each sentence.

The lamp on the table _____ the bed is bent.

beside   through

A basketball is _____ the bed.

behind   on

The broom bumped _____ the table.

across   into

The fish jumped _____ the fishbowl!

under   above

Conjunctions

Use the joining word shown to combine each pair of sentences into one sentence.

Skunks have black fur. Skunks have white stripes. (and)

_____

- -

_____

- -

Skunks have short legs. They move quickly. (but)

_____

- -

_____

- -

Skunks sleep in hollow trees. Skunks sleep underground. (or)

_____

- -

_____

- -

Skunks sleep during the day. They eat at night. (so)

_____

- -

_____

- -

Conjunctions

Circle and write the joining word that best completes each sentence.

Will the goalie catch the ball _____ miss it?

and   **or**

Everyone is hungry, _____ Dad will cook dinner.   **because**   **so**

We all cheered _____ our team won!

because   **but**

Write words after the **conjunction** to complete each sentence.

This is hard for me, but _____
_____.

I made a mistake, but _____
_____.

Telling Sentences

A telling sentence tells something, or gives information. Rewrite the telling sentences. Begin each one with a capital letter. End each one with a period (.).

some children like dogs

_____

_____

some children like cats

_____

_____

some children like snakes

_____

_____

most children like pets

_____

_____

Asking Sentences

An asking sentence asks a question. Rewrite the asking sentences. Begin each one with a capital letter. End each one with a question mark (**?**).

do you like the beach

_____

- - - - - - - - - - - - - - - - - - -

_____

how far can you swim

_____

- - - - - - - - - - - - - - - - - - -

_____

what is under the sand

_____

- - - - - - - - - - - - - - - - - - -

_____

are you cold

_____

- - - - - - - - - - - - - - - - - - -

_____

Exclamations

An exclamation shows a strong feeling. Rewrite each exclamation. Begin each one with a capital letter. End each one with an exclamation mark (!).

school is canceled

_____

- - - - - - - - - - - - - - - - - -

_____

the snow is deep

_____

- - - - - - - - - - - - - - - - - -

_____

it is freezing out here

_____

- - - - - - - - - - - - - - - - - -

_____

this snowman is great

_____

- - - - - - - - - - - - - - - - - -

_____

Commands

A command tells someone to do something. Rewrite the commands. Begin each one with a capital letter. If the command shows a strong feeling, end it with an exclamation mark (**!**). If it does not, end it with a period (**.**).

hit the ball hard

_____

- - - - - - - - - - - - - - - - -

_____

hold out your glove

_____

- - - - - - - - - - - - - - - - -

_____

run to first base

_____

- - - - - - - - - - - - - - - - -

_____

get a home run

_____

- - - - - - - - - - - - - - - - -

_____

Sentences

Write sentences about the picture.

Telling Sentence:

_____

- -

_____

_____

Asking Sentence:

_____

- -

_____

_____

Sentences

Write sentences about the picture.

Exclamation:

_____

- -

_____

_____

- -

_____

Command:

_____

- -

_____

_____

- -

_____

Capitalization

The first and last names of people always begin with capital letters. Write the names correctly. Then, draw a picture of you and write your name.

kyle davis

_____

- -

_____

olivia mendez

_____

- -

_____

howard smith

_____

- -

_____

your name

_____

- -

_____

Capitalization

The names of days of the week and months of the year are always capitalized. Circle the words that are written correctly. Write the other words correctly on the lines.

sunday	July	Wednesday	may	december
friday	tuesday	june	august	Monday
February	March	thursday	April	September

Days of the Week

_____

_____

_____

_____

_____

Months of the Year

_____

_____

_____

_____

_____

135

Commas

Commas are used to separate words in a series of three or more. Look at this example:

My favorite fruits are apples, bananas, and oranges.

Write commas where they are needed in each sentence.

Please buy milk eggs bread and cheese.

I need a folder paper and pencils
for school.

Some good pets are cats dogs gerbils
and rabbits.

We can go by plane train or car.

136

Commas

When you write a date, use a comma between the number that tells the day and the number that tells the year. Write the dates. Use capital letters and commas where needed. The first one is done for you.

june 19 1980

June 19, 1980

december 13 2017

_____

April 17 2020

_____

october 22, 1996

_____

On what day were you born? Complete the sentence. Do not forget to use a capital letter and a **comma**.

I was born on

month	day	year

All About Me

Sequence

The pig is getting ready to go to a party. Number the pictures **1** to **4** to show the order.

_ _ _ _ _ _

_ _ _ _ _ _

_ _ _ _ _ _

_ _ _ _ _ _

Use Picture Clues

Write words from the box to answer the questions. Use the picture for clues.

bear	cat	dog	elephant
giraffe	hippo	pig	tiger

Which animals have bow ties?

_____   _____

- - - - - - - - - - - - -   - - - - - - - - - - - - -

_____   _____

Which animal has a hat?

_____

- - - - - - - - - - - - -

_____

Which animal has a striped shirt?

_____

- - - - - - - - - - - - -

_____

139

Classify

Draw a square around objects that are food for the party. Draw a triangle around the party guests. Draw a circle around the objects used for fun at the party.

hippo

pretzels

giraffe

bear

pig

balloons

juice

fruit

hat

noise makers

cake

games

Comprehension

Read about the party. Then, complete the invitation.

The party for Bear's birthday will be at Dog's house on Saturday, April 10. It will start at 1:00. It will last for two hours.

You Are Invited!

_____

Come to a birthday party for _____ .

_____

Where: _____

_____

Date: _____

_____

Time It Begins: _____

_____

Time It Ends: _____

141

Use Picture Clues

Read about the cats. Look at the picture. Write the correct name beside each cat.

Fluffy, Blackie, and Tiger are playing. Tom is sleeping. Blackie has spots. Tiger has stripes.

Same & Different

Use the names you wrote on page 142. Write words from the box to tell what is different about each cat.

| purple ball   green bow   blue brush   red collar |

Tom is wearing a _____.

Blackie has a _____.

Fluffy is wearing a _____.

Tiger has a _____.

Think about someone you know. What words name things that are the **same** about the two of you? Color the boxes **red**. What words name things that are **different** about the two of you? Color the boxes blue. Why is it good that not everyone is the same?

heights	ages	pets
families	favorite books	favorite movies
favorite TV shows	favorite colors	favorite sports

Social Skills

Sequence

Read the story. Write words from the story to give the directions in order.

Do you like cats? I do. To pet a cat, move slowly. Hold out your hand. The cat will come to you. Then, pet its head. Do not grab a cat! It will run away.

To pet a cat . . .

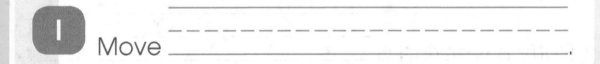

1 Move _____ .

2 Hold out your _____ .

3 The cat will come to _____ .

4 Pet the cat's _____ .

5 Do not _____ a cat.

Comprehension

Read the story on page 144 again. Then, answer the questions.

The story tells you how to _____.

What part of your body should you pet a cat with?

_____

_____

Why should you move slowly to pet a cat?

_____

_____

_____

_____

Why do you think a cat will run away if you grab it?

_____

_____

_____

_____

145

Predict

Follow the order of the numbers. Read the story. In the last box, draw a picture to complete the story.

1

That's my ball.

2

I got it first.

3

It's mine!

4

Predict

Read each story. Circle the sentence that tells how the story will probably end.

Ann was riding her bike. She saw a dog in the park. She stopped to pet it. Ann left to go home.

The dog went swimming.

The dog followed Ann.

The dog went home with a cat.

Antonio went to a baseball game. A baseball player hit a ball toward him. He reached out his hands.

The player caught the ball.

The ball bounced on a car.

Antonio caught the ball.

Draw Conclusions

Read the story about Tess. Then, circle the correct answers.

Tess plays baseball. She likes it when her team wins games. Today, Tess's team did not win.

Tess likes

football. soccer. baseball.

Tess likes to

win.   lose.

Tess uses a bat.

yes   no

Tess is

happy.   sad.

Comprehension

Read the directions for playing "Simon Says." Then, answer the questions.

Simon Says

SIMON SAYS, CLAP YOUR HANDS!

This is how to play "Simon Says." One kid is Simon. Simon is the leader. Everyone must do what Simon says and does, but only if Simon says, "Simon says" first. Let's try it. Simon says: Pat your head. Simon says: Point to your nose. Touch your toes. Oops! Did you touch your toes? I did not say, "Simon says" first. If you touched your toes, you are out!

Who is the leader in this game?

_____

_____

What must the leader say first each time?

_____

_____

What happens if you do something and the leader did not say, "Simon says"?

_____

_____

149

Comprehension

Read each sentence. Look at the picture. Circle the picture if the boy is playing "Simon Says" correctly.

Simon says: Put your hands up.

Stand on one leg.

Simon says: Put your hands on your head.

Simon says: Turn around.

Make a big smile.

Follow Directions

Read the sentences. If Simon tells you to do something, follow the directions. If Simon does not tell you to do something, go to the next sentence.

1 Simon says: Cross out all the numbers.

2 Simon says: Cross out the vowel in the word **sun**.

3 Cross out the letter **B**.

4 Cross out the vowels **A** and **E**.

5 Simon says: Cross out the consonants in the word **cup**.

6 Cross out the letter **Z**.

7 Simon says: Cross out all the **K**s.

8 Simon says: Read your message.

C 3 G U 7 P R U C P E K C P A 8 K K
6 T P U P J C 5 P O K 9 P B U P K K

Write a Story

Write words to finish the sentences. Read the story you wrote!

It is a _____ day on the farm.

First, the farmers _____.

Then, the farmers _____.

All day long, the ducks _____.

There is lots to do every day on the farm.

Write a Story

Write words to finish the sentences. Read the story you wrote!

Ant
Construction

The ants are building _____.

_____

At first, they _____.

Later, they _____.

Finally, the ants _____.

The ants made something amazing by working together!

Write a Story

Write a sentence beside each picture to tell what is happening. Read the story you wrote!

Write a Story

Write a story about the picture. Include a beginning, a middle, and an ending.

_____

- -

_____

- -

_____

_____

- -

_____

- -

_____

_____

- -

_____

- -

Everyone's life tells a different **story**. Your story is about where you live, where your family comes from in the world, and what you choose to do each day. Each person you meet has a different story! Tolerance means understanding and appreciating that everyone is different.

Write to Inform

Imagine you met someone who had never eaten an ice cream cone. Could you teach the person how to do it? Think about each step you take when you eat an ice cream cone. Write them in order.

How to Eat an Ice Cream Cone

First, you _____
_____
_____.

Then, you _____
_____
_____.

Finally, you _____
_____
_____.

Do not forget to _____
_____
_____!

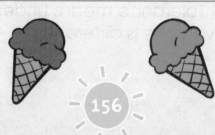

156

Write to Inform

Think about how to wash a dog. Write the steps in order.

How to Wash a Dog

First, _____

_____

_____

Next, _____

_____

_____

Next, _____

_____

_____

Last, _____

_____

_____

157

Write to Inform

With an adult, research facts about your favorite animal. Draw and write to tell what you learned.

My favorite animal is _____.

This animal lives _____.

This animal eats _____.

This animal has _____.

This animal likes to _____.

Write to Inform

Circle one topic from the list. With an adult, do some research to learn more about it. Draw a picture to illustrate your topic. Write facts about your topic.

tornadoes	volcanoes	bees
Mars	Grand Canyon	Australia

Fact #1

Fact #2

Fact #3

159

Write an Opinion

Which season of the year is the best? Write its name to complete the sentence and give your opinion. Then, write three good reasons why you think that season is best.

_____

_____ is the best season of the year.

Reason #1

Reason #2

Reason #3

Write an Opinion

Do you think first graders should have homework? Circle **should** or **should not** to complete the first sentence and give your opinion. Then, write three good reasons why you feel the way you do.

First graders (should/should not) have homework.

Reason #1

_____

- -

_____

- -

_____

Reason #2

- -

_____

- -

_____

Reason #3

_____

- -

_____

- -

_____

Write an Opinion

Which holiday is the best one? Write its name to complete the first sentence and give your opinion. Then, write three good reasons why you think that holiday is best.

_____

_ _ _ _ _ _ _ _ _ _ _ _ _

_____ is the best holiday.

Reason #1

Reason #2

Reason #3

Write an Opinion

Circle a topic from the list. Write a sentence that gives your opinion about it.

> funniest book   most interesting school subject
> most fun sport   most entertaining board game
> best TV show   tastiest dessert

_____
- -
_____
- -
_____
- -
_____

A hero is someone you admire and respect. Finish the sentence to tell your **opinion** about someone who is a hero to you. It can be someone you know or someone you would like to meet.

_____
- -
_____ is a true hero because
_____
- -
_____
- -
_____.

Count Ahead

Write a number to answer each question. Use the number line to help you.

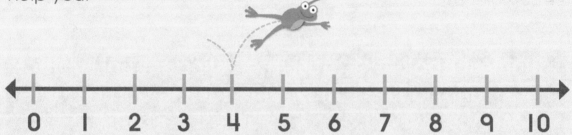

0 1 2 3 4 5 6 7 8 9 10

What is 3 more than 5? _____

What is 2 more than 4? _____

What is 1 more than 3? _____

What is 5 more than 0? _____

What is 6 more than 3? _____

What is 9 more than 1? _____

Count Ahead

Count forward. Write the missing numbers in each row.

_____ 16 _____ 18 19 _____

4 _____ 6 _____ _____ 9

_____ _____ 9 _____ _____ 12

_____ 14 _____ _____ _____ _____

Picture Problems

Solve the addition problems. Use the pictures to help you.

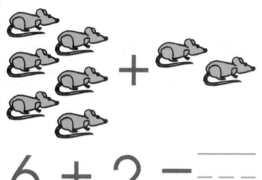

6 + 2 = ____

3 + 6 = ____

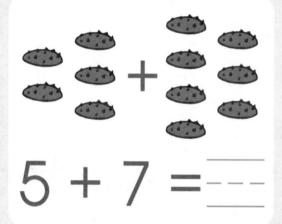

5 + 7 = ____

1 + 9 = ____

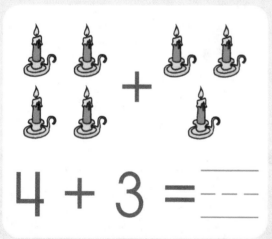

4 + 3 = ____

7 + 8 = ____

Picture Problems

Solve the addition problems. Use the pictures to help you.

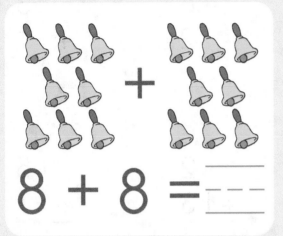

$8 + 8 = $ _ _ _

$5 + 9 = $ _ _ _

$3 + 8 = $ _ _ _

$6 + 7 = $ _ _ _

$8 + 4 = $ _ _ _

$14 + 6 = $ _ _ _

Addition Practice

Find the sums.

$$
\begin{array}{r} 2 \\ + 5 \\ \hline \end{array}
\qquad
\begin{array}{r} 6 \\ + 4 \\ \hline \end{array}
\qquad
\begin{array}{r} 8 \\ + 2 \\ \hline \end{array}
\qquad
\begin{array}{r} 3 \\ +11 \\ \hline \end{array}
$$

$$
\begin{array}{r} 6 \\ + 8 \\ \hline \end{array}
\qquad
\begin{array}{r} 9 \\ + 1 \\ \hline \end{array}
\qquad
\begin{array}{r} 2 \\ +13 \\ \hline \end{array}
\qquad
\begin{array}{r} 15 \\ + 1 \\ \hline \end{array}
$$

$$
\begin{array}{r} 5 \\ + 5 \\ \hline \end{array}
\qquad
\begin{array}{r} 7 \\ + 8 \\ \hline \end{array}
\qquad
\begin{array}{r} 9 \\ + 5 \\ \hline \end{array}
\qquad
\begin{array}{r} 6 \\ +10 \\ \hline \end{array}
$$

Being a leader means sharing what you have and helping others. With an adult, collect food items to donate to a food pantry or pet food for an animal shelter. **Add** the number of items you collect. Write the number to complete the sentence.

_____

I collected _____ items.

Commutative Property

The commutative property of addition is a rule. It says that if you change the order of the numbers being added, the sum stays the same. Use this rule to help you write the missing numbers.

Example: $2 + 3 = 5$

$3 + \underline{2} = 5$

$5 + 4 = 9$

$4 + \underline{} = 9$

$3 + 1 = 4$

$1 + \underline{} = 4$

$6 + 8 = 14$

$8 + \underline{} = 14$

$6 + 4 = 10$

$\underline{} + \underline{} = 10$

$10 + 6 = 16$

$\underline{} + \underline{} = 16$

$8 + 9 = 17$

$\underline{} + \underline{} = 17$

$7 + 4 = 11$

$\underline{} + \underline{} = 11$

$6 + 9 = 15$

$\underline{} + \underline{} = 15$

Missing Numbers

Draw the missing dots on the blank side of each domino. Write a matching number to complete the equation.

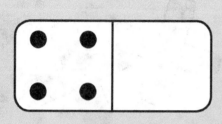

$4 + \underline{} = 9$

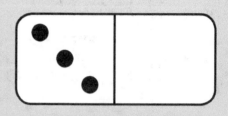

$3 + \underline{} = 6$

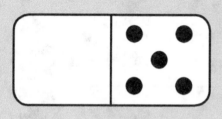

$\underline{} + 5 = 8$

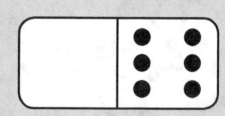

$\underline{} + 6 = 12$

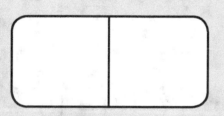

$0 + \underline{} = 5$

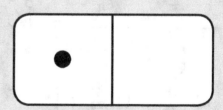

$1 + \underline{} = 7$

Missing Numbers

Write the missing number to complete each equation.

_____ + 6 = 18

13 + _____ = 14

7 + _____ = 8

_____ + 4 = 6

_____ + 9 = 15

3 + _____ = 16

8 + _____ = 9

_____ + 5 = 6

_____ + 4 = 11

9 + _____ = 14

12 + _____ = 15

_____ + 1 = 17

171

Add Three or More Numbers

Add all the numbers to find the sum. Draw pictures to help you.

Example:

```
   1   ●
   2   ● ●
 + 3   ● ● ●
 ───
   6
```

```
   2          3          2
   7          9          4
 + 4        + 6        + 6
 ───        ───        ───
```

```
   7          8          6
   1          3          5
   4          1          2
 + 2        + 5        + 3
 ───        ───        ───
```

Get together with two friends so there are **three** of you. You are all different, but you are probably a lot alike, too. Do you like the same school subjects, sports, movies, or foods? Add all the things you have in common to find the sum.

Social Skills

Associative Property

The associative property of addition is a rule. It says that when you add three or more numbers, you can group the numbers being added in different ways, but the sum stays the same. Use this rule to draw a line between matching equations. One is done for you.

$(3 + 6) + 2 = 11$

$(6 + 5) + 1 = 12$

$8 + (5 + 4) = 17$

$(3 + 7) + 8 = 18$

$9 + (2 + 8) = 19$

$3 + (2 + 6) = 11$

$(5 + 1) + 6 = 12$

$(2 + 9) + 8 = 19$

$7 + (8 + 3) = 18$

$(4 + 8) + 5 = 17$

173

Make 10

When you add three or more numbers, use this strategy. Look for two numbers that make 10. Then, add the rest. Make a 10 as you solve each problem.

Example:

$$6 + 4 + 8 =$$
$$10 + 8 = 18$$

$5 + 5 + 4 =$

$5 + 8 + 2 =$

$2 + 8 + 3 =$

$4 + 1 + 6 =$

$3 + 7 + 8 =$

$6 + 9 + 1 =$

$3 + 3 + 7 =$

$4 + 4 + 6 =$

174

Make 10

Here is another strategy for solving addition problems. Break apart one of the numbers being added into smaller numbers. Then, look at all the numbers. Can you make a 10? Use this strategy to solve the problems.

Example:

$8 + 6 =$

② ④

$8 + 2 + 4 =$

$10 + 4 = 14$

$7 + 5 =$

◯   ◯

$8 + 4 =$

◯   ◯

$9 + 5 =$

◯   ◯

$7 + 8 =$

◯   ◯

Equations

An equation has two sides: the numbers before the equal sign (=) and the numbers after the equal sign (=). In equations that are true, both sides equal the same number. In equations that are false, both sides do not equal the same number.

Examples:
$$1 + 2 = 3 \qquad 1 + 3 = 3$$
$$3 = 3 \qquad\qquad 4 = 3$$
$$\text{True} \qquad\qquad \text{False}$$

Circle the true equations.

$$10 = 10 \qquad 9 = 3 + 5 \qquad 8 + 7 = 15$$

$$3 + 12 = 14 \qquad 4 = 5 \qquad 6 + 9 = 15$$

$$10 + 10 = 20 \qquad 2 + 5 = 8 \qquad 9 = 9$$

Write the number that makes each equation true.

$$12 + 3 = \underline{} + 5 \qquad 9 + 6 = \underline{} + 7$$

Addition Word Problems

Read the problem. Write an equation to help you find the sum. Use the pictures to help you.

Brynn's dog, Max, has 5 bones. She gave him 2 more bones for his birthday. Then, he found 4 bones in the backyard. How many bones does Max have in all?

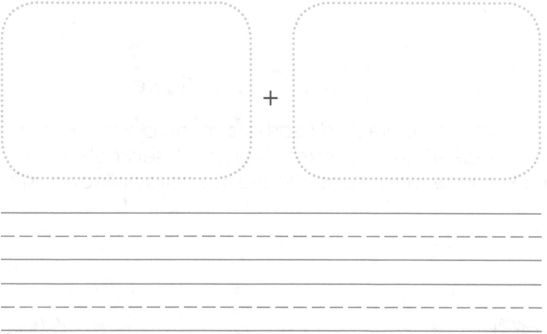

_____ + _____ + _____ = _____ bones

Some people collect keychains, postcards, or rocks. What do you collect? Write and solve a **word problem** about your collection. Draw pictures to illustrate your problem.

+

_____
- - - - - - - - - - - - - - - - - -
_____
- - - - - - - - - - - - - - - - - -
_____

All About Me

Addition Word Problems

Read each problem. Write and solve an equation to find the sum. Draw pictures to help you.

Elena and her dad made 5 cakes for the festival. Sam and his mom made 9 cakes for the festival. How many cakes did the kids and their parents make in all?

[   ] + [   ]

 ____ + ____ = ____ cakes

Ollie planted 12 flowers on Saturday and 8 flowers on Sunday. How many flowers did he plant in all?

[   ] + [   ]

 ____ + ____ = ____ flowers

Eric and Evan collected seashells at the beach. Eric put 8 seashells in his bucket. Evan put 9 seashells in his bucket. How many seashells did the boys collect in all?

[   ] + [   ]

 ____ + ____ = ____ seashells

Addition Word Problems

Read each problem. Write and solve an equation to find the sum. Draw pictures to help you.

Simon, Jessie, and Graham shared a pizza. Simon ate 2 pieces. Jessie ate 2 pieces. Graham ate 4 pieces. How many pieces of pizza did they eat in all?

[   ] + [   ] + [   ]

____ + ____ + ____ = ____ pieces of pizza

Dad bought 6 bananas, 4 lemons, and 9 apples at the store. How many pieces of fruit did he buy in all?

[   ] + [   ] + [   ]

____ + ____ + ____ = ____ pieces of fruit

At the beach, Shari counted 3 crabs, 12 seashells, and 2 boats. How many objects did Shari count at the beach?

[   ] + [   ] + [   ]

____ + ____ + ____ = ____ objects

Count Back

Write a number to answer each question. Use the number line to help you.

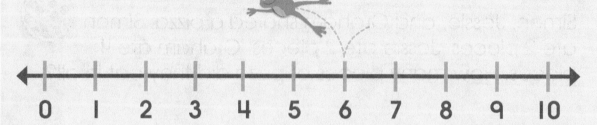

0 1 2 3 4 5 6 7 8 9 10

What is 2 less than 6? _____

What is 4 less than 9? _____

What is 9 less than 10? _____

What is 3 less than 7? _____

What is 8 less than 8? _____

What is 5 less than 6? _____

Count Back

Count backward. Write the missing numbers in each row.

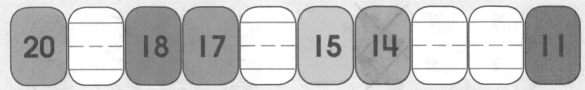

| 20 | | 18 | 17 | | 15 | 14 | | | 11 |

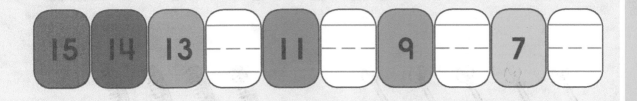

| 15 | 14 | 13 | | 11 | | 9 | | 7 | |

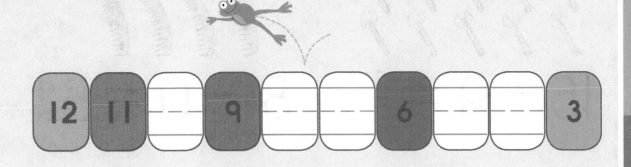

| 12 | 11 | | 9 | | | 6 | | | 3 |

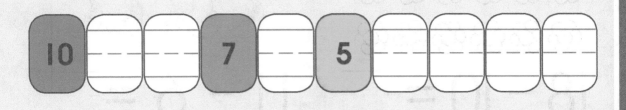

| 10 | | | 7 | | 5 | | | | |

181

Picture Problems

Solve the subtraction problems. Cross out the pictures to help you. The first one is done for you.

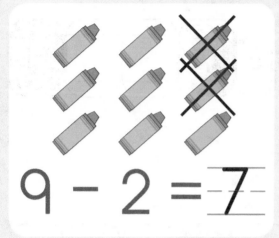

9 - 2 = 7

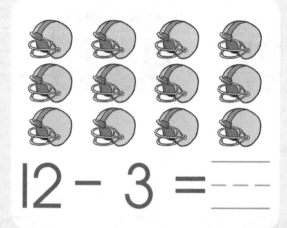

12 - 3 = ___

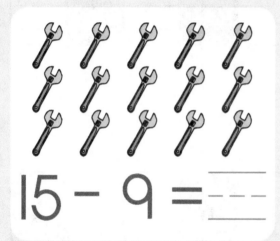

15 - 9 = ___

8 - 0 = ___

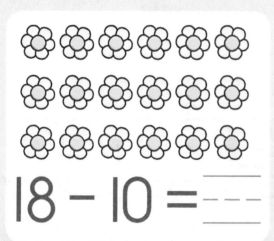

18 - 10 = ___

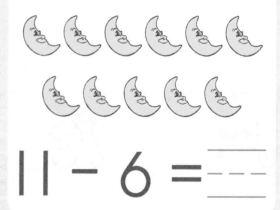

11 - 6 = ___

Picture Problems

Solve the subtraction problems. Cross out the pictures to help you.

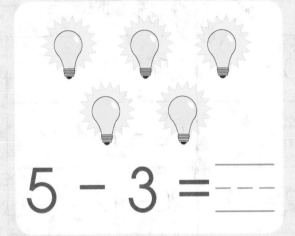

$$5 - 3 = \text{\_\_\_}$$

$$14 - 11 = \text{\_\_\_}$$

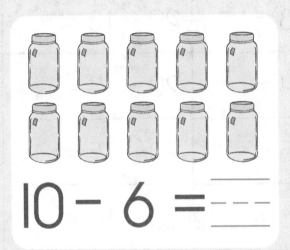

$$10 - 6 = \text{\_\_\_}$$

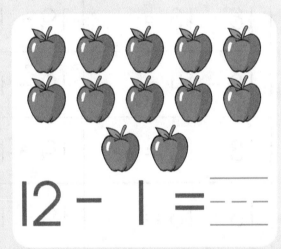

$$12 - 1 = \text{\_\_\_}$$

$$6 - 2 = \text{\_\_\_}$$

$$20 - 5 = \text{\_\_\_}$$

Subtraction Practice

Solve the problems to complete the chart. What patterns do you see?

18 – 10 =	19 – 10 =	20 – 10 =
18 – 11 =	19 – 11 =	20 – 11 =
18 – 12 =	19 – 12 =	20 – 12 =
18 – 13 =	19 – 13 =	20 – 13 =
18 – 14 =	19 – 14 =	20 – 14 =
18 – 15 =	19 – 15 =	20 – 15 =
18 – 16 =	19 – 16 =	20 – 16 =
18 – 17 =	19 – 17 =	20 – 17 =
18 – 18 =	19 – 18 =	20 – 18 =
	19 – 19 =	20 – 19 =
		20 – 20 =

Subtraction Practice

Find the differences.

```
  12        16         8       13
-  6      - 14       - 2      - 11
____      ____      ____      ____


  16         9        12       15
-  7      -  1       - 3      -  1
____      ____      ____      ____


   5        17        19       16
-  4      -  8      - 15      - 10
____      ____      ____      ____
```

With practice, you can become a **subtraction** super star! Think of a way to practice subtraction problems. It could be worksheets you make yourself, flash cards, or a computer game. Then, practice solving 15 problems each day for five days. If you make a mistake, include that problem in the next day's practice. Are your subtraction skills growing?

Growth Mindset

Use Addition for Subtraction

Use this strategy to help solve subtraction problems. Think of an addition problem with the same numbers. Write each difference. Then, draw a line to the addition problem that helped you. Use the color clues.

16 - 7 = _____

2 + 10 = 12

9 - 3 = _____

9 + 9 = 18

12 - 2 = _____

3 + 6 = 9

20 - 14 = _____

7 + 9 = 16

18 - 9 = _____

14 + 6 = 20

Use Addition for Subtraction

Solve the problem pairs. What pattern do you see?

$$12 - 7 = \underline{\quad}$$

$$7 + \underline{\quad} = 12$$

$$8 - 4 = \underline{\quad}$$

$$\underline{\quad} + 4 = 8$$

$$20 - 11 = \underline{\quad}$$

$$11 + \underline{\quad} = 20$$

$$15 - 8 = \underline{\quad}$$

$$\underline{\quad} + 8 = 15$$

Missing Numbers

Use the dominoes to help you write the missing number in each equation.

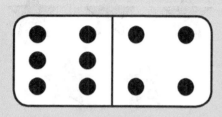

$$10 - \underline{\quad} = 6$$

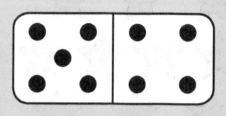

$$9 - \underline{\quad} = 4$$

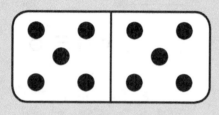

$$\underline{\quad} - 5 = 5$$

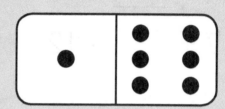

$$7 - 6 = \underline{\quad}$$

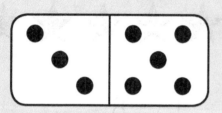

$$\underline{\quad} - 3 = 5$$

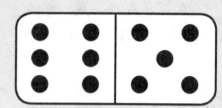

$$11 - \underline{\quad} = 5$$

Missing Numbers

Write the missing number to complete each equation.

_____ − 3 = 6

8 − _____ = 4

12 − _____ = 1

_____ − 5 = 12

_____ − 3 = 13

19 − _____ = 15

20 − _____ = 19

_____ − 1 = 3

_____ − 2 = 4

16 − _____ = 8

13 − _____ = 5

_____ − 7 = 2

Make 10

Use this strategy to help solve subtraction problems. Break apart one of the numbers before the equal sign (=) into an addition problem. Then, try to make 10 from two of the numbers. Use this strategy to solve the problems.

Example:

$$13 - 4 =$$

③ ①

$$13 - 3 - 1 =$$

$$10 - 1 = 9$$

$$11 - 6 =$$

◯ ◯

$$13 - 7 =$$

◯ ◯

$$15 - 8 =$$

◯ ◯

$$16 - 9 =$$

◯ ◯

Here is one way to practice self-control. When you feel angry or frustrated, stop. Do not react. Count to **10**. With each count, take a deep breath. Then, you will be able to think more clearly and decide what to do.

Make 10

Break apart one of the numbers before the equal sign (=) into an addition problem. Then, try to make 10 from two of the numbers. Use this strategy to solve the problems. Follow the example on page 190.

17 – 9 =

◯ ◯

20 – 12 =

◯ ◯

16 – 7 =

◯ ◯

15 – 8 =

◯ ◯

Equations

Circle the true equations.

10 − 1 = 10   5 = 10 − 5   11 = 1

12 − 2 = 14   5 = 5   16 − 7 = 8

6 − 3 = 3   15 − 4 = 11   11 − 5 = 7

Write the number that makes each equation true.

14 − 3 = ____ − 5   19 − 4 = ____ − 1

Circle the **true** statements about good table manners.
Cross out the **false** statements.

You should put your napkin on your lap.

It is polite to kick your feet under the table.

You should say that the food is gross.

It is nice to chew with your mouth closed.

It is polite to pass food to the next person.

Subtraction Word Problems

Read the problem. Write and solve an equation to find the difference. Cross out the pictures to help you.

There were 12 flowers growing by the pond. Finley's little brother, Brad, picked 3 flowers to give to their mother. How many flowers were left?

$$\underline{\quad\quad} - \underline{\quad\quad} = \underline{\quad\quad} \text{ flowers}$$

Read the problem. Write and solve an equation to find the difference. Draw pictures to help you.

Asher and Beckett played with 15 toys at Asher's house. Beckett took 7 toys to his house. How many toys did Asher have left?

$$\underline{\quad\quad} - \underline{\quad\quad} = \underline{\quad\quad} \text{ toys}$$

Subtraction Word Problems

Read each problem. Write and solve an equation to find the difference. Draw pictures to help you.

Ella's dad cut 12 celery sticks. Ella ate 4. How many celery sticks were left?

$$\underline{\hspace{2em}} - \underline{\hspace{2em}} = \underline{\hspace{2em}}$$ celery sticks

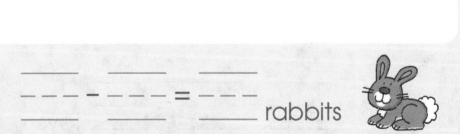

Anna's first grade classroom had 19 chairs, but 5 chairs were taken to another room. How many chairs were left in Anna's classroom?

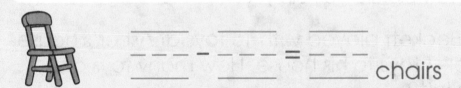

$$\underline{\hspace{2em}} - \underline{\hspace{2em}} = \underline{\hspace{2em}}$$ chairs

Nick counted 14 rabbits in the field. When an owl hooted, 7 rabbits ran away. How many rabbits were left in the field?

$$\underline{\hspace{2em}} - \underline{\hspace{2em}} = \underline{\hspace{2em}}$$ rabbits

Subtraction Word Problems

Read each problem. Write and solve an equation to find the difference. Draw pictures to help you.

On the Grady's farm, there were 18 cows. 7 cows were brown. How many cows were not brown?

_____ _ _____ = _____ cows

Derek earned 9 stickers this week. He earned 3 star stickers, and the rest were smiley faces. How many stickers were smiley faces?

_____ _ _____ = _____ smiley face stickers

There were 16 children at Bea's birthday party. 9 children ate cake, and the rest ate ice cream cones. How many children ate ice cream cones?

_____ _ _____ = _____ children

Fact Families

Write the missing problem in each fact family. The first one is done for you. Use the color clues.

$10 + 3 = 13$

$3 + 10 = 13$

$13 - 10 = 3$

$13 - 3 = 10$

$4 + 5 = 9$

$5 + 4 = 9$

$9 - 5 = 4$

$\bigcirc - \bigcirc = \bigcirc$

$8 + 9 = 17$

$\bigcirc + \bigcirc = \bigcirc$

$17 - 9 = 8$

$17 - 8 = 9$

$12 + 4 = 16$

$4 + 12 = 16$

$\bigcirc - \bigcirc = \bigcirc$

$16 - 12 = 4$

Fact Families

Complete the fact families.

③ ⑦ ⑩ ⑨ ② ⑪

_ _ _ _ + _ _ _ _ = _ _ _ _   _ _ _ _ + _ _ _ _ = _ _ _ _

_ _ _ _ + _ _ _ _ = _ _ _ _   _ _ _ _ + _ _ _ _ = _ _ _ _

_ _ _ _ − _ _ _ _ = _ _ _ _   _ _ _ _ − _ _ _ _ = _ _ _ _

_ _ _ _ − _ _ _ _ = _ _ _ _   _ _ _ _ − _ _ _ _ = _ _ _ _

⑭ ③ ⑰ ⑧ ⑦ ⑮

_ _ _ _ + _ _ _ _ = _ _ _ _   _ _ _ _ + _ _ _ _ = _ _ _ _

_ _ _ _ + _ _ _ _ = _ _ _ _   _ _ _ _ + _ _ _ _ = _ _ _ _

_ _ _ _ − _ _ _ _ = _ _ _ _   _ _ _ _ − _ _ _ _ = _ _ _ _

_ _ _ _ − _ _ _ _ = _ _ _ _   _ _ _ _ − _ _ _ _ = _ _ _ _

Addition & Subtraction Word Problems

Read the problems. Circle to tell whether you should add or subtract to solve each one. Use the space provided to draw pictures and write equations. Then, write the sum or difference.

Sam bought 6 fish. The next day, Dad gave her 2 more fish. How many fish did she have in all?

Circle one: **add** or **subtract**

Sam had _____ fish.

Connor had 20 quarters in his piggy bank. He spent 3 quarters on a piece of candy. How many quarters did Connor have left?

Circle one: **add** or **subtract**

Connor had _____ quarters left.

Addition & Subtraction Word Problems

Use both addition and subtraction to solve the word problems. Write the missing numbers in the equations.

Georgia has 20 books on her bookshelf. 9 books are fiction, and the rest are nonfiction. How many books are nonfiction?

$9 + \underline{} = 20$ books in all

$20 - 9 = \underline{}$ nonfiction books

Of the 16 cars in the school parking lot, 8 cars are red. The other cars are different colors. How many cars are colors other than red?

$8 + \underline{} = 16$ cars in all

$16 - 8 = \underline{}$ cars with colors other than red

Count by Tens

Write the number for each group of tens.

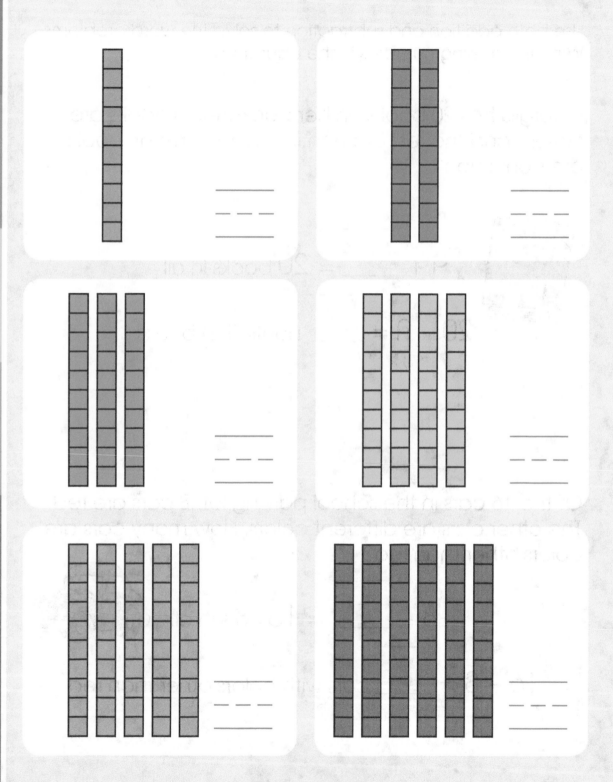

Count by Tens

Count by tens. Write the missing numbers.

10 ___ 30

___ ___ 60 70

___ ___ ___

Have you heard the saying, "An apple a day keeps the doctor away"? Eating lots of fruits and vegetables is a good way to stay healthy. Read the names of fruits and vegetables. Circle **ten** you like best.

apples	corn	pineapples	peaches
pears	bananas	lettuce	onions
broccoli	celery	peppers	tomatoes
peas	green beans	oranges	kiwis

Health & Fitness

Count by Tens

Count by tens. Write the missing numbers in each row.

60   ___   80   ___

10   ___   ___   40

List **ten** of your favorite things. They could be places, books, movies, animals, or something else.

1 _____   6 _____

2 _____   7 _____

3 _____   8 _____

4 _____   9 _____

5 _____   10 _____

Count by Tens

Write the missing numbers. **Hint:** Each number you write will end with **0**.

1	2	3	4	5	6	7	8	9	
11	12	13	14	15	16	17	18	19	
21	22	23	24	25	26	27	28	29	
31	32	33	34	35	36	37	38	39	
41	42	43	44	45	46	47	48	49	
51	52	53	54	55	56	57	58	59	
61	62	63	64	65	66	67	68	69	
71	72	73	74	75	76	77	78	79	
81	82	83	84	85	86	87	88	89	
91	92	93	94	95	96	97	98	99	

203

Count to 120

Count the objects. Write the number.

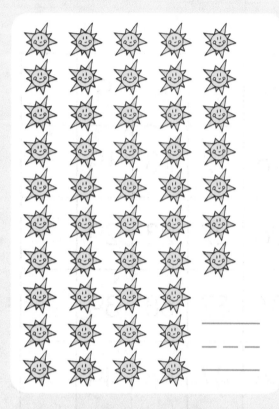

_____

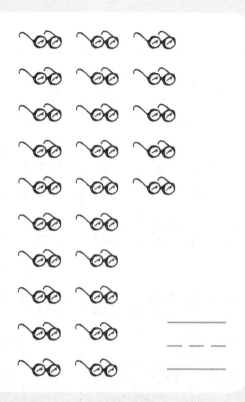

_____

_____

_____

Count to 120

Draw more circles to make the number shown.

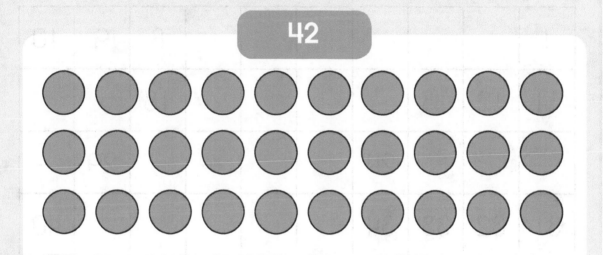

42

98

Count to 120

Write the missing numbers.

1							8	9	10
11	12	13					18		
			24					29	
31	32	33	34						40
41					46	47	48	49	
						57	58		60
61	62				67				
	72			75			78	79	80
		83			86				
91	92	93						98	99
									110
				115					120

Count to 120

Write the missing numbers.

___ 52 53   69 ___ 71

22 ___ 24   76 77 ___

___ 90 91   100 101 ___

109 110 ___   ___ 119 120

Two-Digit Numbers

Color the tens blocks and ones blocks to show the numbers.

12

16

13

15

208

Two-Digit Numbers

Color the tens blocks and ones blocks to show the numbers.

14

17

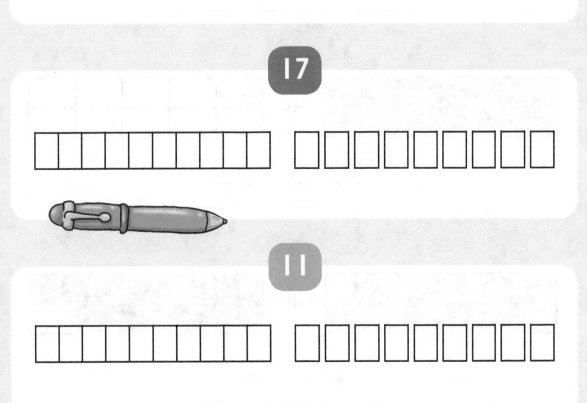

11

19

Two-Digit Numbers

Write the addition problems shown by the ten frames.

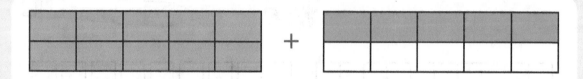

_____ _____
_ _ _ _ + _ _ _ _ = _ _ _ _
_____

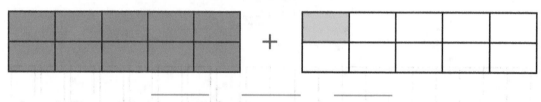

_____ _____
_ _ _ _ + _ _ _ _ = _ _ _ _
_____

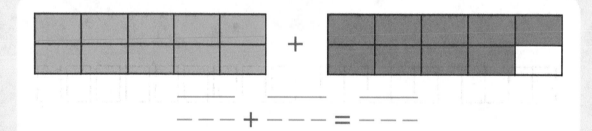

_____ _____
_ _ _ _ + _ _ _ _ = _ _ _ _
_____

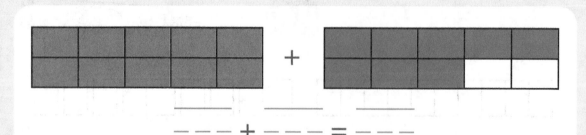

_____ _____
_ _ _ _ + _ _ _ _ = _ _ _ _
_____

Two-Digit Numbers

Write the addition problems shown by the ten frames.

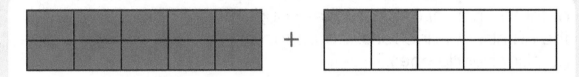

_____ _____ _____
_ _ _ _ + _ _ _ _ = _ _ _ _

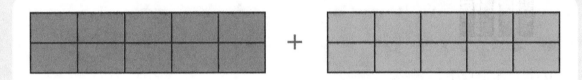

_____ _____ _____
_ _ _ _ + _ _ _ _ = _ _ _ _

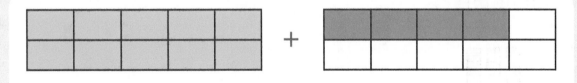

_____ _____ _____
_ _ _ _ + _ _ _ _ = _ _ _ _

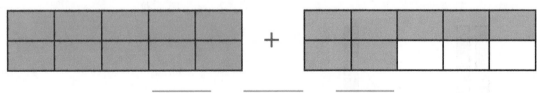

_____ _____ _____
_ _ _ _ + _ _ _ _ = _ _ _ _

Two-Digit Numbers

What is place value? It is the value of each numeral in its place. In the number **23**, the **2** is in the tens place. It has the value of two tens, or **20**. The **3** is in the ones place. It has the value of three ones, or **3**. Count the groups of tens blocks and write the number beside **tens**. Count the ones blocks and write the number beside **ones**.

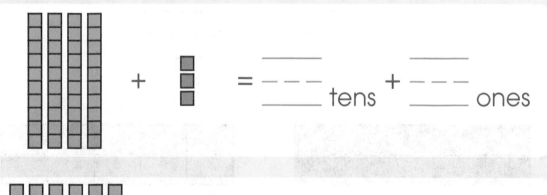

$$\underline{\hspace{1.5cm}} \text{ tens} + \underline{\hspace{1.5cm}} \text{ ones}$$

$$\underline{\hspace{1.5cm}} \text{ tens} + \underline{\hspace{1.5cm}} \text{ ones}$$

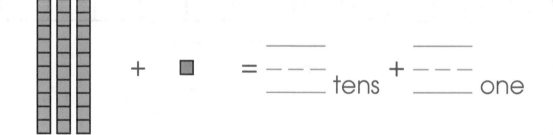

$$\underline{\hspace{1.5cm}} \text{ tens} + \underline{\hspace{1.5cm}} \text{ one}$$

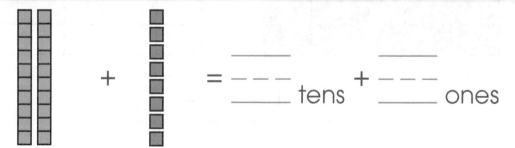

$$\underline{\hspace{1.5cm}} \text{ tens} + \underline{\hspace{1.5cm}} \text{ ones}$$

Two-Digit Numbers

Count the groups of tens blocks and write the number beside **tens**. Count the ones blocks and write the number beside **ones**. Then, write the whole number. The first one is done for you.

$$\underline{1}\ \text{ten} + \underline{2}\ \text{ones} = \underline{12}$$

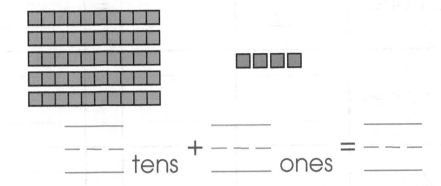

_____ tens + _____ ones = _____

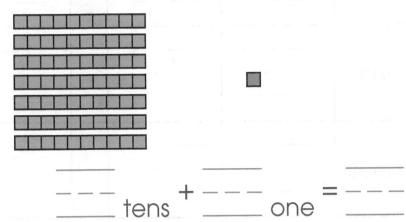

_____ tens + _____ ones = _____

_____ tens + _____ one = _____

213

Two-Digit Numbers

Complete the chart. The first row is done for you.

	Tens	Ones	=	Two-Digit Number
3 tens, 2 ones	3	2	=	32
1 ten, 7 ones			=	
9 tens, 1 one			=	
5 tens, 6 ones			=	
6 tens, 5 ones			=	
1 ten, 1 one			=	
7 tens, 9 ones			=	

Two-Digit Numbers

Complete the chart.

		Tens	Ones
28	=	_____ tens	_____ ones
64	=	_____ tens	_____ ones
56	=	_____ tens	_____ ones
72	=	_____ tens	_____ ones
17	=	_____ ten	_____ ones
34	=	_____ tens	_____ ones
98	=	_____ tens	_____ ones
15	=	_____ ten	_____ ones
22	=	_____ tens	_____ ones
57	=	_____ tens	_____ ones

Two-Digit Numbers

Circle the numbers that have **9** in the tens place.

51 94 58 19 93 96 45

Circle the numbers that have **2** in the ones place.

12 84 21 63 92 42 76

Circle the numbers that have **3** in the tens place.

83 36 90 85 37 63 34

Write a **two-digit number** to complete each goal. Then, make a plan to practice and improve each skill.

I want to read _____ _____ chapter books.
tens   ones

I want to learn to spell _____ _____ tricky words.
tens   ones

I want to jump rope _____ _____ times without missing.
tens   ones

Growth Mindset

Comparing Two-Digit Numbers

Read the examples below. Then, write **<**, **>**, or **=** in the circles to compare the two-digit numbers.

Examples:

> means **greater than**.   **<** means **less than**.   **=** means **equal to**.

$$50 > 40$$ $$40 < 50$$ $$40 = 40$$

50 is greater than 40.   40 is less than 50.   40 is equal to 40.

32 ◯ 33   36 ◯ 87

44 ◯ 55   95 ◯ 84

54 ◯ 54   31 ◯ 40

16 ◯ 17   50 ◯ 50

217

Comparing Two-Digit Numbers

Write <, >, or = in the circles to compare the two-digit numbers.

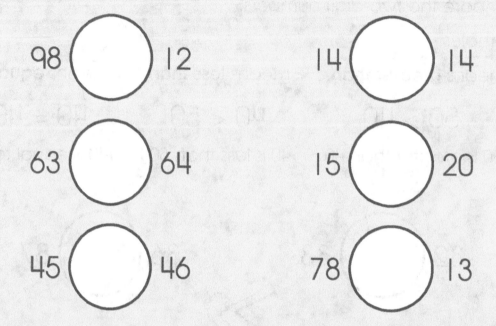

98 ◯ 12   14 ◯ 14

63 ◯ 64   15 ◯ 20

45 ◯ 46   78 ◯ 13

Write numbers in the correct spaces to compare the amounts. Then, answer the questions.

Keith has 48 dollars. Brady has 40 dollars.

_____ _____

- - - - > - - - -

_____ _____

_____

Who has more money? _____

Kerry has 13 pairs of shoes. George has 18 pairs of shoes.

_____ _____

- - - - < - - - -

_____ _____

_____

Who has more shoes? _____

Comparing Two-Digit Numbers

Cut out the numbers. Tape or glue them in the spaces to make comparisons that are true.

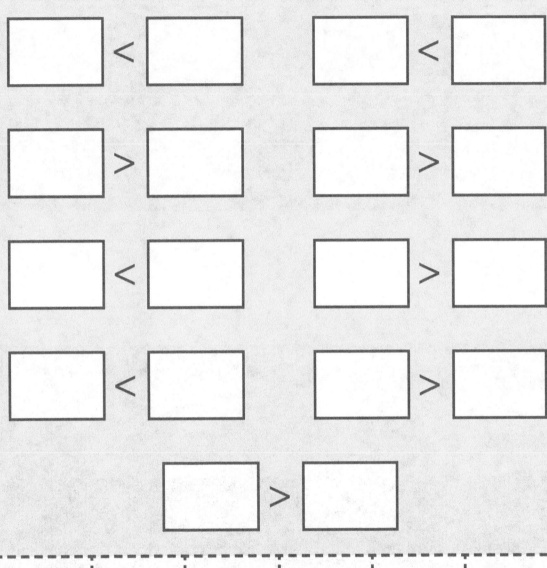

	<			<	
	>			>	
	<			>	
	<			>	

| | > | |

15	51	76	82	32	67
10	31	22	45	35	65
87	43	94	81	99	14

BLANK PAGE FOR CUTTING ACTIVITY

Add 10

Draw a line from each bee to the flower with a number that is 10 more.

Add 10

Add 10 to each number on a cloud. Write the sum on the sun.

15

72

31

89

76

40

49

19

Subtract 10

Draw a line from each frog to the lily pad with a number that is 10 less.

 34

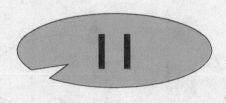 11

 66

 33

 21

 56

 43

 70

 80

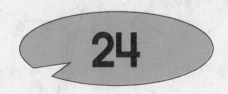 24

Subtract 10

Subtract 10 from each number on a raindrop. Write the difference on the umbrella.

Add & Subtract 10

Write the numbers that are 10 more and 10 less than each number shown.

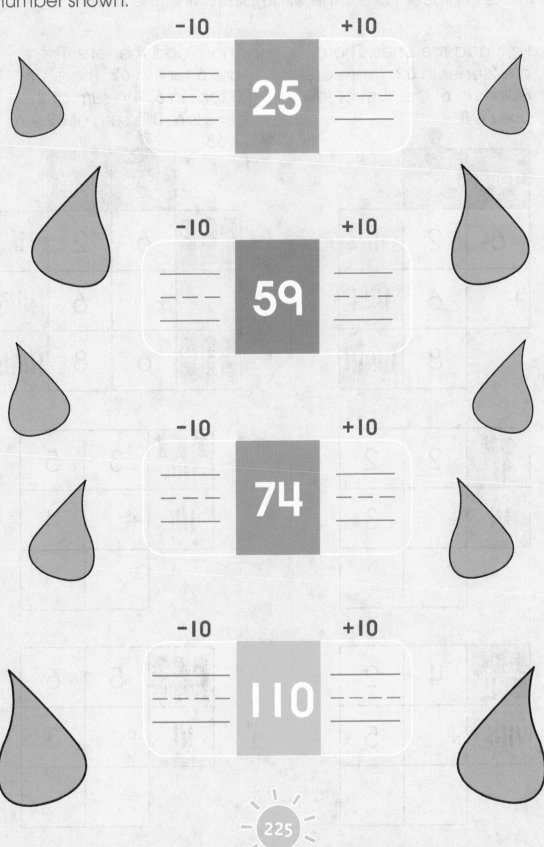

-10   +10

25

-10   +10

59

-10   +10

74

-10   +10

110

225

Add One Digit to Two Digits

First, add the numbers in the ones place. Then, add the numbers in the tens place. Follow the example to find the sums.

1. First, add the ones. There are **2** ones in **62**. There are **6** ones in **6**. The sum of the ones is **8**.

Tens	Ones	
6	2	
+	6	
	8	

2. Then, add the tens. There are **6** tens in **62**. There are **0** tens in **6**. The sum of the tens is **6**. The sum of **62 + 6** is **68**.

	Tens	Ones	
	6	2	
	+	6	
	6	8	

	2	2
	+	3

	3	5
	+	4

	4	2
	+	5

	5	6
	+	3

226

Add One Digit to Two Digits

Add to find the total points scored in each game.

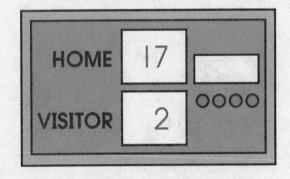

HOME 28
VISITOR 1

Total _____

HOME 17
VISITOR 2

Total _____

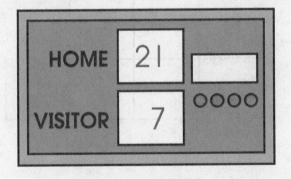

HOME 21
VISITOR 7

Total _____

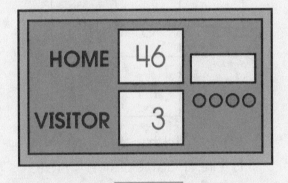

HOME 46
VISITOR 3

Total _____

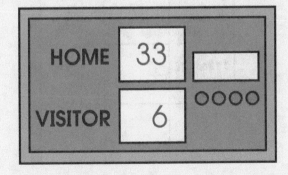

HOME 33
VISITOR 6

Total _____

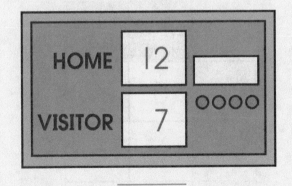

HOME 12
VISITOR 7

Total _____

Regroup

Sometimes when you add, the sum of the ones is more than 9. When that happens, you need to regroup 10 ones as 1 ten. Follow the example.

1. First, add the ones. There are **6** ones in **56**. There are **5** ones in **5**. The sum of the ones is **11**.

Tens	Ones
5	6
+	5
	11

2. Next, regroup **11** as **1** ten and **1** one. Move **1** ten into the tens place.

Tens	Ones
5	6
+	5
	1

3. Last, add the tens. There is **1** regrouped ten. There are **5** tens in **56**. There are **0** tens in **5**. The sum of the tens is **6**. The sum of **56 + 5** is **61**.

Tens	Ones
5	6
+	5
6	1

Find the sum.

Tens	Ones
7	5
+	8

Regroup

Add. As you solve each problem, regroup 10 ones as 1 ten.

	1	2
	+	9

	7	5
	+	9

	4	8
	+	6

	1	3
	+	8

	8	9
	+	9

	5	5
	+	5

229

Regroup

Add to find the total points scored in each game. As you solve each problem, regroup 10 ones as 1 ten.

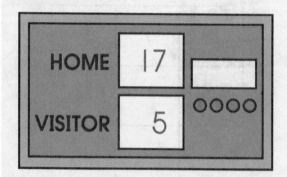

HOME 17
VISITOR 5
oooo

Total _____

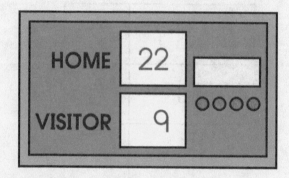

HOME 22
VISITOR 9
oooo

Total _____

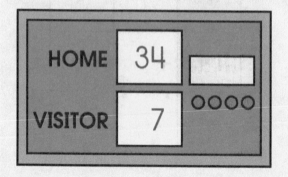

HOME 34
VISITOR 7
oooo

Total _____

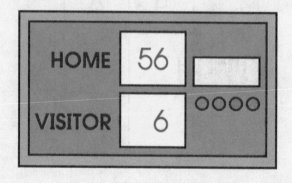

HOME 56
VISITOR 6
oooo

Total _____

You **regroup** numbers in math problems. Did you know that regrouping can help you solve other problems, too? **Regroup** can mean "to stop, think, and get ready." When you make a mistake, do not blame yourself or give up. Instead, regroup! Stop and think about what you can do differently before you try again.

Growth Mindset

Regroup

Write the addition problems in the boxes. Then, add. Regroup when needed.

78 + 6	29 + 3	44 + 4
53 + 6	54 + 5	95 + 5
15 + 8	11 + 9	18 + 7

Tens	Ones
+	

Tens	Ones
+	

Tens	Ones
+	

Tens	Ones
+	

Tens	Ones
+	

Tens	Ones
+	

Tens	Ones
+	

Tens	Ones
+	

Tens	Ones
+	

Add Multiples of 10

Add the ones. Then, add the tens.

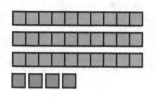

$$\begin{array}{r} 34 \\ +30 \\ \hline \end{array}$$

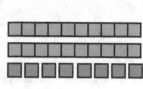

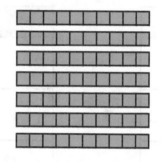

$$\begin{array}{r} 28 \\ +70 \\ \hline \end{array}$$

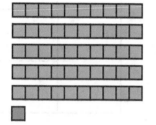

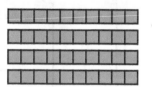

$$\begin{array}{r} 51 \\ +40 \\ \hline \end{array}$$

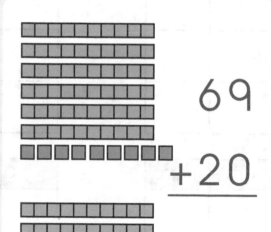

$$\begin{array}{r} 69 \\ +20 \\ \hline \end{array}$$

Add Multiples of 10

Use the sums in the shapes to answer the problems below.

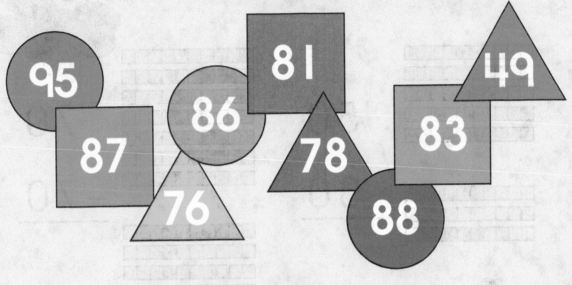

```
  56          45          18
+ 30        + 50        + 60
```

```
  67          33          29
+ 20        + 50        + 20
```

```
  71          58          16
+ 10        + 30        + 60
```

233

Subtract Multiples of 10

Subtract the ones. Then, subtract the tens.

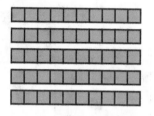

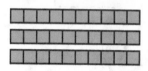

50
−30

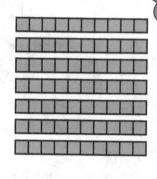

70
−70

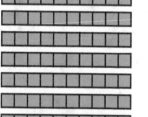

90
−40

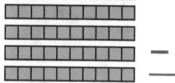

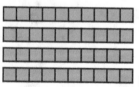

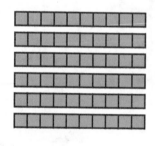

60
−30

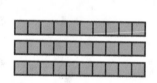

Subtract Multiples of 10

Use the differences in the shapes to answer the problems below.

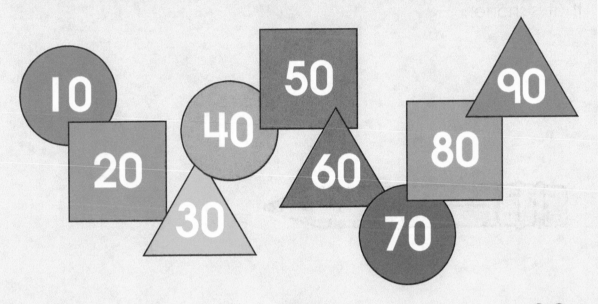

70	40	90
− 50	− 10	− 10

90	90	70
− 20	− 30	− 30

30	70	100
− 20	− 20	− 10

Compare Lengths

Look at the pencil. Draw a pencil that is longer. Draw a pencil that is shorter.

Look at the crayon. Draw a crayon that is longer. Draw a crayon that is shorter.

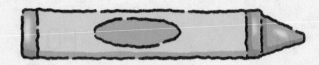

Order Lengths

In each group, write **1** beside the shortest object, write **2** beside the object that is the next longest, and write **3** beside the object that is the longest.

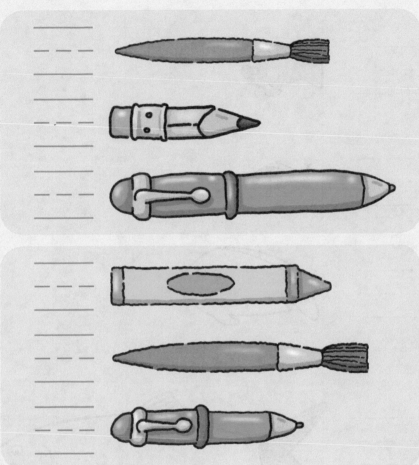

Read the steps for solving a problem in a group.
Number them **1**, **2**, **3** to put them in **order**.

_____ Choose a solution that everyone likes.

_____ Stop! Take deep breaths and calm down.

_____ Let everyone talk. Listen to others. Think of ways to solve the problem.

Social Skills

Order Lengths

In each group, write **1** beside the shortest fish, write **2** beside the fish that is the next longest, and write **3** beside the fish that is the longest.

Compare Lengths

Look at the fish in the fish tank. Draw a fish in the tank that is shorter. Draw a fish in the tank that is longer.

Measure Length

Measure the objects by counting the boxes (units).

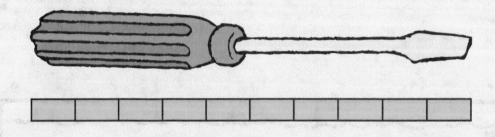

The screwdriver is _____ units long.

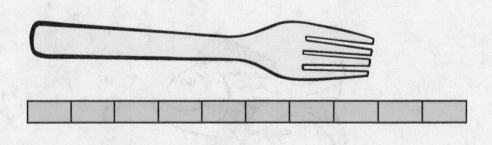

The fork is _____ units long.

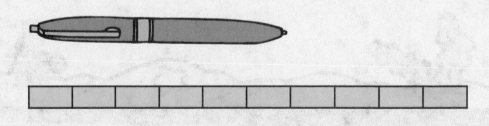

The pen is _____ units long.

Measure Length

Cut out the ruler from the bottom of the page. Measure each pencil by lining up the ruler with the left edge of the pencil. Then, write the number of boxes (units) you count. Finally, circle the longest pencil.

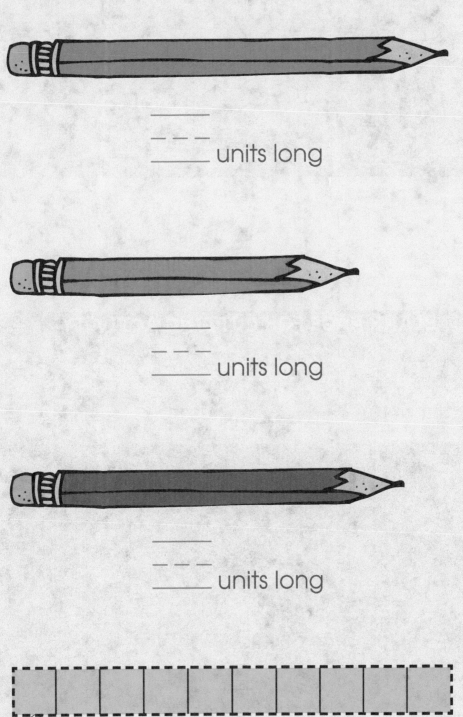

_____ units long

_____ units long

_____ units long

BLANK PAGE FOR CUTTING ACTIVITY

Measure Length

Count the paper clips (units) to measure each drinking straw.
Circle the shortest straw.

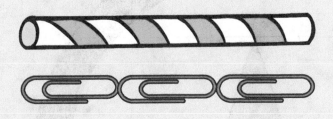

_____
_ _ _
_____ units long

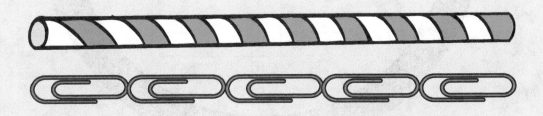

_____
_ _ _
_____ units long

_____
_ _ _
_____ units long

Tell Time

Write the missing numbers.

Do you take **time** each day to do the things you are responsible for? Check the sentences that are true. Then, complete the last sentence.

Character Development

☐ I am responsible for doing my homework.

☐ I am responsible for putting away my toys.

☐ I am responsible for brushing my teeth.

☐ I am responsible for getting myself dressed.

I am responsible for _____.

Tell Time

On a clock face, the short hand tells the hour. When the long hand is on **12**, it is the beginning of the hour. Write the time shown on each clock. The first one is done for you.

__3__ o'clock

_____ o'clock

_____ o'clock

_____ o'clock

_____ o'clock

_____ o'clock

Tell Time

When the short hand is on **3** and the long hand is on **12**, it is three o'clock or 3:00. Write the time shown on each clock in two different ways. The first one is done for you.

eight o'clock

8 : 00

_____ o'clock

____ : 00

_____ o'clock

____ : 00

_____ o'clock

____ : 00

Tell Time

Match the analog and digital clocks that show the same times.

5:00

10:00

2:00

Draw a picture to show what you do at each **time** of day.

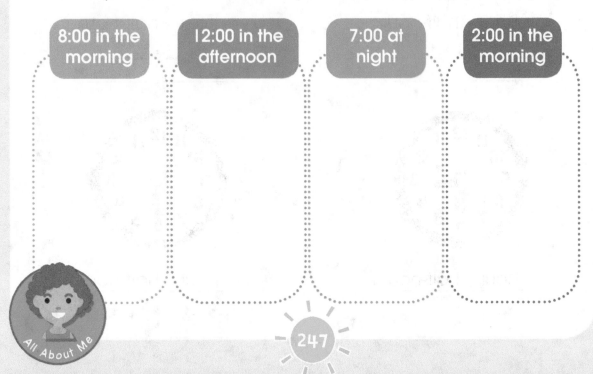

| 8:00 in the morning | 12:00 in the afternoon | 7:00 at night | 2:00 in the morning |

All About Me

247

Tell Time

On a clock face, the short hand tells the hour. The long hand tells how many minutes after the hour. When the long hand is on **6**, it shows **30** minutes after the hour, or a half-hour. Write the time shown on each clock. The first one is done for you.

hour   half-hour

I : 30

hour   half-hour

____ : ____

hour   half-hour

____ : ____

hour   half-hour

____ : ____

hour   half-hour

____ : ____

hour   half-hour

____ : ____

Tell Time

Write the time shown on each clock in two different ways. The first one is done for you.

half past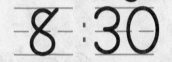

half past _____

___ : ___

half past _____

___ : ___

half past _____

___ : ___

Tell Time

Match the analog and digital clocks that show the same times.

Tell Time

Match the analog and digital clocks that show the same times.

Tell Time

Draw hands on each clock to show the time.

2:30

9:00

7:00

4:30

3:00

1:30

Tell Time

Draw hands on the clock faces to match the times shown on the digital clocks.

Kids need at least 60 minutes (1 hour) of physical activity each day. Have a fun fitness evening with your family. Watch the **time**. When the clock shows the hour or half past the hour, spend 10 minutes playing soccer, playing tag, or doing another physical activity together. If you do this six times, you will have spent a whole hour exercising!

Health & Fitness

Bar Graphs

Count the banana peels in each column. Color the boxes to show how many bananas were eaten by the monkey.

Bar Graphs

Kayla is counting how many school supplies she has left. Color the boxes to show how many of each item. Then, answer the questions.

Kayla has the most _____. Circle your answer.

Kayla has the least _____. Circle your answer.

Bar Graphs

Kirsten made a bar graph to show how many books she read over the summer. Use the graph to answer the questions.

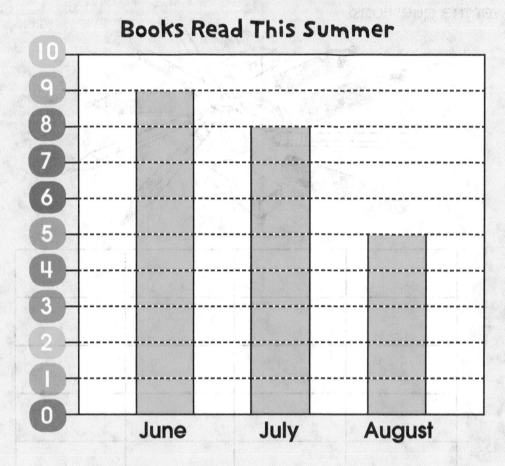

Books Read This Summer

During which month did Kirsten read the most books? Circle your answer.

June   July   August

During which month did Kirsten read 8 books? Circle your answer.

June   July   August

How many more books did Kirsten read in June than in August?

_____ books

Bar Graphs

Use the bar graph to answer the questions.

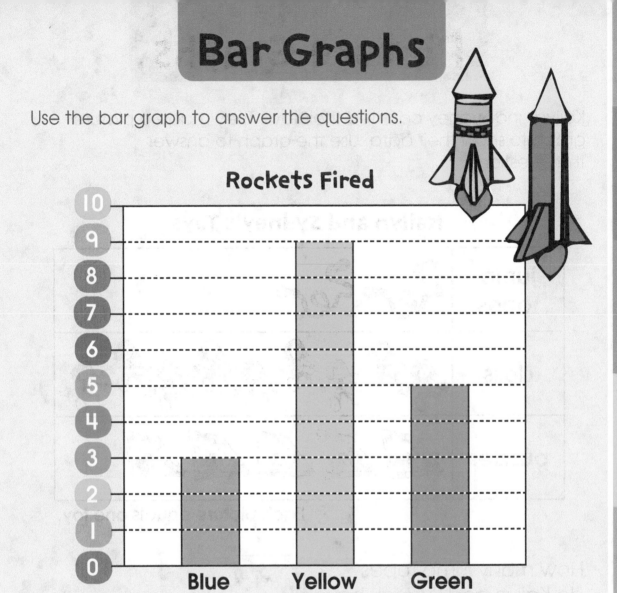

Rockets Fired

How many rockets did the Green Club fire? _____

How many rockets did the Yellow Club fire? _____

How many more rockets did the
Yellow Club fire than the Blue Club? _____

How many rockets were fired in all? _____

Picture Graphs

Kailyn and Sydney counted their toys. They made a picture graph to show their data. Use the graph to answer the questions.

Kailyn and Sydney's Toys

jump ropes	
dolls	
puzzles	

Each picture equals one toy.

How many jump ropes do Kailyn and Sydney have? _____

How many toys do they have altogether? _____

Do Kailyn and Sydney have more dolls or more puzzles? Circle your answer.

dolls   puzzles

Do Kailyn and Sydney have more puzzles or more jump ropes? Circle your answer.

puzzles   jump ropes

Picture Graphs

Hayden asked his first grade classmates to vote for their favorite fruit. Each student chose one fruit. Use the picture graph to answer the questions.

Grade 1 Favorite Fruits

watermelon	
grapes	
peaches	

Each picture equals one student's vote.

How many classmates chose watermelon as their favorite fruit? _____

How many classmates chose grapes as their favorite fruit? _____

Which fruit was the favorite of Hayden's classmates? Circle your answer.

watermelon   **grapes**   **peaches**

Which fruit was the least favorite of Hayden's classmates? Circle your answer.

watermelon   **grapes**   **peaches**

259

Tally Charts

Use the examples to make tally marks in the chart as you read the story.

| | | | | = 3 | ||| ||| = 5 | ||| ||| | | | | = 9 |

Jake and his mom went to the store to buy food for a party. They bought 3 pizzas, 5 cartons of milk, and 12 cupcakes.

Food for Jake's Party

🍕	
🥛 MILK	
🧁	

Read each message that will help you grow and reach your goals. Make a **tally mark** each time you tell yourself the message.

Try Again!	
Mistakes Are Ok!	
I Am Learning!	

Growth Mindset

Tally Charts

Write the total number of tally marks in each row. Then, use the chart to answer the questions.

On Mr. Johnson's Farm

Animal	Tally	Total
	ⅣⅢ III	_ _ _
	ⅣⅢ ⅣⅢ ⅣⅢ IIII	_ _ _
	ⅣⅢ ⅣⅢ II	_ _ _

Which animal does Mr. Johnson have the most of? Circle your answer.

How many rabbits does Mr. Johnson have? _____

How many more chicks than sheep does Mr. Johnson have? _____

Flat Shapes

Write the name of each flat (two-dimensional) shape.

rectangle   rhombus   oval   circle
trapezoid   triangle   hexagon   square

_____   _____

- - - - - - - - - - -   - - - - - - - - - - -

_____   _____

_____   _____

- - - - - - - - - - -   - - - - - - - - - - -

_____   _____

_____   _____

- - - - - - - - - - -   - - - - - - - - - - -

_____   _____

_____   _____

- - - - - - - - - - -   - - - - - - - - - - -

_____   _____

Flat Shapes

Use the code to color the shapes.

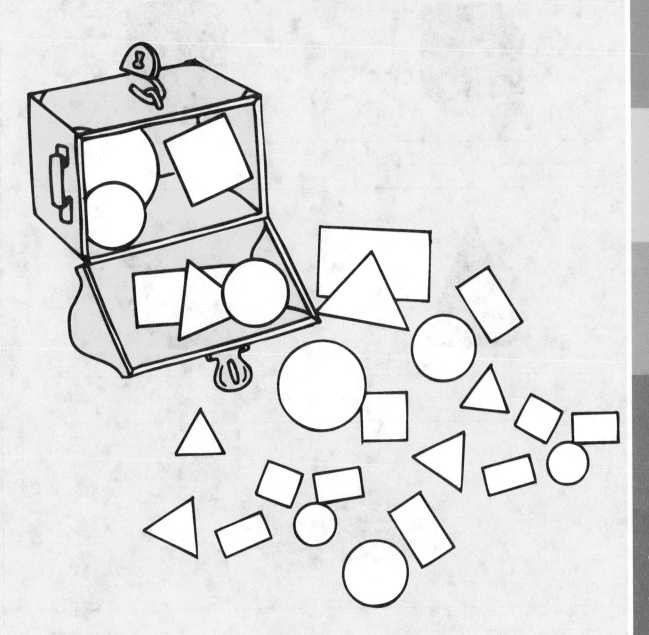

Solid Shapes

Write the name of each solid (three-dimensional) shape.

cone　　rectangular prism　　cylinder
cube　　　　　sphere

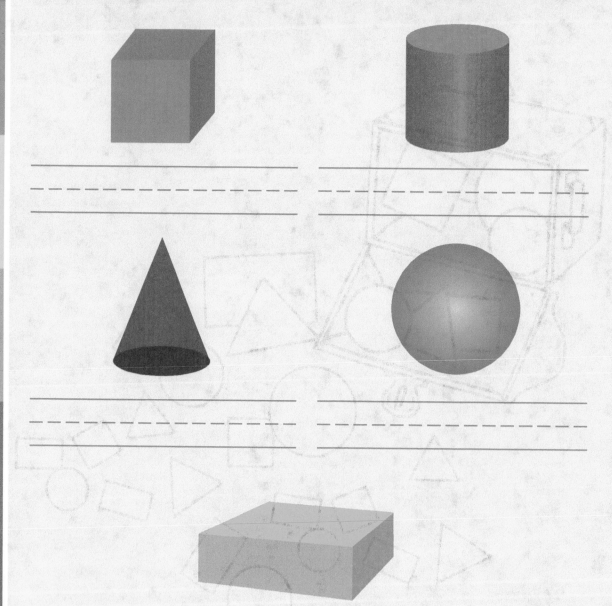

_____　_____
- - - - - - - - - - - - - - -　- - - - - - - - - - - - - - -
_____　_____

_____
- - - - - - - - - - - - - - -
_____

_____
- - - - - - - - - - - - - - -
_____

Flat & Solid Shapes

Draw a line from each shape to an object that has the same shape.

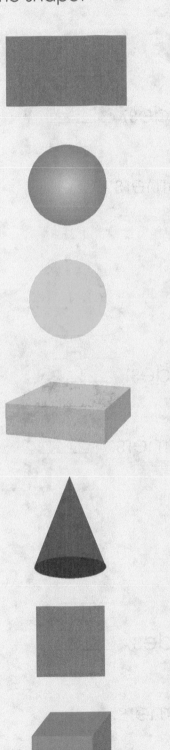

Describe Shapes

Write the number of sides and corners for each flat shape.

Sides: _____

Corners: _____

Sides: _____

Corners: _____

Sides: _____

Corners: _____

Sides: _____

Corners: _____

Sides: _____

Corners: _____

Sides: _____

Corners: _____

Describe Shapes

Solid (three-dimensional) shapes are made up of flat surfaces called faces. Cut out the solid shapes. Tape or glue each one above its description.

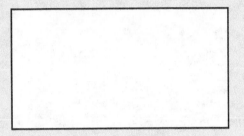

I have 2 faces shaped
like circles.

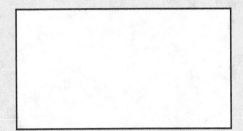

I have 0 faces.

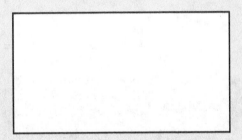

I have 6 faces shaped
like squares.

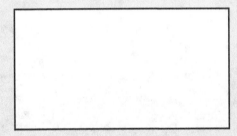

I have 6 faces shaped
like rectangles.

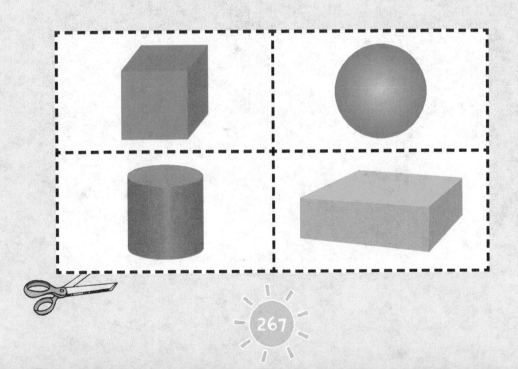

BLANK PAGE FOR CUTTING ACTIVITY

Make Shapes

Cut out the shapes and mix up the pieces. Use all the pieces to create one large square on a tabletop.

BLANK PAGE FOR CUTTING ACTIVITY

Make Shapes

In each box, use all the shapes shown to draw a new shape.

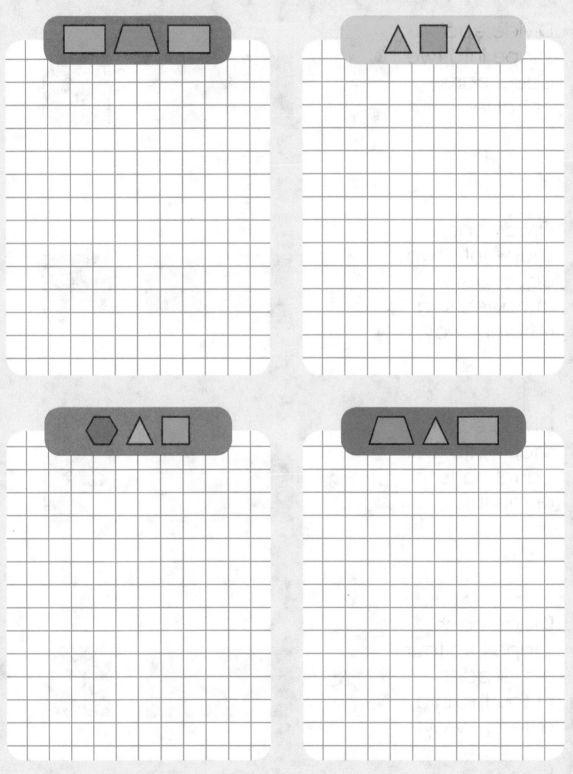

Equal Shares

Draw one or more lines to divide each shape into equal parts.

Divide each shape into two equal parts, or halves.

Divide each shape into two equal parts, or halves, in a different way.

Divide each shape into four equal parts, or fourths.

Divide each shape into four equal parts, or fourths, in a different way.

Equal Shares

Cut out the shapes. Then, cut them into the equal parts shown. Put the pieces together on a tabletop. How many halves equal one whole shape? How many fourths equal one whole shape? How many fourths equal one-half shape?

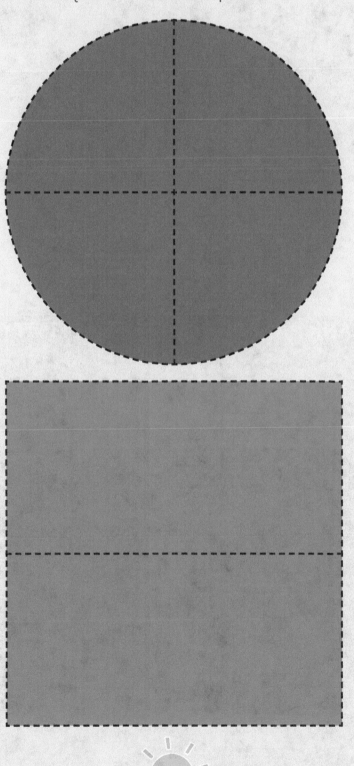

BLANK PAGE FOR CUTTING ACTIVITY

Equal Shares

Follow the directions to color equal parts of each shape.

Color one-half.

Color
one-fourth, or
one quarter.

 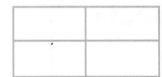

Color
two-fourths, or
two quarters.

 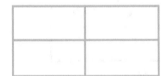

Color two halves,
or one whole.

 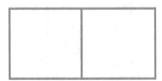

Answer key

Write Aa, Bb, Cc

Trace and write.

6

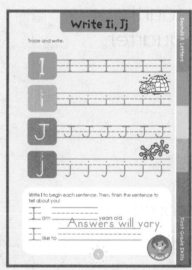

Write Dd, Ee

Trace and write.

When you have a growth mindset, you know that if you try and work hard, you learn and improve. Check sentences that show a growth mindset. In each one, find a word that begins with **d**.

- [ ] I will never learn this.
- [x] This is difficult, but I will get better at it.
- [ ] She is talented at this, but I am not.
- [x] I made a mistake, so I will do it again.

7

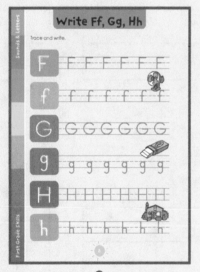

Write Ff, Gg, Hh

Trace and write.

8

Write Ii, Jj

Trace and write.

Write I to begin each sentence. Then, finish the sentence to tell about you!

I am ___ years old. Answers will vary.
I like to ___

9

Write Kk, Ll, Mm

Trace and write.

10

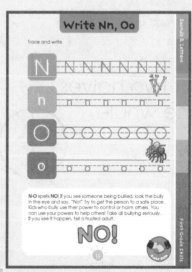

Write Nn, Oo

Trace and write.

N-O spells NO! If you see someone being bullied, look the bully in the eye and say, "No!" Try to get the person to a safe place. Kids who bully use their power to control or harm others. You can use your powers to help others! Take all bullying seriously. If you see it happen, tell a trusted adult.

NO!

11

276

Answer key

12

Sounds & Letters

Write Pp, Qq, Rr

Trace and write.

P — P P P P P P P

p — p p p p p p p

Q — Q Q Q Q Q Q

q — q q q q q q q

R — R R R R R R

r — r r r r r r r

First Grade Skills

13

Sounds & Letters

Write Ss, Tt

Trace and write.

S — S S S S S S S

s — s s s s s s s

T — T T T T T T T

t — t t t t t t t

Write s or t in each car safety rule.

Wear a seatbelt during every __T__rip.

Buckle up righ __T__ away.

Never __S__ hare a seatbelt.

First Grade Skills

14

Sounds & Letters

Write Uu, Vv, Ww

Trace and write.

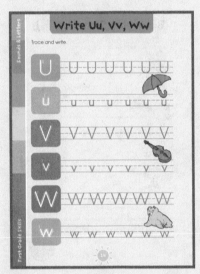

U — U U U U U U U

u — u u u u u u u

V — V V V V V V V

v — v v v v v v v

W — W W W W W W W

w — w w w w w w w

First Grade Skills

15

Sounds & Letters

Write Xx, Yy, Zz

Trace and write.

X — X X X X X X X

x — x x x x x x x

Y — Y Y Y Y Y Y

y — y y y y y y y

Z — Z Z Z Z Z Z

z — z z z z z z z

First Grade Skills

16

Sounds & Letters

Uppercase & Lowercase Letters

Write the missing letter in each pair.

Aa Bb Cc Dd Ee

Ff Gg Hh Ii Jj

Kk Ll Mm Nn Oo

Pp Qq Rr Ss Tt

Uu Vv Ww

Xx Yy Zz

First Grade Skills

17

Sounds & Letters

Write Your Name

Circle the letters in your first and last names.

Aa	Bb	Cc	Dd	Ee	Ff	Gg
Hh	Ii	Jj	Kk	Ll	Mm	Nn
Oo	Pp	Qq	Rr	Ss	Tt	Uu
Vv	Ww	Xx	Yy	Zz		

Write your first and last names.

Answers will vary.

When you introduce yourself, tell your full **name**. Stand up straight, look the person in the eye, and give a firm handshake. Imagine you are meeting one of your heroes. Complete the introduction.

Hi, I am __Answers will vary.__
your name

It is nice to meet you, _____
your hero's name

First Grade Skills

277

Answer key

18

19

20

21

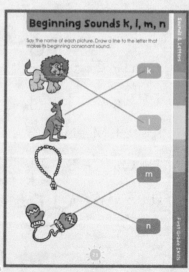

22

278

23

Answer key

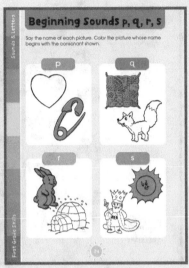

24

25

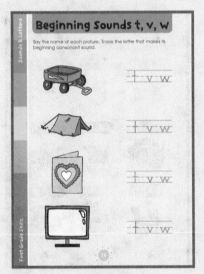

26

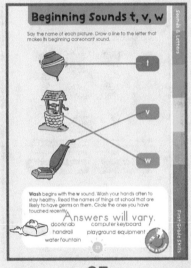

27

28

29

279

Answer key

30

31

32

33

34

280

35

Answer key

36

Answer each riddle by writing a word with a consonant blend.

| sleep | clap | clock | blow | glass |

I have two hands on my face. What am I?

clock

I can be empty or full. What am I?

glass

I am the opposite of **wake**. What am I?

sleep

I am what you do with a whistle or bubble gum. What am I?

blow

I am what people do after a good show. What am I?

clap

37

38

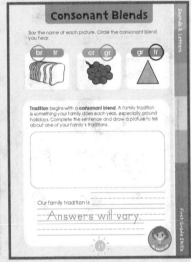

39

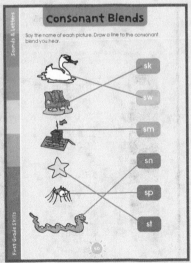

40

Write a consonant blend to complete each word.

skunk   snow

sled   slide

skate   snake

41

Answer key

Consonant Blends

Write a consonant blend to complete each word.

she**lf**   be**lt**

ra**ft**   mi**lk**

ma**sk**   qui**lt**

42

Consonant Blends

Say the name of each picture. Draw a line to the consonant blend you hear at the end of the word.

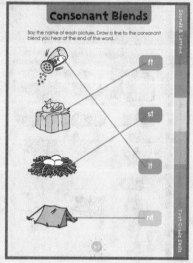

ft

st

lt

nt

43

Consonant Digraphs

A consonant digraph is two or more consonant letters that come together to make one sound in a word. The word at the top of each column has a consonant digraph. Circle pictures in the column whose names have the same consonant digraph.

sh — shoe   ch — chin   th — thumb

44

Consonant Digraphs

Write a consonant digraph to complete each word.

sheep   **wh**ale

chair   **th**orn

ship   **ch**icken

45

Consonant Digraphs

Underline a consonant digraph in each word in the box. Then, write a word to name each picture.

bench whale shoe wheel brush chair

shoe

wheel

chair

whale

bench

brush

46

Consonant Digraphs

Underline a consonant digraph in each word in the box. Then, write a word to name each picture.

watch shell peach thimble teeth match

thimble

watch

peach

match

shell

teeth

47

282

Answer key

Short a

Short **a** is the vowel sound you hear in the middle of **bat**. In each column, circle the picture whose name has the short **a** sound.

48

Short a

Write a short **a** word to name each picture.

| rat | grass | can | bag | man | bat |

bag
grass
bat
can
rat
man

49

Short e

Short **e** is the vowel sound you hear in the middle of **pet**. Color the pictures whose names have the short **e** sound.

50

Short e

Write a short **e** word to name each picture.

| ten | net | bell | beg |

net
bell
beg
ten

You hear the short **e** sound in **help**. Circle ways that you help at home.   Answers will vary.

feed my pet   weed the garden   set the table
sweep the floor   wash dishes   make my bed
carry groceries   put toys away
turn out lights

51

Short i

Short **i** is the vowel sound you hear in the middle of **six**. In each sentence, find and circle two words that have the short **i** sound.

(Is) that a shark's (fin?)

Dante put cans (in) the (bin.)

The (chick) ran to (its) mother.

(Lift) the jar's (lid.)

52

Short i

Write a short **i** word to name each picture.

| pig | bib | wig | pin | gift | hit |

gift
pin
hit
bib
wig
pig

53

Short o

Short **o** is the vowel sound you hear in the middle of **hot**. Write a short **o** word that rhymes with each word shown. Draw a picture to match the word you wrote.

frog

Answers and drawings will vary.

sock

You hear the short **o** sound in **not**. Cross out **not** in each sentence. Then, read the sentences about learning and trying hard.

I am ~~not~~ getting better at this.

It is ~~not~~ OK to make mistakes.

I do ~~not~~ want to try again.

54

Short o

Write a short **o** word to name each picture.

box   pot   ox   rod   rock   lock

rock
pot
ox
lock
rod
box

55

Short u

Short **u** is the vowel sound you hear in the middle of **pup**. Draw a line from **u** to pictures whose names have the short **u** sound.

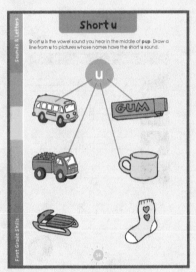

u

56

Short u

Write a short **u** word to name each picture.

cup   hug   cut   rug   duck   sun

duck
hug
rug
cup
cut
sun

57

Long a

Long **a** is the vowel sound you hear in **hay**. It says its own name. Circle the pictures whose names have the long **a** sound.

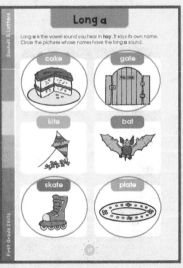

cake   gate
kite   bat
skate   plate

58

Long a

Write a long **a** word to name each picture.

rake   plane   chain   snake   mane   cape

chain
snake
plane
rake
mane
cape

59

284

Answer Key

Long e

Long e is the vowel sound you hear in **bee**. It says its own name. Draw lines from the bee to the pictures whose names have the long e sound.

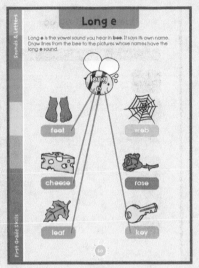

feet — web
cheese — rose
leaf — key

60

Long e

Write a long e word to name each picture.

beans   sheep   green

sheep
beans
green

You hear the long e sound in **feeling**. Draw a face to match each feeling. Then, play a game with a friend. Act out a feeling. Can your partner guess what it is?

happy   surprised   angry
○   ○   ○
confused sad   proud
○   ○   ○

Drawings will vary.

61

Long i

Long i is the vowel sound you hear in **kite**. It says its own name. In each sentence, circle two words that have the long i sound.

Five friends shared the pie.

Are you ready to ride down the slide?

I rode a bike to the park.

The mice ran from the light.

62

Long i

Write a long i word to name each picture.

kite   ice   tie   nine

tie
kite
ice
nine

You hear the long i sound in **bike**. Color only the boxes with letters. You will find a hidden message about bike safety!

63

Long o

Long o is the vowel sound you hear in **rope**. It says its own name. Circle the long o word in each column.

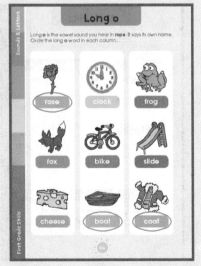

rose   clock   frog
fox   bike   slide
cheese boat   coat

64

Long o

Write a long o word to name each picture.

smoke throne bone soap goat globe

bone
globe
throne
smoke
soap
goat

65

285

Answer key

66

Long u & Long oo

Long u and long oo are the vowel sounds you hear in **cute** and **rule**. Color pictures whose names have the long **u** and long **oo** sounds.

mule — hive
moose — drum
cube — moon

67

Long u & Long oo

Write a long u or long oo word to name each picture.

fruit   tube   juice   glue   music   suit

music
juice
glue
tube
suit
fruit

68

Super Silent e

When you add **e** to the end of some words, the vowel sound changes from short to long. The **e** is silent. That is why it is called super silent e! Rewrite each short vowel word, but add **e** to the end. Listen for a long vowel sound in each word you write. The first one is done for you.

tub — tube
kit — kite
pin — pine
cap — cape

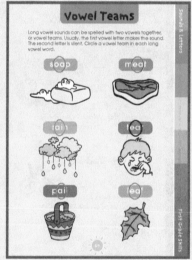

69

Vowel Teams

Long vowel sounds can be spelled with two vowels together, or vowel teams. Usually, the first vowel letter makes the sound. The second letter is silent. Circle a vowel team in each long vowel word.

soap — meat
rain — tear
pail — leaf

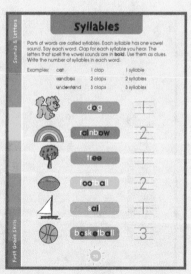

70

Syllables

Parts of words are called syllables. Each syllable has one vowel sound. Say each word. Clap for each syllable you hear. The letters that spell the vowel sounds are in **bold**. Use them as clues. Write the number of syllables in each word.

Examples:
cat — 1 clap — 1 syllable
sandbox — 2 claps — 2 syllables
understand — 3 claps — 3 syllables

d**o**g — 1
r**ai**nb**ow** — 2
tr**ee** — 1
ootb**a**l — 2
s**ai**l — 1
b**a**sk**e**tb**a**ll — 3

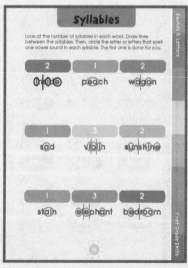

71

Syllables

Look at the number of syllables in each word. Draw lines between the syllables. Then, circle the letter or letters that spell one vowel sound in each syllable. The first one is done for you.

2 — t**o**m**a**t**o**   1 — p**ea**ch   2 — w**a**g**o**n
1 — s**a**d   3 — v**i**(**o**)l**i**n   2 — s**u**nsh**i**ne
1 — st**ai**n   3 — **e**l**e**ph**a**nt   2 — b**e**dr**oo**m

Answer key

Sight Words: after & again

Write **after** or **again** to complete each sentence.

after   again

Pedro came to my house __again__ today.

What will we do __after__ lunch?

I was ready for bed __after__ a long day.

We left the door open, and Bruno
ran away __again__

72

Sight Words: any & ask

Look at the word at the top of each box. Circle the same word in the list below.

ask
as
(ask)
task
sack

any
many
ant
an
(any)

ask
(ask)
mask
act
ash

any
money
(any)
anyway
yam

73

Sight Words: by & fly

Color the leaves with **by** orange. Color the leaves with **fly** green.

by · fly · fly · by · fly · fly · by · by · by · fly

74

Sight Words: could & every

Write **could** or **every** to complete each sentence.

could   every

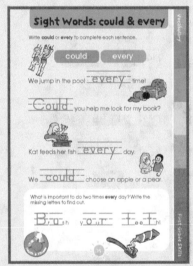

We jump in the pool __every__ time!

__Could__ you help me look for my book?

Kat feeds her fish __every__ day.

We __could__ choose an apple or a pear.

What is important to do two times **every** day? Write the missing letters to find out.

__Brush__ __your__ __Teeth__

75

Sight Words: from & give

Color the boxes with **from** purple. Color the boxes with **give** pink.

from	fort	give	from
five	give	grime	hive
frame	gave	from	frog
give	from	gave	fright
from	give	have	give

When you respect others, you let them know that they are important to you. Check the ways you **give** respect to people you know.

Answers will vary.
☐ Be on time.
☐ Listen carefully.
☐ Follow the rules.
☐ Say "please" and "thank you."
☐ Offer to help.
☐ Try hard.

76

Sight Words: had & has

Decide whether each sentence is missing **had** or **has**. Then, write **d** or **s** to complete the word.

Last year, Trey ha __d__ two cats.

Now, Trey ha __s__ a third cat, Ginger.

Ginger ha __s__ brown fur.

Trey's friend Antonio ha __d__ one cat, but it ran away.

Antonio ha __s__ a new cat now.

77

287

Sight Words: her & his

Write **her** or **his** in each sentence. Then, draw a line to the correct object.

Jared brought lunch.
This is ___his___ lunch.

It is Kara's birthday.
This is ___her___ cake.

Travon's jacket is green.
This is ___his___ jacket.

Sheila's shoes are old.
These are ___her___ shoes.

78

Sight Words: know & let

Circle **know** or **let** in each sentence.

(Let) me tell you a story about yesterday.

Maria wanted to (know) if I would skate with her.

I love to skate, but I (know) my mom had already made plans.

I asked Mom if I could go, and she (let) me!

When you talk, you want others to listen to you. Then, it is your turn to **let** others talk while you listen. Practice with a partner. Tell a story while your partner interrupts. How do you feel? Then, tell a story while your partner listens carefully. How do you feel now?

79

Sight Words: live & may

In each row, color the letters that spell **live**.

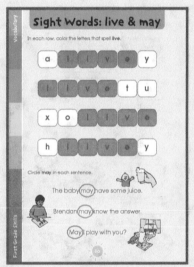

Circle **may** in each sentence.

The baby (may) have some juice.

Brendan (may) know the answer.

(May) I play with you?

80

Sight Words: of & put

Color the books with **of** blue. Color the books with **put** green. Color the other books red.

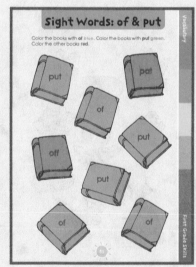

81

Sight Words: old & once

Circle the picture that matches each sentence. Pay attention to the **bold** word.

Is it time to replace my **old** shoes?

We will go outside **once** it stops raining.

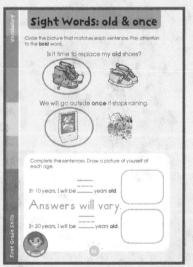

Complete the sentences. Draw a picture of yourself at each age.

In 10 years, I will be ___ years **old**.

Answers will vary.

In 20 years, I will be ___ years **old**.

82

Sight Words: round & stop

Draw a picture to match each sentence. Pay attention to the **bold** word.

The ducks swim in the (round) pond.

Drawings will vary.

Cars **stop** at the red light.

83

Sight Words: some & them

Circle the chicks with **some**.

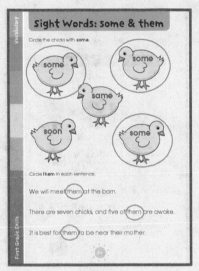

Circle **them** in each sentence.

We will meet them at the barn.

There are seven chicks, and five of them are awake.

It is best for them to be near their mother.

84

Sight Words: take & thank

Find words in the puzzle. Circle **take** six times in green. Circle **thank** six times in blue. Look across and down.

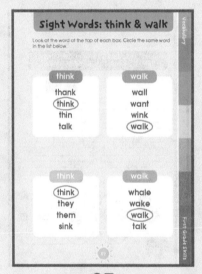

It is polite to **thank** someone who does something for you. When someone is nice to you, be nice in return! Emilie's mom brought her grapes for a snack. Write what Emilie should say.

Thank you!

85

Sight Words: then & were

Write **then** or **were** to complete each sentence.

then   were

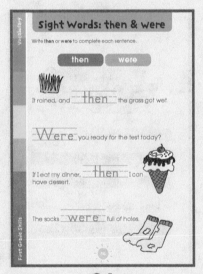

It rained, and ___then___ the grass got wet.

___Were___ you ready for the test today?

If I eat my dinner, ___then___ I can have dessert.

The socks ___were___ full of holes.

86

Sight Words: think & walk

Look at the word at the top of each box. Circle the same word in the list below.

think	walk
thank	wall
(think)	want
thin	wink
talk	(walk)

think	walk
(think)	whale
they	wake
them	(walk)
sink	talk

87

Sight Words

Write the missing letters to complete the words.

| ask | from | think | put | then |
| round | give | old | some | thank |

ol_d_   so_me_

_th_ank   from

_a_sk   _t_hin_k_

p_ut_   _g_ive

_r_ound   _t_hen

88

Sight Words

Write the missing letters to complete the words.

| after know once could take walk |

w_al_k   _o_nce

_t_ake   kn_o_w

a_fte_r   c_o_ul_d_

Write **sight words** from the box to complete the safety rules.

Always __walk__ outside with a buddy.

Do not go anywhere with a person you do not __know__

Never __take__ something from a person you do not know.

89

289

Answer key

Context Clues

Write words from the box to complete the story. Use clues in the story to help you.

cloudy   grow   rain   water   wet

"May I please go outside?" I asked.

"It is too __cloudy__," Dad told me.

Later, the sun came out, but then it began to

__rain__. "May I go out now?" I

asked again.

Dad looked out the window. "You will get

__wet__," he said.

"But I want to see if the rain helped our

flowers __grow__," I said.

"You mean you want to play in the

__water__," Dad said with a

smile. How did he know that?

90

Context Clues

Write words from the box to complete the story. Use clues in the story to help you.

practice   teach   finish   write   read

James was trying to __teach__ his little sister how to write her name.

"Watch what I do," James said. He took

the pencil and got ready to __write__. He

showed her how to make **W**, then **e, n, d,** and **y.**

At first, Wendy's letters were large and

shaky. But with __practice__ and hard work,

Wendy's letters became more and more clear.

"I can do it!" Wendy said with a smile. "I can

write my name from start to __finish__.

Would you teach me how to __read__

now, James?"

James laughed. "Of course! But

let's do it tomorrow."

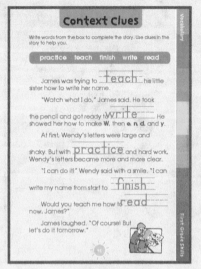

91

Classify

Write words from the box under the pictures they describe.

day   night   rays   moon
sun   dark   light   stars

__sun__   __stars__

__rays__   __moon__

__light__   __dark__

__day__   __night__

Classify the children's actions. Circle the pictures that show kindness. Draw a box around the pictures that show curiosity.

reading   sharing   giving a gift   asking a question

92

Classify

Draw an **X** on the word in each row that does not belong.

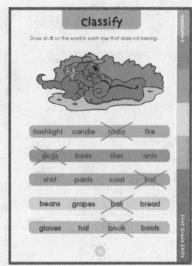

flashlight   candle   ~~radio~~   fire

~~dogs~~   bees   flies   ants

shirt   pants   coat   ~~ball~~

beans   grapes   ~~ball~~   bread

gloves   hat   ~~book~~   boots

93

Prefixes

Write a prefix in front of each base word. Then, match the new word to its meaning.

un   dis   re   over

__un__ real — not real

__re__ heat — heat again

__dis__ like — do not like

__over__ coat — coat worn over clothes

__re__ turn — turn back

94

Prefixes

Write a prefix in front of the base word in each sentence.

un   dis   re   over

The magician made the rabbit __dis__ appear.

That bucket is about to __over__ flow with water.

He will __re__ take the blurry photo.

Jasmine was __un__ happy
when the snowman melted.

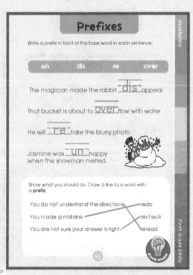

Show what you should do. Draw a line to a word with a **prefix.**

You do not understand the directions. — redo

You made a mistake. — recheck

You are not sure your answer is right. — reread

95

Answer Key

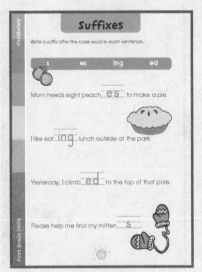

Suffixes

Write a suffix after the base word in each sentence.

s   es   ing   ed

Mom needs eight peach**es** to make a pie.

I like eat**ing** lunch outside at the park.

Yesterday, I climb**ed** to the top of that pole.

Please help me find my mitten**s**.

96

Suffixes

Write a suffix after the base word in each sentence.

s   es   ing   ed

Where are you go**ing** after lunch?

I jump**ed** even higher than Brady!

Ms. Moore mix**es** paints for art class.

Cupcake**s** are my favorite treat.

97

Shades of Meaning

Write each word in the list where it belongs.

scream sprint whisper run flutter glide

say	fly
shout	soar
scream	flutter
whisper	glide

| jog |
| gallop |
| sprint |
| run |

98

Shades of Meaning

Write each word in the list where it belongs.

speedy afraid spooked quick

fast	scared
rapid	frightened
speedy	afraid
quick	spooked

Read the words with similar **meanings**. Choose one to describe yourself. Then, finish the sentence.

| honest | truthful | reliable |
| fair | trustworthy | dependable |

I am Answers will vary. because

99

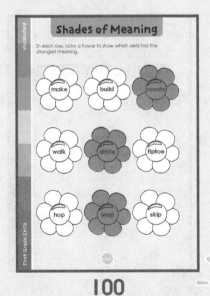

Shades of Meaning

In each row, color a flower to show which verb has the strongest meaning.

make build **create**

walk **stride** tiptoe

hop **leap** skip

100

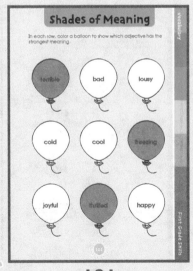

Shades of Meaning

In each row, color a balloon to show which adjective has the strongest meaning.

terrible bad lousy

cold cool **freezing**

joyful **thrilled** happy

101

291

Common Nouns

A noun names a person, place, or thing. Read the story and circle all the nouns. Then, write the nouns you circled under the pictures.

Our family likes to go to the park. We play on the swings. We eat sandwiches. We throw the ball to our dog. Then, we go home.

family   sandwiches

park   dog

swings   ball

home

102

Common Nouns

Draw the missing pictures to match the nouns. Write the missing nouns to match the pictures.

astronaut   beach

Drawings will vary.

plane   snake

103

Plural Nouns

Plural nouns name more than one person, place, or thing. To form most plurals, add s or es to the end of the word. If a word ends in y, change y to i before adding es. Examples: **baby/babies, story/stories.** Read each noun. Write the plural.

desk   desks   wish   wishes

lady   ladies   dress   dresses

bunny   bunnies   pencil   pencils

Community helpers keep people safe and healthy. Write a **plural** to complete each sentence.

police officers   doctors   firefighters

Doctors care for the sick and injured.

Police officers make sure people follow the law.

Firefighters put out fires and rescue people from danger.

104

Proper Nouns

Proper nouns name specific people, places, and things. Proper nouns always begin with a capital letter. Write the proper nouns.

denver, colorado
Denver Colorado

miss davis
Miss Davis

aiden james
Aiden James

patches
Patches

For each common noun, write a **proper noun** that names a person or place you know.

school
friend   Answers will vary
pet
park

105

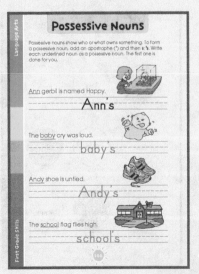

Possessive Nouns

Possessive nouns show who or what owns something. To form a possessive noun, add an apostrophe (') and then s's. Write each underlined noun as a possessive noun. The first one is done for you.

Ann gerbil is named Happy.
Ann's

The baby cry was loud.
baby's

Andy shoe is untied.
Andy's

The school flag flies high.
school's

106

Personal Pronouns

Pronouns are words that can take the place of nouns. Read the first sentence in each pair. Complete the second sentence by writing a pronoun to replace the underlined noun.

he   she   it   they

Oliver likes funny jokes.
He likes funny jokes.

Mei and Sam are on the trampoline.
They are on the trampoline.

Sarah is a very good dancer.
She is a very good dancer.

The dolphin dove into the water.
It dove into the water.

107

Answer key

Possessive Pronouns

Possessive pronouns take the place of nouns and tell who or what owns something. Circle and write a possessive pronoun to complete each sentence.

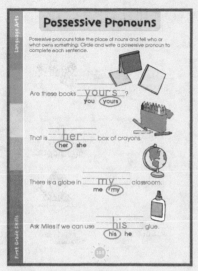

Are these books **yours**?
you (yours)

That is **her** box of crayons.
(her) she

There is a globe in **my** classroom.
me (my)

Ask Miles if we can use **his** glue.
(his) he

108

Indefinite Pronouns

An indefinite pronoun does not take the place of a specific (or definite) person, place, or thing. Write the indefinite pronoun that best completes each sentence.

everything anyone someone something

Can **someone** please turn on the lights?

Does **anyone** know where I left my umbrella?

I can carry **everything** in one bag.

Do you see **something** you can buy with your money?

109

Present-Tense Verbs

Some verbs tell what actions are happening now. Write verbs to complete the sentences.

make race jump watch ride rest

The girls **watch** the frogs **jump**

The boys **race** to the park, then they **rest**

They **make** cars to **ride** in.

110

Present-Tense Verbs

The underlined verb in each sentence is wrong. Add s to write the correct verb that tells what is happening now.

The baby sleep with a teddy bear.
sleeps

Sari cook breakfast for us.
cooks

Chad stop and looks both ways.
stops

Match each **verb** with the character trait it shows.

share ⎯⎯ patience
wait ⎯⎯ courage
try ⎯⎯ kindness

111

Use Verbs with Nouns

Nouns (or pronouns) and verbs go together. Rewrite each verb that tells what is happening now. Make it go with each pronoun shown. The first one is done for you.

ride
I **ride**
She **rides**
They **ride**

sleep
We **sleep**
He **sleeps**
You **sleep**

make
He **makes**
They **make**
I **make**

play
We **play**
He **plays**
She **plays**

112

Use Verbs with Nouns

These sentences need a verb to tell what is happening now. Circle and write the verb that goes with the noun to complete each sentence.

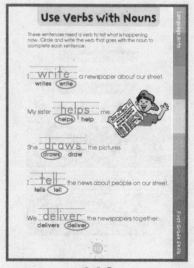

I **write** a newspaper about our street.
writes (write)

My sister **helps** me.
(helps) help

She **draws** the pictures.
(draws) draw

I **tell** the news about people on our street.
tells (tell)

We **deliver** the newspapers together.
delivers (deliver)

113

293

Past-Tense Verbs

Some verbs tell what already happened. Look at each pair of verbs. Circle the verb that tells what already happened. Then, write letters to answer the question.

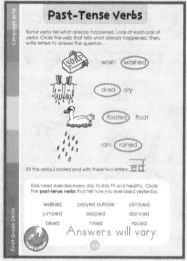

wash (washed)

(dried) dry

(floated) float

rain (rained)

All the verbs I circled end with these two letters: **ed**.

Kids need exercise every day to stay fit and healthy. Circle the **past-tense verbs** that tell how you exercised yesterday.

walked	played outside	climbed
jumped	skipped	danced
biked	hiked	raced

Answers will vary.

114

Past-Tense Verbs

The underlined verb in each sentence is wrong. Write the correct verb that tells what already happened. **Hint:** The verbs you write will end with **ed**.

It <u>snow</u>, so I made a snowman.

snowed

Ben <u>rake</u> the leaves when they fell off the tree.

raked

My brother <u>bake</u> a cake on my birthday.

baked

My family <u>visit</u> the beach last summer.

visited

115

Future-Tense Verbs

Some verbs tell what has not happened yet. These verbs are made up of two words. The first word is **will**. In each sentence, write **will** in front of the underlined verb.

We ___will___ <u>wash</u> our dog Fritz later today.

First, we ___will___ <u>fill</u> the tub with soapy water.

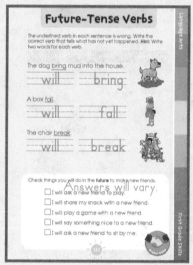

Then, I ___will___ <u>call</u> Fritz.

He ___will___ <u>cry</u> at first.

Then, he ___will___ <u>like</u> his bath.

Fritz ___will___ <u>look</u> a lot better after his bath!

116

Future-Tense Verbs

The underlined verb in each sentence is wrong. Write the correct verb that tells what has not yet happened. **Hint:** Write two words for each verb.

The dog <u>bring</u> mud into the house.

will bring

A box <u>fall</u>.

will fall

The chair <u>break</u>.

will break

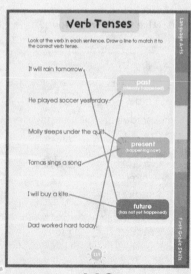

Check things you will do in the **future** to make new friends.

Answers will vary.

☐ I will ask a new friend To play.

☐ I will share my snack with a new friend.

☐ I will play a game with a new friend.

☐ I will say something nice to a new friend.

☐ I will ask a new friend to sit by me.

117

Verb Tenses

Look at the verb in each sentence. Use the key to color the box around the sentence.

present (happening now)

past (already happened)

future (has not yet happened)

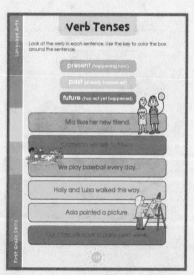

Mia likes her new friend.

Cameron will walk to Mom's.

We play baseball every day.

Holly and Luisa walked this way.

Ada painted a picture.

Our class will have a party.

118

Verb Tenses

Look at the verb in each sentence. Draw a line to match it to the correct verb tense.

It will rain tomorrow

He played soccer yesterday

past (already happened)

Molly sleeps under the quilt

Tomas sings a song

present (happening now)

I will buy a kite

future (has not yet happened)

Dad worked hard today

119

Adjectives

Adjectives are describing words. They tell more about a noun. Write two adjectives that could describe each noun.

shiny horned bright scaly giant slow sweet juicy

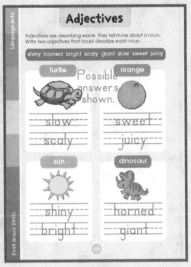

Possible answers shown.

turtle
slow
scaly

orange
sweet
juicy

sun
shiny
bright

dinosaur
horned
giant

120

Adjectives

Circle the adjective in each sentence. Draw a line from the sentence to a picture.

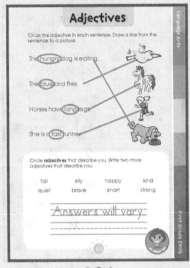

The (hungry) dog is eating.

The (blue) bird flies.

Horses have (long) legs.

She is a (fast) runner.

Circle **adjectives** that describe you. Write two more adjectives that describe you.

| tall | silly | happy | kind |
| quiet | brave | smart | strong |

Answers will vary

121

Articles

The small word **the** is often used before nouns. Write **the** to complete each sentence.

Spread ___the___ peanut butter on each slice of bread.

Put ___the___ two slices of bread together.

Eat ___the___ sandwich for a yummy lunch.

Remember to clean up ___the___ kitchen!

122

Articles

The small words **a** and **an** are often used before nouns. Use **an** before a word that begins with a vowel. Use **a** before a word that begins with a consonant. Write **a** or **an** to complete each sentence.

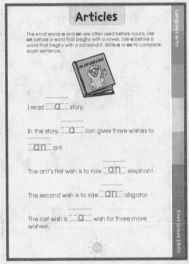

I read ___a___ story.

In the story, ___a___ lion gives three wishes to ___an___ ant.

The ant's first wish is to ride ___an___ elephant.

The second wish is to ride ___an___ alligator.

The last wish is ___a___ wish for three more wishes!

123

Prepositions

Prepositions are words that can describe position or direction. Circle and write a preposition to complete each sentence.

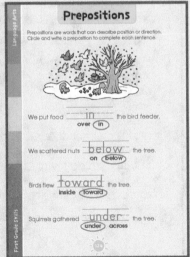

We put food ___in___ the bird feeder.
over (in)

We scattered nuts ___below___ the tree.
on (below)

Birds flew ___toward___ the tree.
inside (toward)

Squirrels gathered ___under___ the tree.
(under) across

124

Prepositions

Circle and write a preposition to complete each sentence.

The lamp on the table ___beside___ the bed is bent.
(beside) through

A basketball is ___on___ the bed.
behind (on)

The broom bumped ___into___ the table.
across (into)

The fish jumped ___above___ the fishbowl!
under (above)

125

Answer key

Conjunctions

Use the joining word shown to combine each pair of sentences into one sentence.

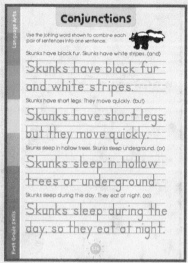

Skunks have black fur. Skunks have white stripes. (and)

Skunks have black fur and white stripes.

Skunks have short legs. They move quickly. (but)

Skunks have short legs, but they move quickly.

Skunks sleep in hollow trees. Skunks sleep underground. (or)

Skunks sleep in hollow trees or underground.

Skunks sleep during the day. They eat at night. (so)

Skunks sleep during the day, so they eat at night.

126

Conjunctions

Circle and write the joining word that best completes each sentence.

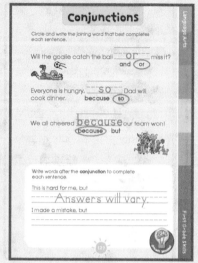

Will the goalie catch the ball **or** miss it?
and (or)

Everyone is hungry. **so** Dad will cook dinner. because (so)

We all cheered **because** our team won!
(because) but

Write words after the **conjunction** to complete each sentence.

This is hard for me, but

Answers will vary.

I made a mistake, but

127

Telling Sentences

A telling sentence tells something, or gives information. Rewrite the telling sentences. Begin each one with a capital letter. End each one with a period (.).

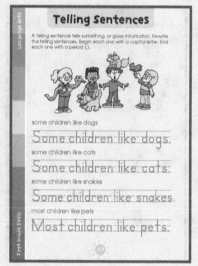

some children like dogs

Some children like dogs.

some children like cats

Some children like cats.

some children like snakes

Some children like snakes.

most children like pets

Most children like pets.

128

Asking Sentences

An asking sentence asks a question. Rewrite the asking sentences. Begin each one with a capital letter. End each one with a question mark (?).

do you like the beach

Do you like the beach?

how far can you swim

How far can you swim?

what is under the sand

What is under the sand?

are you cold

Are you cold?

129

Exclamations

An exclamation shows a strong feeling. Rewrite each exclamation. Begin each one with a capital letter. End each one with an exclamation mark (!).

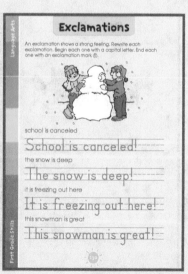

school is canceled

School is canceled!

the snow is deep

The snow is deep!

it is freezing out here

It is freezing out here!

this snowman is great

This snowman is great!

130

Commands

A command tells someone to do something. Rewrite the commands. Begin each one with a capital letter. If the command shows a strong feeling, end it with an exclamation mark (!). If it does not, end it with a period (.).

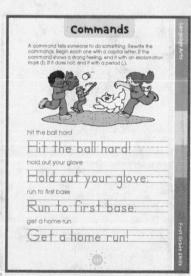

hit the ball hard

Hit the ball hard!

hold out your glove

Hold out your glove.

run to first base

Run to first base.

get a home run

Get a home run!

131

Answer key

Sentences

Write sentences about the picture.

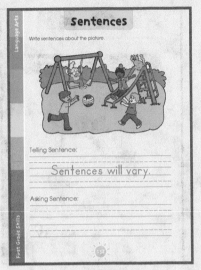

Telling Sentence:

Sentences will vary.

Asking Sentence:

132

Sentences

Write sentences about the picture.

Exclamation:

Sentences will vary.

Command:

133

Capitalization

The first and last names of people always begin with capital letters. Write the names correctly. Then, draw a picture of you and write your name.

kyle davis

Kyle Davis

olivia mendez

Olivia Mendez

howard smith

Howard Smith

your name

Drawings and names will vary.

134

Capitalization

The names of days of the week and months of the year are always capitalized. Circle the words that are written correctly. Write the other words correctly on the lines.

sunday (July) (Wednesday) may december
friday tuesday june august (Monday)
(February) (March) thursday (April) (September)

Days of the Week

Sunday
Friday
Tuesday
Thursday

Months of the Year

May
December
June
August

135

Commas

Commas are used to separate words in a series of three or more. Look at this example:

My favorite fruits are apples, bananas, and oranges.

Write commas where they are needed in each sentence.

Please buy milk, eggs, bread, and cheese.

I need a folder, paper, and pencils for school.

Some good pets are cats, dogs, gerbils, and rabbits.

We can go by plane, train, or car.

136

Commas

When you write a date, use a comma between the number that tells the day and the number that tells the year. Write the dates. Use capital letters and commas where needed. The first one is done for you.

june 19 1980

June 19, 1980

december 13 2017

December 13, 2017

April 17 2020

April 17, 2020

october 22, 1996

October 22, 1996

On what day were you born? Complete the sentence. Do not forget to use a capital letter and a **comma**.

I was born on

Answers will vary.

month day year

137

297

Answer key

138

139

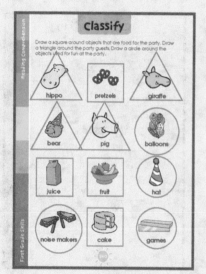

140

141

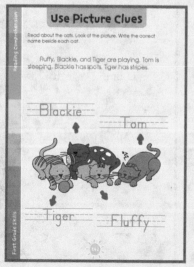

142

143

Answer key

First Grade Skills

298

Answer key

Sequence

Read the story. Write words from the story to give the directions in order.

Do you like cats? I do. To pet a cat, move slowly. Hold out your hand. The cat will come to you. Then, pet its head. Do not grab a cat! It will run away.

To pet a cat . . .

1. Move ___slowly___
2. Hold out your ___hand___
3. The cat will come to ___you___.
4. Pet the cat's ___head___
5. Do not ___grab___ a cat.

144

Comprehension

Read the story on page 144 again. Then, answer the questions.

The story tells you how to ___pet a cat___

What part of your body should you pet a cat with?
___your hand___

Why should you move slowly to pet a cat?
___Answers will vary___

Why do you think a cat will run away if you grab it?
___Answers will vary___

145

Predict

Follow the order of the numbers. Read the story. In the last box, draw a picture to complete the story.

1. That's my ball.
2. I got it first.
3. It's mine!
4. Drawings will vary.

146

Predict

Read each story. Circle the sentence that tells how the story will probably end.

Ann was riding her bike. She saw a dog in the park. She stopped to pet it. Ann left to go home.

The dog went swimming.

(The dog followed Ann.)

The dog went home with a cat.

Antonio went to a baseball game. A baseball player hit a ball toward him. He reached out his hands.

The player caught the ball.

The ball bounced on a car.

(Antonio caught the ball.)

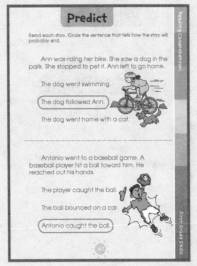

147

Draw Conclusions

Read the story about Tess. Then, circle the correct answers.

Tess plays baseball. She likes it when her team wins games. Today, Tess's team did not win.

Tess likes

football.　soccer.　(baseball.)

Tess likes to

(win.)　lose.

Tess uses a bat.

(yes)　no

Tess is

happy.　(sad.)

148

Comprehension

Read the directions for playing "Simon Says." Then, answer the questions.

Simon Says

This is how to play "Simon Says." One kid is Simon. Simon is the leader. Everyone must do what Simon says and does, but only if Simon says, "Simon says" first. Let's try it. Simon says: Pat your head. Simon says: Point to your nose. Touch your toes. Oops! Did you touch your toes? I did not say, "Simon says" first. If you touched your toes, you are out!

Who is the leader in this game?
___Simon___

What must the leader say first each time?
___Simon says___

What happens if you do something and the leader did not say, "Simon says"?
___You are out___

149

299

Comprehension

Read each sentence. Look at the picture. Circle the picture if the boy is playing "Simon Says" correctly.

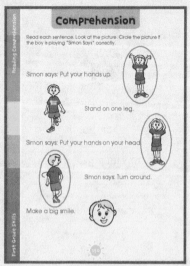

Simon says: Put your hands up.

Stand on one leg.

Simon says: Put your hands on your head.

Simon says: Turn around.

Make a big smile.

150

Follow Directions

Read the sentences. If Simon tells you to do something, follow the directions. If Simon does not tell you to do something, go to the next sentence.

1. Simon says: Cross out all the numbers.
2. Simon says: Cross out the vowel in the word **sun**.
3. Cross out the letter **B**.
4. Cross out the vowels **A** and **E**.
5. Simon says: Cross out the consonants in the word **cup**.
6. Cross out the letter **Z**.
7. Simon says: Cross out all the Ks.
8. Simon says: Read your message.

G R E A
T J O B

151

Write a Story

Write words to finish the sentences. Read the story you wrote!

Answers will vary.

It is a _____ day on the farm.

First, the farmers _____

Then, the farmers _____

All day long, the ducks _____

There is lots to do every day on the farm.

152

Write a Story

Write words to finish the sentences. Read the story you wrote!

Answers will vary.

The ants are building _____

At first, they _____

Later, they _____

Finally, the ants _____

The ants made something amazing by working together!

153

Write a Story

Write a sentence beside each picture to tell what is happening. Read the story you wrote!

Stories will vary.

154

Write a Story

Write a story about the picture. Include a beginning, a middle, and an ending.

Stories will vary

Everyone's life tells a different **story**. Your story is about where you live, where your family comes from in the world, and what you choose to do each day. Each person you meet has a different story! Tolerance means understanding and appreciating that everyone is different.

155

Answer key

156

Write to Inform

Imagine you met someone who had never eaten an ice cream cone. Could you teach the person how to do it? Think about each step you take when you eat an ice cream cone. Write them in order.

How to Eat an Ice Cream Cone

First, you _Answers will vary._

Then, you

Finally, you

Do not forget to

157

Write to Inform

Think about how to wash a dog. Write the steps in order.

How to Wash a Dog

First, _Answers will vary._

Next,

Next,

Last,

158

Write to Inform

With an adult, research facts about your favorite animal. Draw and write to tell what you learned.

My favorite animal is

Answers will vary.

This animal lives

This animal eats

This animal has

This animal likes to

159

Write to Inform

Circle one topic from the list. With an adult, do some research to learn more about it. Draw a picture to illustrate your topic. Write facts about your topic.

| tornadoes | volcanoes | bees |
| Mars | Grand Canyon | Australia |

Drawings will vary.

Fact #1

Fact #2 _Answers will vary._

Fact #3

160

Write an Opinion

Which season of the year is the best? Write its name to complete the sentence and give your opinion. Then, write three good reasons why you think that season is best.

_____ is the best season of the year.

Reason #1

Reason #2 _Answers will vary._

Reason #3

161

Write an Opinion

Do you think first graders should have homework? Circle **should** or **should not** to complete the first sentence and give your opinion. Then, write three good reasons why you feel the way you do.

First graders (should/should not) have homework.

Reason #1

Reason #2 _Answers will vary._

Reason #3

Answer key

Write an Opinion

Which holiday is the best one? Write its name to complete the first sentence and give your opinion. Then, write three good reasons why you think that holiday is best.

_____ is the best holiday.

Reason #1

_____

Reason #2

Answers will vary.

Reason #3

_____

162

Write an Opinion

Circle a topic from the list. Write a sentence that gives your opinion about it.

funniest book | most interesting school subject
most fun sport | most entertaining board game
best TV show | tastiest dessert

Answers will vary

A hero is someone you admire and respect. Finish the sentence to tell your **opinion** about someone who is a hero to you. It can be someone you know or someone you would like to meet.

Answers _____ is a true hero because
will vary.

163

Count Ahead

Write a number to answer each question. Use the number line to help you.

0 1 2 3 4 5 6 7 8 9 10

What is 3 more than 5? — 8

What is 2 more than 4? — 6

What is 1 more than 3? — 4

What is 5 more than 0? — 5

What is 6 more than 3? — 9

What is 9 more than 1? — 10

164

Count Ahead

Count forward. Write the missing numbers in each row.

15 16 17 18 19 20

4 5 6 7 8 9

7 8 9 10 11 12

13 14 15 16 17 18

165

Picture Problems

Solve the addition problems. Use the pictures to help you.

6 + 2 = 8   3 + 6 = 9

5 + 7 = 12   1 + 9 = 10

4 + 3 = 7   7 + 8 = 15

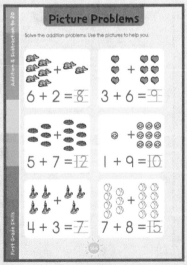

166

Picture Problems

Solve the addition problems. Use the pictures to help you.

8 + 8 = 16   5 + 9 = 14

3 + 8 = 11   6 + 7 = 13

8 + 4 = 12   14 + 6 = 20

167

Answer Key

Addition Practice

Find the sums.

$$\begin{array}{r} 2 \\ +5 \\ \hline 7 \end{array} \quad \begin{array}{r} 6 \\ +4 \\ \hline 10 \end{array} \quad \begin{array}{r} 8 \\ +2 \\ \hline 10 \end{array} \quad \begin{array}{r} 3 \\ +11 \\ \hline 14 \end{array}$$

$$\begin{array}{r} 6 \\ +8 \\ \hline 14 \end{array} \quad \begin{array}{r} 9 \\ +1 \\ \hline 10 \end{array} \quad \begin{array}{r} 2 \\ +13 \\ \hline 15 \end{array} \quad \begin{array}{r} 15 \\ +1 \\ \hline 16 \end{array}$$

$$\begin{array}{r} 5 \\ +5 \\ \hline 10 \end{array} \quad \begin{array}{r} 7 \\ +8 \\ \hline 15 \end{array} \quad \begin{array}{r} 9 \\ +5 \\ \hline 14 \end{array} \quad \begin{array}{r} 6 \\ +10 \\ \hline 16 \end{array}$$

Being a leader means sharing what you have and helping others. With an adult, collect food items to donate to a food pantry or pet food for an animal shelter. **Add** the number of items you collect. Write the number to complete the sentence.

Answers will vary.

I collected _____ items.

168

Commutative Property

The commutative property of addition is a rule. It says that if you change the order of the numbers being added, the sum stays the same. Use this rule to help you write the missing numbers.

Example: $2 + 3 = 5$

$3 + \boxed{2} = 5$

$5 + 4 = 9$ $3 + 1 = 4$
$4 + \boxed{5} = 9$ $1 + \boxed{3} = 4$

$6 + 8 = 14$ $6 + 4 = 10$
$8 + \boxed{6} = 14$ $\boxed{4} + \boxed{6} = 10$

$10 + 6 = 16$ $8 + 9 = 17$
$\boxed{6} + \boxed{10} = 16$ $\boxed{9} + \boxed{8} = 17$

$7 + 4 = 11$ $6 + 9 = 15$
$\boxed{4} + \boxed{7} = 11$ $\boxed{9} + \boxed{6} = 15$

169

Missing Numbers

Draw the missing dots on the blank side of each domino. Write a matching number to complete the equation.

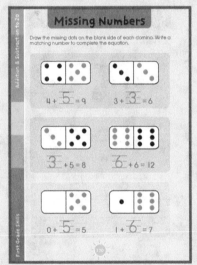

$4 + \boxed{5} = 9$ $3 + \boxed{3} = 6$

$\boxed{3} + 5 = 8$ $\boxed{6} + 6 = 12$

$0 + \boxed{5} = 5$ $1 + \boxed{6} = 7$

170

Missing Numbers

Write the missing number to complete each equation.

$\boxed{12} + 6 = 18$ $13 + \boxed{1} = 14$

$7 + \boxed{1} = 8$ $\boxed{2} + 4 = 6$

$\boxed{6} + 9 = 15$ $3 + \boxed{13} = 16$

$8 + \boxed{1} = 9$ $\boxed{1} + 5 = 6$

$\boxed{7} + 4 = 11$ $9 + \boxed{5} = 14$

$12 + \boxed{3} = 15$ $\boxed{16} + 1 = 17$

171

Add Three or More Numbers

Add all the numbers to find the sum. Draw pictures to help you.

Example:
$$\begin{array}{r} 1 \\ 2 \\ +3 \\ \hline 6 \end{array}$$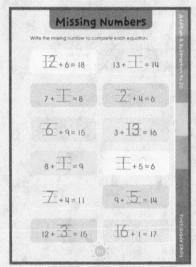

$$\begin{array}{r} 2 \\ 7 \\ +4 \\ \hline 13 \end{array} \quad \begin{array}{r} 3 \\ 9 \\ +6 \\ \hline 18 \end{array} \quad \begin{array}{r} 2 \\ 4 \\ +6 \\ \hline 12 \end{array}$$

$$\begin{array}{r} 7 \\ 1 \\ 4 \\ +2 \\ \hline 14 \end{array} \quad \begin{array}{r} 8 \\ 3 \\ 1 \\ +5 \\ \hline 17 \end{array} \quad \begin{array}{r} 6 \\ 5 \\ 2 \\ +3 \\ \hline 16 \end{array}$$

Get together with two friends so there are **three** of you. You are all different, but you are probably a lot alike, too. Do you like the same school subjects, sports, movies, or foods? Add all the things you have in common to find the sum.

172

Associative Property

The associative property of addition is a rule. It says that when you add three or more numbers, you can group the numbers being added in different ways, but the sum stays the same. Use this rule to draw a line between matching equations. One is done for you.

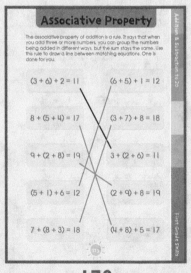

$(3 + 6) + 2 = 11$ $(6 + 5) + 1 = 12$

$8 + (5 + 4) = 17$ $(3 + 7) + 8 = 18$

$9 + (2 + 8) = 19$ $3 + (2 + 6) = 11$

$(5 + 1) + 6 = 12$ $(2 + 9) + 8 = 19$

$7 + (8 + 3) = 18$ $(4 + 8) + 5 = 17$

173

Answer key

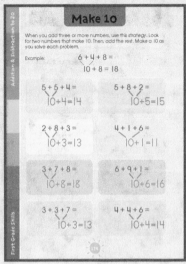

Make 10

When you add three or more numbers, use this strategy. Look for two numbers that make 10. Then, add the rest. Make a 10 as you solve each problem.

Example:
$6 + 4 + 8 =$
$10 + 8 = 18$

$5 + 5 + 4 =$
$10 + 4 = 14$

$5 + 8 + 2 =$
$10 + 5 = 15$

$2 + 8 + 3 =$
$10 + 3 = 13$

$4 + 1 + 6 =$
$10 + 1 = 11$

$3 + 7 + 8 =$
$10 + 8 = 18$

$6 + 9 + 1 =$
$10 + 6 = 16$

$3 + 3 + 7 =$
$10 + 3 = 13$

$4 + 4 + 6 =$
$10 + 4 = 14$

174

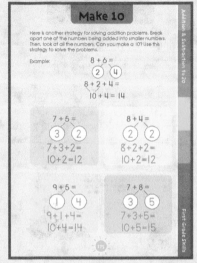

Make 10

Here is another strategy for solving addition problems. Break apart one of the numbers being added into smaller numbers. Then, look at all the numbers. Can you make a 10? Use this strategy to solve the problems.

Example:
$8 + 6 =$
② ④
$8 + 2 + 4 =$
$10 + 4 = 14$

$7 + 5 =$
③ ②
$7 + 3 + 2 =$
$10 + 2 = 12$

$8 + 4 =$
② ②
$8 + 2 + 2 =$
$10 + 2 = 12$

$9 + 5 =$
① ④
$9 + 1 + 4 =$
$10 + 4 = 14$

$7 + 8 =$
③ ⑤
$7 + 3 + 5 =$
$10 + 5 = 15$

175

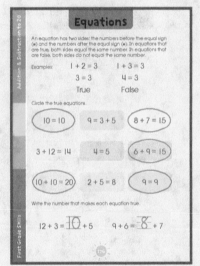

Equations

An equation has two sides: the numbers before the equal sign (=) and the numbers after the equal sign (=). In equations that are true, both sides equal the same number. In equations that are false, both sides do not equal the same number.

Examples:
$1 + 2 = 3$ $1 + 3 = 3$
$3 = 3$ $4 = 3$
True   False

Circle the true equations.

$10 = 10$ $9 = 3 + 5$ $8 + 7 = 15$

$3 + 12 = 14$ $4 = 5$ $6 + 9 = 15$

$10 + 10 = 20$ $2 + 5 = 8$ $9 = 9$

Write the number that makes each equation true.

$12 + 3 = 10 + 5$ $9 + 6 = 8 + 7$

176

Addition Word Problems

Read the problem. Write an equation to help you find the sum. Use the pictures to help you.

Brynn's dog, Max, has 5 bones. She gave him 2 more bones for his birthday. Then, he found 4 bones in the backyard. How many bones does Max have in all?

$5 + 2 + 4 = 11$ bones

Some people collect keychains, postcards, or rocks. What do you collect? Write and solve a **word problem** about your collection. Draw pictures to illustrate your problem.

Answers will vary.

177

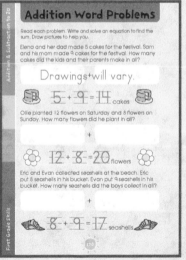

Addition Word Problems

Read each problem. Write and solve an equation to find the sum. Draw pictures to help you.

Elena and her dad made 5 cakes for the festival. Sam and his mom made 9 cakes for the festival. How many cakes did the kids and their parents make in all?

Drawings will vary.

$5 + 9 = 14$ cakes

Ollie planted 12 flowers on Saturday and 8 flowers on Sunday. How many flowers did he plant in all?

___ + ___

$12 + 8 = 20$ flowers

Eric and Evan collected seashells at the beach. Eric put 8 seashells in his bucket. Evan put 9 seashells in his bucket. How many seashells did the boys collect in all?

___ + ___

$8 + 9 = 17$ seashells

178

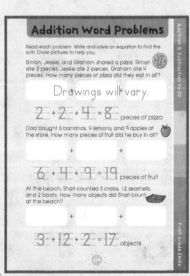

Addition Word Problems

Read each problem. Write and solve an equation to find the sum. Draw pictures to help you.

Simon, Jessie, and Graham shared a pizza. Simon ate 2 pieces. Jessie ate 2 pieces. Graham ate 4 pieces. How many pieces of pizza did they eat in all?

Drawings will vary.

$2 + 2 + 4 = 8$ pieces of pizza

Dad bought 6 bananas, 4 lemons, and 9 apples at the store. How many pieces of fruit did he buy in all?

___ + ___ + ___

$6 + 4 + 9 = 19$ pieces of fruit

At the beach, Shari counted 3 crabs, 12 seashells, and 2 boats. How many objects did Shari count at the beach?

___ + ___ + ___

$3 + 12 + 2 = 17$ objects

179

Answer key

Count Back

Write a number to answer each question. Use the number line to help you.

0 1 2 3 4 5 6 7 8 9 10

What is 2 less than 6? **4**

What is 4 less than 9? **5**

What is 9 less than 10? **1**

What is 3 less than 7? **4**

What is 8 less than 8? **0**

What is 5 less than 6? **1**

180

Count Back

Count backward. Write the missing numbers in each row.

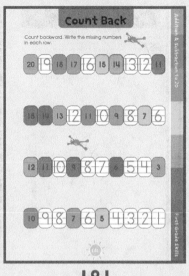

20 19 18 17 16 15 14 13 12 11

15 14 13 12 11 10 9 8 7 6

12 11 10 9 8 7 6 5 4 3

10 9 8 7 6 5 4 3 2 1

181

Picture Problems

Solve the subtraction problems. Cross out the pictures to help you. The first one is done for you.

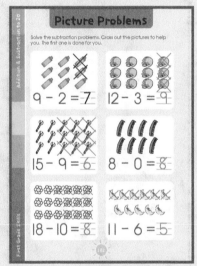

9 − 2 = **7**   12 − 3 = **9**

15 − 9 = **6**   8 − 0 = **8**

18 − 10 = **8**   11 − 6 = **5**

182

Picture Problems

Solve the subtraction problems. Cross out the pictures to help you.

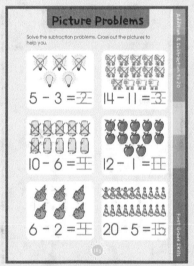

5 − 3 = **2**   14 − 11 = **3**

10 − 6 = **4**   12 − 1 = **11**

6 − 2 = **4**   20 − 5 = **15**

183

Subtraction Practice

Solve the problems to complete the chart. What patterns do you see?

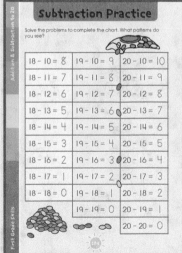

18 − 10 = 8	19 − 10 = 9	20 − 10 = 10
18 − 11 = 7	19 − 11 = 8	20 − 11 = 9
18 − 12 = 6	19 − 12 = 7	20 − 12 = 8
18 − 13 = 5	19 − 13 = 6	20 − 13 = 7
18 − 14 = 4	19 − 14 = 5	20 − 14 = 6
18 − 15 = 3	19 − 15 = 4	20 − 15 = 5
18 − 16 = 2	19 − 16 = 3	20 − 16 = 4
18 − 17 = 1	19 − 17 = 2	20 − 17 = 3
18 − 18 = 0	19 − 18 = 1	20 − 18 = 2
	19 − 19 = 0	20 − 19 = 1
		20 − 20 = 0

184

Subtraction Practice

Find the differences.

$$\begin{array}{r} 12 \\ -\ 6 \\ \hline 6 \end{array} \qquad \begin{array}{r} 16 \\ -14 \\ \hline 2 \end{array} \qquad \begin{array}{r} 8 \\ -\ 2 \\ \hline 6 \end{array} \qquad \begin{array}{r} 13 \\ -11 \\ \hline 2 \end{array}$$

$$\begin{array}{r} 16 \\ -\ 7 \\ \hline 9 \end{array} \qquad \begin{array}{r} 9 \\ -\ 1 \\ \hline 8 \end{array} \qquad \begin{array}{r} 12 \\ -\ 3 \\ \hline 9 \end{array} \qquad \begin{array}{r} 15 \\ -\ 1 \\ \hline 14 \end{array}$$

$$\begin{array}{r} 5 \\ -\ 4 \\ \hline 1 \end{array} \qquad \begin{array}{r} 17 \\ -\ 8 \\ \hline 9 \end{array} \qquad \begin{array}{r} 19 \\ -15 \\ \hline 4 \end{array} \qquad \begin{array}{r} 16 \\ -10 \\ \hline 6 \end{array}$$

With practice, you can become a **subtraction** super star! Think of a way to practice subtraction problems. It could be worksheets you make yourself, flash cards, or a computer game. Then, practice solving 15 problems each day for five days. If you make a mistake, include that problem in the next day's practice. Are your subtraction skills growing?

185

305

Answer key

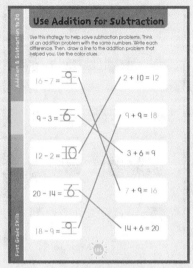

186

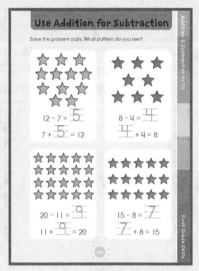

187

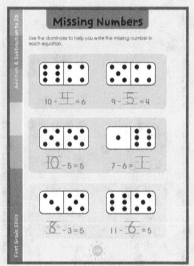

188

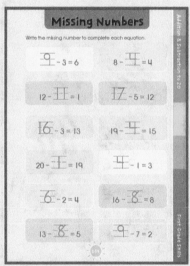

189

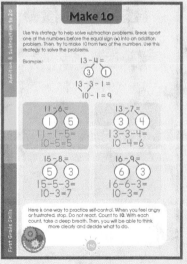

190

191

Answer key

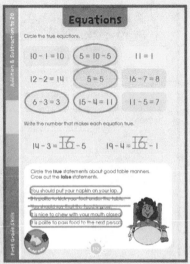

Equations

Circle the true equations.

10 − 1 = 10   (5 = 10 − 5)   11 = 1

12 − 2 = 14   (5 = 5)   16 − 7 = 8

(6 − 3 = 3)   (15 − 4 = 11)   11 − 5 = 7

Write the number that makes each equation true.

14 − 3 = 16 − 5   19 − 4 = 16 − 1

Circle the **true** statements about good table manners. Cross out the **false** statements.

(You should put your napkin on your lap.)

~~It is polite to tuck your feet under the table.~~

~~You should say that the food is yucky.~~

~~It is nice to chew with your mouth closed.~~

(It is polite to pass food to the next person.)

192

Subtraction Word Problems

Read the problem. Write and solve an equation to find the difference. Cross out the pictures to help you.

There were 12 flowers growing by the pond. Finley's little brother, Brad, picked 3 flowers to give to their mother. How many flowers were left?

12 − 3 = 9 flowers

Read the problem. Write and solve an equation to find the difference. Draw pictures to help you.

Asher and Beckett played with 15 toys at Asher's house. Beckett took 7 toys to his house. How many toys did Asher have left?

Drawings will vary.

15 − 7 = 8 toys

193

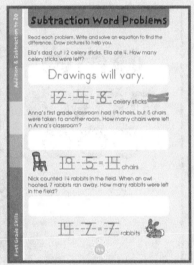

Subtraction Word Problems

Read each problem. Write and solve an equation to find the difference. Draw pictures to help you.

Ella's dad cut 12 celery sticks. Ella ate 4. How many celery sticks were left?

Drawings will vary.

12 − 4 = 8 celery sticks

Anna's first grade classroom had 19 chairs, but 5 chairs were taken to another room. How many chairs were left in Anna's classroom?

19 − 5 = 14 chairs

Nick counted 14 rabbits in the field. When an owl hooted, 7 rabbits ran away. How many rabbits were left in the field?

14 − 7 = 7 rabbits

194

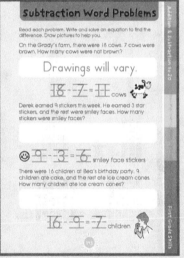

Subtraction Word Problems

Read each problem. Write and solve an equation to find the difference. Draw pictures to help you.

On the Grady's farm, there were 18 cows. 7 cows were brown. How many cows were not brown?

Drawings will vary.

18 − 7 = 11 cows

Derek earned 9 stickers this week. He earned 3 star stickers, and the rest were smiley faces. How many stickers were smiley faces?

9 − 3 = 6 smiley face stickers

There were 16 children at Bea's birthday party. 9 children ate cake, and the rest ate ice cream cones. How many children ate ice cream cones?

16 − 9 = 7 children

195

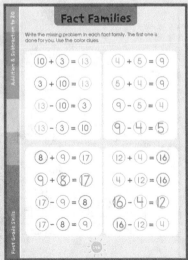

Fact Families

Write the missing problem in each fact family. The first one is done for you. Use the color clues.

(10) + (3) = (13)   (4) + (5) = (9)

(3) + (10) = (13)   (5) + (4) = (9)

(13) − (10) = (3)   (9) − (5) = (4)

(13) − (3) = (10)   (9) − (4) = (5)

(8) + (9) = (17)   (12) + (4) = (16)

(9) + (8) = (17)   (4) + (12) = (16)

(17) − (9) = (8)   (16) − (4) = (12)

(17) − (8) = (9)   (16) − (12) = (4)

196

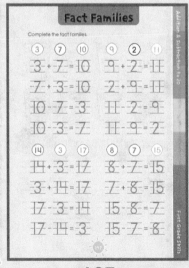

Fact Families

Complete the fact families.

(3) (7) (10)   (9) (2) (11)

3 + 7 = 10   9 + 2 = 11

7 + 3 = 10   2 + 9 = 11

10 − 7 = 3   11 − 2 = 9

10 − 3 = 7   11 − 9 = 2

(14) (3) (17)   (8) (7) (15)

14 + 3 = 17   8 + 7 = 15

3 + 14 = 17   7 + 8 = 15

17 − 3 = 14   15 − 8 = 7

17 − 14 = 3   15 − 7 = 8

197

Answer key

Addition & Subtraction Word Problems

Read the problems. Circle to tell whether you should add or subtract to solve each one. Use the space provided to draw pictures and write equations. Then, write the sum or difference.

Sam bought 6 fish. The next day, Dad gave her 2 more fish. How many fish did she have in all?

Circle one: (add) or subtract

Drawings will vary.

Sam had **8** fish.

Connor had 20 quarters in his piggy bank. He spent 3 quarters on a piece of candy. How many quarters did Connor have left?

Circle one: add or (subtract)

Connor had **17** quarters left.

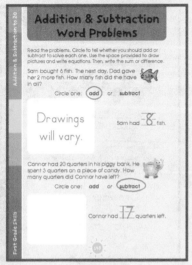

198

Addition & Subtraction Word Problems

Use both addition and subtraction to solve the word problems. Write the missing numbers in the equations.

Georgia has 20 books on her bookshelf. 9 books are fiction, and the rest are nonfiction. How many books are nonfiction?

$9 + 11 = 20$ books in all

$20 - 9 = 11$ nonfiction books

Of the 16 cars in the school parking lot, 8 cars are red. The other cars are different colors. How many cars are colors other than red?

$8 + 8 = 16$ cars in all

$16 - 8 = 8$ cars with colors other than red

199

Count by Tens

Write the number for each group of tens.

10

20

30

40

50

60

200

Count by Tens

Count by tens. Write the missing numbers.

10 · 20 · 30

40 · 50 · 60 · 70

80 · 90 · 100

Have you heard the saying, "An apple a day keeps the doctor away"? Eating lots of fruits and vegetables is a good way to stay healthy. Read the names of fruits and vegetables. Circle **ten** you like best.

Answers will vary.

apples	corn	pineapples	peaches
pears	bananas	lettuce	onions
broccoli	celery	peppers	tomatoes
peas	green beans	oranges	kiwis

201

Count by Tens

Count by tens. Write the missing numbers in each row.

60 · 70 · 80 · 90

10 · 20 · 30 · 40

List **ten** of your favorite things. They could be places, books, movies, animals, or something else.

1 _____ 6 Answers
2 _____ 7 will vary.
3 _____ 8 _____
4 _____ 9 _____
5 _____ 10 _____

202

Count by Tens

Write the missing numbers. **Hint:** Each number you write will end with **0**.

1	2	3	4	5	6	7	8	9	10
11	12	13	14	15	16	17	18	19	20
21	22	23	24	25	26	27	28	29	30
31	32	33	34	35	36	37	38	39	40
41	42	43	44	45	46	47	48	49	50
51	52	53	54	55	56	57	58	59	60
61	62	63	64	65	66	67	68	69	70
71	72	73	74	75	76	77	78	79	80
81	82	83	84	85	86	87	88	89	90
91	92	93	94	95	96	97	98	99	100

203

Answer Key

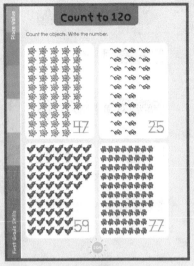

204

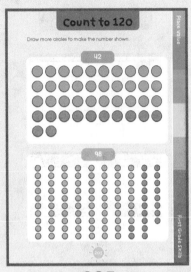

205

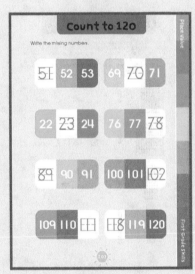

206

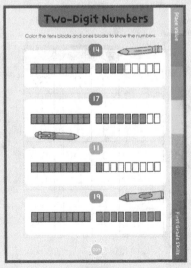

207

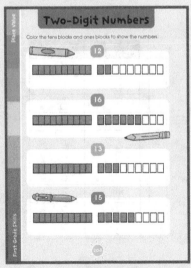

208

309

209

Answer key

First Grade skills

210

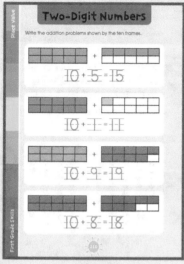

Two-Digit Numbers

Write the addition problems shown by the ten frames.

$10 + 5 = 15$

$10 + 1 = 11$

$10 + 9 = 19$

$10 + 8 = 18$

211

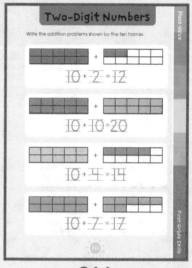

Two-Digit Numbers

Write the addition problems shown by the ten frames.

$10 + 2 = 12$

$10 + 10 = 20$

$10 + 4 = 14$

$10 + 7 = 17$

212

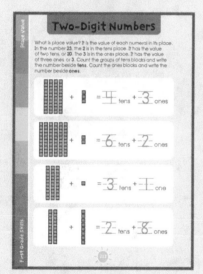

Two-Digit Numbers

What is place value? It is the value of each numeral in its place. In the number 23, the 2 is in the tens place. It has the value of two tens, or 20. The 3 is in the ones place. It has the value of three ones, or 3. Count the groups of tens blocks and write the number beside **tens**. Count the ones blocks and write the number beside **ones**.

$= 4$ tens $+ 3$ ones

$= 6$ tens $+ 2$ ones

$= 3$ tens $+ 1$ one

$= 2$ tens $+ 8$ ones

213

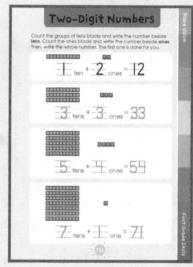

Two-Digit Numbers

Count the groups of tens blocks and write the number beside **tens**. Count the ones blocks and write the number beside **ones**. Then, write the whole number. The first one is done for you.

1 ten $+ 2$ ones $= 12$

3 tens $+ 3$ ones $= 33$

5 tens $+ 4$ ones $= 54$

7 tens $+ 1$ one $= 71$

214

Two-Digit Numbers

Complete the chart. The first row is done for you.

	Tens	Ones	=	Two-Digit Number
3 tens, 2 ones	3	2	=	32
1 ten, 7 ones	1	7	=	17
9 tens, 1 one	9	1	=	91
5 tens, 6 ones	5	6	=	56
6 tens, 5 ones	6	5	=	65
1 ten, 1 one	1	1	=	11
7 tens, 9 ones	7	9	=	79

215

Two-Digit Numbers

Complete the chart.

		Tens	Ones
28	=	2 tens	8 ones
64	=	6 tens	4 ones
56	=	5 tens	6 ones
72	=	7 tens	2 ones
17	=	1 ten	7 ones
34	=	3 tens	4 ones
98	=	9 tens	8 ones
15	=	1 ten	5 ones
22	=	2 tens	2 ones
57	=	5 tens	7 ones

First Grade skills

Answer Key

216

Two-Digit Numbers

Circle the numbers that have **9** in the tens place.

51　(94)　58　19　(93)　(96)　45

Circle the numbers that have **2** in the ones place.

(12)　84　(21)　63　(92)　(42)　76

Circle the numbers that have **3** in the tens place.

83　(36)　90　85　(37)　63　(34)

Write a **two-digit number** to complete each goal. Then, make a plan to practice and improve each skill.

I want to read ___ ___ chapter books.
tens ones

~~Answers will vary~~

I want to learn to spell ___ ___ tricky words.
tens ones

I want to jump rope ___ ___ times without missing.
tens ones

217

Comparing Two-Digit Numbers

Read the examples below. Then, write <, >, or = in the circles to compare the two-digit numbers.

Examples:

> means **greater than**.　< means **less than**.　= means **equal to**.

50 > 40　　40 < 50　　40 = 40

50 is greater than 40.　40 is less than 50.　40 is equal to 40.

32　(<)　33　　36　(<)　87

44　(<)　55　　95　(>)　84

54　(=)　54　　31　(<)　40

16　(<)　17　　50　(=)　50

218

Comparing Two-Digit Numbers

Write <, >, or = in the circles to compare the two-digit numbers.

98　(>)　12　　14　(=)　14

63　(<)　64　　15　(<)　20

45　(<)　46　　78　(>)　13

Write numbers in the correct spaces to compare the amounts. Then, answer the questions.

Keith has 48 dollars. Brady has 40 dollars.

48 > 40

Who has more money? __Keith__

Kerry has 13 pairs of shoes. George has 18 pairs of shoes.

13 < 18

Who has more shoes? __George__

219

Comparing Two-Digit Numbers

Cut out the numbers. Tape or glue them in the spaces to make comparisons that are true.

[ ] < [ ]　　[ ] < [ ]

[ ] > [ ]　　[ ] = [ ]

[ ] < [ ]　　[ ] < [ ]

[ ] < [ ]　　[ ] > [ ]

[ ] > [ ]

Answers will vary.

221

Add 10

Draw a line from each bee to the flower with a number that is 10 more.

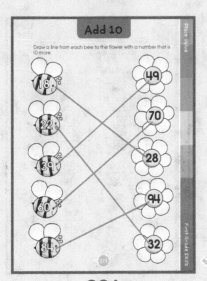

222

Add 10

Add 10 to each number on a cloud. Write the sum on the sun.

15	(25)	72	(82)
31	(41)	89	(99)
76	(86)	40	(50)
49	(59)	19	(29)

Answer key

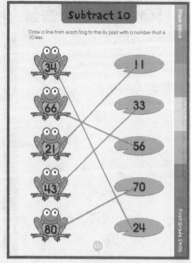

223

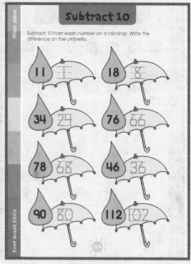

224

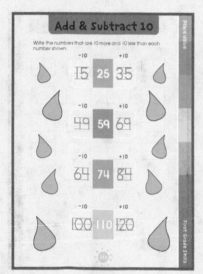

225

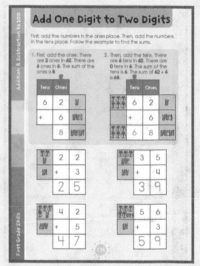

226

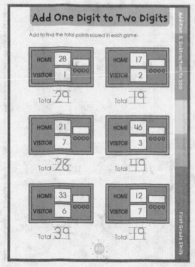

227

228

Answer key

229

Regroup

Add. As you solve each problem, regroup 10 ones as 1 ten.

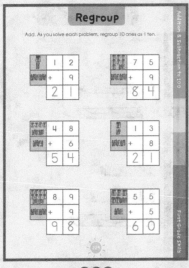

	1	2
+		9
	2	1

	7	5
+		9
	8	4

	4	8
+		6
	5	4

	1	3
+		8
	2	1

	8	9
+		9
	9	8

	5	5
+		5
	6	0

230

Regroup

Add to find the total points scored in each game. As you solve each problem, regroup 10 ones as 1 ten.

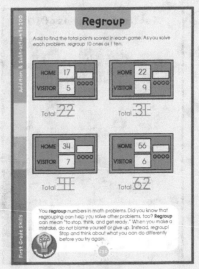

HOME 17 VISITOR 5 Total 22

HOME 22 VISITOR 9 Total 31

HOME 34 VISITOR 7 Total 41

HOME 56 VISITOR 6 Total 62

You **regroup** numbers in math problems. Did you know that regrouping can help you solve other problems, too? **Regroup** can mean "to stop, think, and get ready." When you make a mistake, do not blame yourself or give up. Instead, regroup! Stop and think about what you can do differently before you try again.

231

Regroup

Write the addition problems in the boxes. Then, add. Regroup when needed.

78 + 6	29 + 3	44 + 4
53 + 6	54 + 5	95 + 5
15 + 8	11 + 9	18 + 7

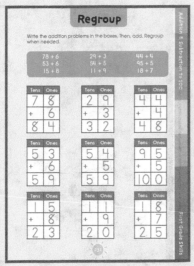

Tens	Ones
7	8
+	6
8	4

Tens	Ones
2	9
+	3
3	2

Tens	Ones
4	4
+	4
4	8

Tens	Ones
5	3
+	6
5	9

Tens	Ones
5	4
+	5
5	9

Tens	Ones
9	5
+	5
10	0

Tens	Ones
1	5
+	8
2	3

Tens	Ones
1	1
+	9
2	0

Tens	Ones
1	8
+	7
2	5

232

Add Multiples of 10

Add the ones. Then, add the tens.

$$34 + 30 = 64$$

$$28 + 70 = 98$$

$$51 + 40 = 91$$

$$69 + 20 = 89$$

233

Add Multiples of 10

Use the sums in the shapes to answer the problems below.

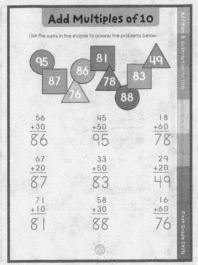

95   81   49
87   86   83
76   78   88

56 +30 = 86	45 +50 = 95	18 +60 = 78
67 +20 = 87	33 +50 = 83	29 +20 = 49
71 +10 = 81	58 +30 = 88	16 +60 = 76

234

Subtract Multiples of 10

Subtract the ones. Then, subtract the tens.

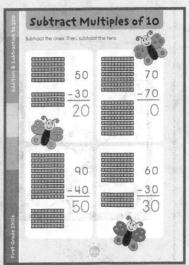

$$50 - 30 = 20$$

$$70 - 70 = 0$$

$$90 - 40 = 50$$

$$60 - 30 = 30$$

Subtract Multiples of 10

Use the differences in the shapes to answer the problems below.

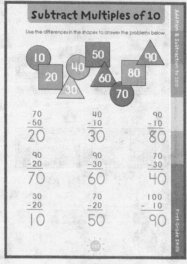

$\begin{array}{r} 70 \\ -50 \\ \hline 20 \end{array}$	$\begin{array}{r} 40 \\ -10 \\ \hline 30 \end{array}$	$\begin{array}{r} 90 \\ -10 \\ \hline 80 \end{array}$
$\begin{array}{r} 90 \\ -20 \\ \hline 70 \end{array}$	$\begin{array}{r} 90 \\ -30 \\ \hline 60 \end{array}$	$\begin{array}{r} 70 \\ -30 \\ \hline 40 \end{array}$
$\begin{array}{r} 30 \\ -20 \\ \hline 10 \end{array}$	$\begin{array}{r} 70 \\ -20 \\ \hline 50 \end{array}$	$\begin{array}{r} 100 \\ -10 \\ \hline 90 \end{array}$

235

Compare Lengths

Look at the pencil. Draw a pencil that is longer. Draw a pencil that is shorter.

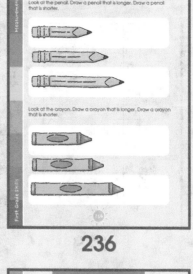

Look at the crayon. Draw a crayon that is longer. Draw a crayon that is shorter.

236

Order Lengths

In each group, write **1** beside the shortest object, write **2** beside the object that is the next longest, and write **3** beside the object that is the longest.

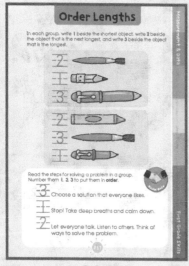

Read the steps for solving a problem in a group. Number them **1, 2, 3** to put them in **order**.

3 Choose a solution that everyone likes.

1 Stop! Take deep breaths and calm down.

2 Let everyone talk. Listen to others. Think of ways to solve the problem.

237

Order Lengths

In each group, write **1** beside the shortest fish, write **2** beside the fish that is the next longest, and write **3** beside the fish that is the longest.

238

Compare Lengths

Look at the fish in the fish tank. Draw a fish in the tank that is shorter. Draw a fish in the tank that is longer.

239

Measure Length

Measure the objects by counting the boxes (units).

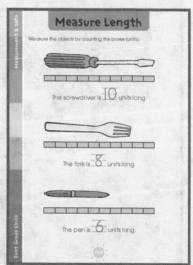

The screwdriver is 10 units long.

The fork is 8 units long.

The pen is 6 units long.

240

314

Answer key

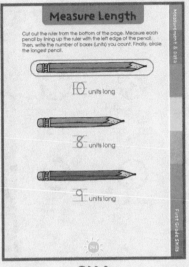

241

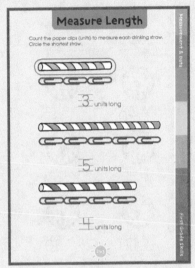

243

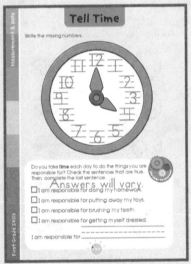

244

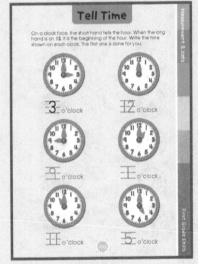

245

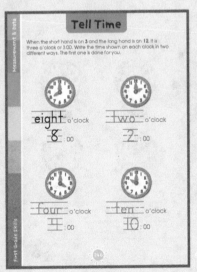

246

315

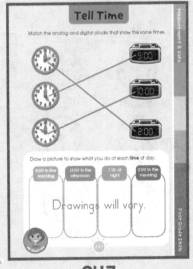

247

Answer key

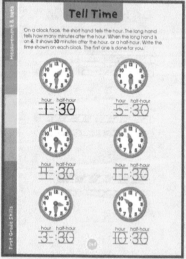

Tell Time

On a clock face, the short hand tells the hour. The long hand tells how many minutes after the hour. When the long hand is on 6, it shows 30 minutes after the hour, or a half-hour. Write the time shown on each clock. The first one is done for you.

1 : 30   5 : 30

4 : 30   11 : 30

3 : 30   10 : 30

248

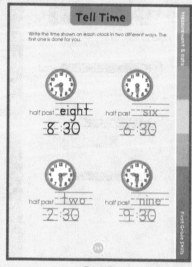

Tell Time

Write the time shown on each clock in two different ways. The first one is done for you.

half past **eight**   half past **six**
8 : 30   6 : 30

half past **two**   half past **nine**
2 : 30   9 : 30

249

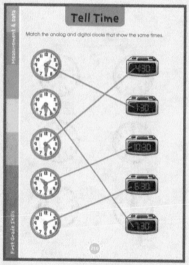

Tell Time

Match the analog and digital clocks that show the same times.

250

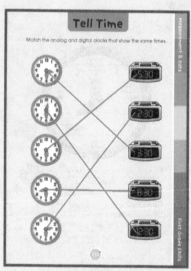

Tell Time

Match the analog and digital clocks that show the same times.

251

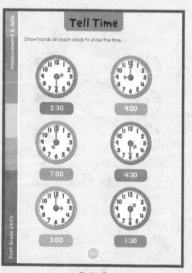

Tell Time

Draw hands on each clock to show the time.

2:30   9:00

7:00   4:30

3:00   1:30

252

Tell Time

Draw hands on the clock faces to match the times shown on the digital clocks.

2:30   1:00

1:00   4:30

Kids need at least 60 minutes (1 hour) of physical activity each day. Have a fun fitness evening with your family. Watch the **time**. When the clock shows the hour or half past the hour, spend 10 minutes playing soccer, playing tag, or doing another physical activity together. If you do this six times, you will have spent a whole hour exercising!

253

Answer key

Bar Graphs

Count the banana peels in each column. Color the boxes to show how many bananas were eaten by the monkey.

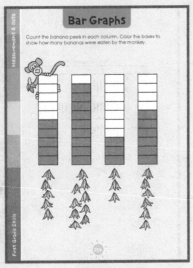

254

Bar Graphs

Kayla is counting how many school supplies she has left. Color the boxes to show how many of each item. Then, answer the questions.

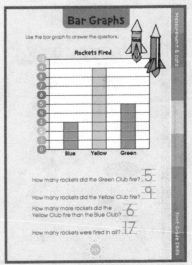

Kayla has the most _____. Circle your answer.

Kayla has the least _____. Circle your answer.

255

Bar Graphs

Kirsten made a bar graph to show how many books she read over the summer. Use the graph to answer the questions.

Books Read This Summer

During which month did Kirsten read the most books? Circle your answer.

(June)   July   August

During which month did Kirsten read 8 books? Circle your answer.

June   (July)   August

How many more books did Kirsten read in June than in August?   4 books

256

Bar Graphs

Use the bar graph to answer the questions.

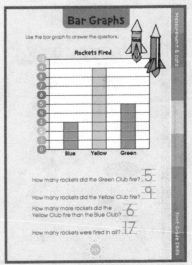

Rockets Fired

How many rockets did the Green Club fire?   5

How many rockets did the Yellow Club fire?   9

How many more rockets did the Yellow Club fire than the Blue Club?   6

How many rockets were fired in all?   17

257

Picture Graphs

Kailyn and Sydney counted their toys. They made a picture graph to show their data. Use the graph to answer the questions.

Kailyn and Sydney's Toys

jump ropes	
dolls	
puzzles	

Each picture equals one toy.

How many jump ropes do Kailyn and Sydney have?   2

How many toys do they have altogether?   16

Do Kailyn and Sydney have more dolls or more puzzles? Circle your answer.

(dolls)   puzzles

Do Kailyn and Sydney have more puzzles or more jump ropes? Circle your answer.

(puzzles)   jump ropes

258

Picture Graphs

Hayden asked his first grade classmates to vote for their favorite fruit. Each student chose one fruit. Use the picture graph to answer the questions.

Grade 1 Favorite Fruits

watermelon	
grapes	
peaches	

Each picture equals one student's vote.

How many classmates chose watermelon as their favorite fruit?   3

How many classmates chose grapes as their favorite fruit?   7

Which fruit was the favorite of Hayden's classmates? Circle your answer.

watermelon   (grapes)   peaches

Which fruit was the least favorite of Hayden's classmates? Circle your answer.

(watermelon)   grapes   peaches

259

Answer key

260
Tally Charts
Use the examples to make tally marks in the chart as you read the story.

III = 3   THL = 5   THL IIII = 9

Jake and his mom went to the store to buy food for a party. They bought 3 pizzas, 5 cartons of milk, and 12 cupcakes.

Food for Jake's Party

🍕	III
🥛	THL
🧁	THL THL II

Read each message that will help you grow and reach your goals. Make a **tally mark** each time you tell yourself the message.

Try Again!
Mistakes Are OK!
I Am Learning!

Answers will vary.

261
Tally Charts
Write the total number of tally marks in each row. Then, use the chart to answer the questions.

On Mr. Johnson's Farm

Animal	Tally	Total
🐑	THL III	8
🐤	THL THL THL IIII	19
🐭	THL THL II	12

Which animal does Mr. Johnson have the most of? Circle your answer.

🐑 (🐤) 🐭

How many rabbits does Mr. Johnson have? 12

How many more chicks than sheep does Mr. Johnson have? 11

262
Flat Shapes
Write the name of each flat (two-dimensional) shape.

rectangle rhombus oval circle
trapezoid triangle hexagon square

rectangle   square
circle   triangle
oval   rhombus
hexagon   trapezoid

263
Flat Shapes
Use the code to color the shapes.

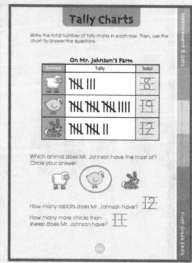

264
Solid Shapes
Write the name of each solid (three-dimensional) shape.

cone rectangular prism cylinder
cube sphere

cube   cylinder
cone   sphere
rectangular prism

265
Flat & Solid Shapes
Draw a line from each shape to an object that has the same shape.

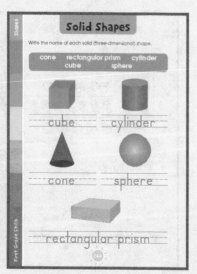

Answer key

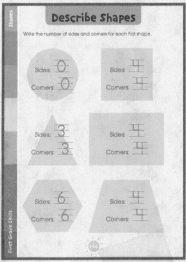

266

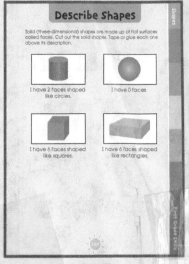

267

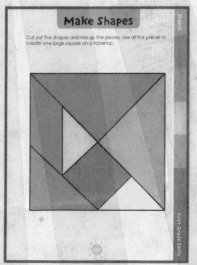

269

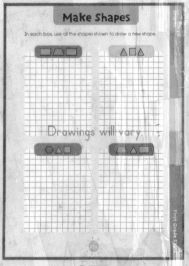

271

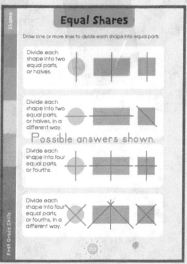

272

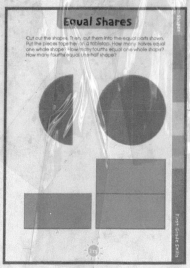

273

Answer key

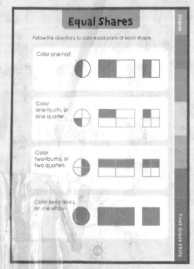

275